W9-DBW-852

BIG BUSINESS, THE STATE, AND FREE TRADE

Constructing Coalitions in Mexico

Existing theories of economic liberalization fail to account for Mexico's experiences. Why has the Mexican government risked alienating its primary constituencies by pursuing trade opening and joining the North American Free Trade Agreement (NAFTA)? *Big Business, the State, and Free Trade* develops a general explanation of trade policy coalition politics and uses it to explain the opening of Mexico's economy. It emphasizes the role of business and state actors in constructing competing trade policy coalitions. The book traces the formation and relative strength of a protectionist and a free trade coalition across a series of policy episodes from the 1970s to the 1990s. It pays particular attention to NAFTA, which consolidated a strong free trade coalition between big business and state elites. The conditions that strengthened the free trade coalition have also contributed to higher levels of political and economic instability since 1994. Coalition politics is likely to become more important as Mexico's political system democratizes.

Strom C. Thacker is Assistant Professor of International Relations at Boston University. He has published articles in journals including *World Politics* and the *Journal of Interamerican Studies and World Affairs*. Professor Thacker is currently conducting research on neoliberalism and democracy in Latin America and on the politics of U.S. bilateral and multilateral aid.

To Isabelle

BIG BUSINESS, THE STATE, AND FREE TRADE

Constructing Coalitions in Mexico

STROM C. THACKER
Boston University

CAMBRIDGE
UNIVERSITY PRESS

PUBLISHED BY THE PRESS SYNDICATE OF THE UNIVERSITY OF CAMBRIDGE
The Pitt Building, Trumpington Street, Cambridge, United Kingdom

CAMBRIDGE UNIVERSITY PRESS
The Edinburgh Building, Cambridge CB2 2RU, UK   http://www.cup.cam.ac.uk
40 West 20th Street, New York, NY 10011-4211, USA   http://www.cup.org
10 Stamford Road, Oakleigh, Melbourne 3166, Australia
Ruiz de Alarcón 13, 28014 Madrid, Spain

© Strom C. Thacker 2000

This book is in copyright. Subject to statutory exception
and to the provisions of relevant collective licensing agreements,
no reproduction of any part may take place without
the written permission of Cambridge University Press.

First published 2000

Printed in the United States of America

Typeface Sabon 10/12 pt.   *System* QuarkXPress™ [BTS]

A catalog record for this book is available from the British Library.

Library of Congress Cataloging in Publication data

Thacker, Strom Cronan.
Big business, the State, and free trade: constructing coalitions in Mexico /
Strom C. Thacker.
p.   cm.
Includes bibliographical references.
ISBN 0-521-78168-X (hb)
1. Mexico – Commercial policy.   2. Business and politics – Mexico.
3. Free trade – Mexico.   4. Canada. Treaties, etc. 1992 Oct. 7.   I. Title.
HF1481.T43 2000
382'.3'0972 – dc21   00-027890

ISBN   0 521 78168 X   hardback

Contents

Contents

List of Figures

List of Figures

List of Tables

List of Tables

List of Abbreviations

AAMA	American Apparel Manufacturers Association
Ajustabonos	Adjustable Treasury Bonds
ALADI	Latin American Integration Association
AMCB	Mexican Association of Brokerage Houses
AMIA	Mexican Association of the Automobile Industry
AMIS	Mexican Association of Insurance Institutions
ANIERM	National Association of Importers and Exporters
ANIQ	National Association of the Chemical Industry
ANIT	National Association of Manufacturing Industries
ANPACT	National Association of Bus, Truck and Tractor Producers
ATMI	American Textile Manufacturers Institute
Banamex	National Bank of Mexico
Bancomext	National Bank of Foreign Trade
Banxico	Bank of Mexico
BIS	Bank for International Settlements
BMV	Mexican Stock Exchange
CACINTE	Advisory Council for the Free Trade Agreement
CANACINTRA	National Chamber of Industries
CANACO	National Chamber of Commerce of Mexico City
CANAINTEX	National Chamber of the Textile Industry
CANIVE	National Chamber of the Apparel Industry
CAP MEX CCI	Mexico Chapter of the International Chamber of Commerce
CCE	Business Coordinating Council
CEESP	Center for Economic Studies of the Private Sector
CEFYL	Center for Fiscal and Legislative Studies
CEMAI	Mexican Business Council for International Affairs

List of Abbreviations

CEMEX	Cementos Mexicanos
CES	Center for Social Studies
Cetes	Treasury Bills
CMHN	Mexican Businessmen's Council
CNA	National Agricultural Council
COECE	Coordinating Council of Foreign Trade Business Organizations
COLMEX	College of Mexico
CONACEX	National Council of Foreign Trade
CONCAMIN	National Federation of Chambers of Industry
CONCANACO	National Chamber of Commerce
COPARMEX	Employers' Federation of the Mexican Republic
CPC	Confederation for Production and Commerce
CPO	Ordinary Participation Certificate
DFI	Direct foreign investment
FDN	National Democratic Front
FICORCA	Fund for Exchange Risk
GATT	General Agreement on Tariffs and Trade
GDP	Gross domestic product
IFI	International financial institution
IMF	International Monetary Fund
IMSS	Mexican Institute of Social Security
INA	National Auto Parts Industry
INEGI	National Institute of Statistics and Geography
IPN	National Polytechnic University
ISI	Import-substituting industrialization
ITAM	Autonomous Technological Institute of Mexico
ITESM	Monterrey Technological Institute
MNC	Multinational corporation
NAFTA	North American Free Trade Agreement
NVAp	National value added in production
PAN	National Action Party
PECE	Pact for Economic Stabilization and Growth
PRD	Democratic Revolutionary Party
PRI	Institutional Revolutionary Party
Pronasol	National Solidarity Program
PSE	Economic Solidarity Pact
SECOFI	Ministry of Trade and Industrial Development
SEDESOL	Ministry of Social Development
SEDUE	Ministry of Urban Development and Ecology
SEMIP	Ministry of Energy, Mines and Parastatals
SHCP	Ministry of Finance and Public Credit
SPP	Ministry of Programming and Budget

List of Abbreviations

Telmex	Teléfonos de México
Tesobonos	Federal Treasury Bonds
UNAM	National Autonomous University of Mexico
USMCOC	United States–Mexico Chamber of Commerce

Acknowledgments

Like many first books, this one would not have been possible without the guidance of my graduate advisor, Tim McKeown, and the other members of my dissertation committee: Jonathan Hartlyn, Evelyne Huber, Thomas Oatley, and Lars Schoultz. Collectively and individually, they provided a balance of support and constructive criticism that improved the first iterations of this book immeasurably.

Generous financial support from a Fulbright–García Robles grant, a University of North Carolina Off-Campus Dissertation grant, and pre-dissertation grants sponsored by the Tinker Foundation and the Mellon Foundation and administered by the Institute of Latin American Studies at the University of North Carolina, Chapel Hill, funded this research. Many people provided assistance in Mexico and the United States. The members of the Department of International Relations at the Autonomous Technological Institute of Mexico (ITAM), which hosted my field research in Mexico City in 1993–94 and employed me as a faculty member in 1995–96, provided a congenial atmosphere and valuable suggestions as I modified my approach to the empirical research after my arrival in Mexico. Rafael Fernández de Castro, chair of the department, was especially welcoming and helpful in coordinating institutional support and in securing contacts for the interviews that provide the empirical backbone of this research. Blanca Heredia first invited me to ITAM in 1992 and has been an important sounding board for the ideas that guide my research. Sergio Merino, a student at ITAM, provided excellent research assistance. Carlos Alba, Carlos Rico, and Gustavo Vega at the Colegio de México welcomed me to Mexico during my first visits there in 1990 and 1992 and encouraged me to think about business-state relations and Mexico's economic reforms in new ways. Cristina Puga in the Political and Social Sciences Department at the National Autonomous University of Mexico (UNAM) gave me access to the archives and publications of POEM, the Program on Business

Acknowledgments

Organizations in Mexico. Stephanie R. Golob, a fellow Fulbright grantee and ITAM affiliate, provided fresh insight into my research and the field work experience more generally, as well as a friendship that has extended to each of our families. Ken Shadlen, another Mexico City field researcher and friend, gave great feedback on early drafts of chapters. Economist Jay Bryson helped me understand some of the more esoteric implications of economic theory for my project. Above all else, I would like to express my gratitude to my interview subjects, who took time out of their very tight schedules to share their experiences with a young visiting researcher. Without their openness, candor, and cooperation I would not have been able to conduct this research.

Colleagues in the Department of International Relations at Boston University have welcomed me and provided a stimulating environment for research and teaching. My brother-in-law, Lincoln P. Paine, tutored me in the world of publishing. Alex Holzman at Cambridge University Press has been an extremely supportive and helpful editor. Two anonymous reviewers gave uncommonly insightful feedback on the previous version of the manuscript. Without the help of all these people, I would have made far more mistakes than I have. Any remaining errors of fact or interpretation are my responsibility alone.

On a personal note, my parents, Terry K. Strom and Roger D. Thacker, instilled in me a passion for reading, learning, and discovery. My children, Matthew and Caroline, gave the smiles and good cheer that sustained me during the final writing and revision of the manuscript. This book is dedicated to my wife, Isabelle Paine Thacker. From the very beginning of this project, her faithful support, timely prodding, and endless encouragement have improved the book and made writing it far more enjoyable.

Boston, Massachusetts
January 2000

I

Introduction: International Context, Domestic Interests, and Mexican Trade Reform

THE PROBLEM

The inauguration of the North American Free Trade Agreement (NAFTA) on January 1, 1994, ushered in a new era in trade relations for Mexico, the United States, and Canada. This date also marked an end of sorts, the culmination of a dramatic turnaround in Mexican trade policy that transformed the Mexican economy from one of the most closed to one of the most open in the developing world. This process began in 1983, accelerated between 1985 and 1988, and has been consolidated since 1990 with the emergence, negotiation, approval, and implementation of NAFTA. Over a span of scarcely a decade, the governments of Miguel de la Madrid and Carlos Salinas de Gortari reversed four decades of trade policy predicated on an import-substituting industrialization (ISI) model of development intended to promote the industrialization of the Mexican economy through the restriction of most imports by a variety of high trade barriers, including tariffs, quantitative restrictions, import licenses, and official pricing mechanisms.

Trade is not the only aspect of the Mexican economy that has undergone important changes since the early 1980s. Recent governments have freed domestic prices, relaxed exchange controls, stabilized inflation, opened the foreign investment regime and domestic capital markets, privatized nearly 90 percent of the country's state-owned enterprises, cut government spending, and reformed the tax system (see Edwards 1995). But what is perhaps most surprising about the post-1982 period is that trade protection, which historically had been one of the most consistent elements of Mexican development policy, was effectively dismantled in almost all sectors of the economy. Macroeconomic policy has fluctuated widely in the postrevolutionary period, ranging from the statist policies initiated by Lázaro Cárdenas in the 1930s, through the more conservative fiscal and monetary policies of the Stabilizing Development period

(1954–70), to Luis Echeverriía's more activist Shared Development model in the early 1970s and José López Portillo's oil and debt led spending boom of the late 1970s (see Maxfield 1990). Despite these periodic vacillations, trade protection remained at the center of an ISI development strategy that dominated Mexican policy making for most of the postrevolutionary period. The development of the border-processing maquiladora plants and the occasional, temporary attempt to open trade did not significantly alter the general tendency of high and rising trade barriers through the 1970s (Zabludovsky 1990, Buffie 1989).[1]

Only after 1985 did Mexico significantly alter the basic direction of trade policy, undertaking a wide-ranging program of liberalization. By any measure, the breadth, depth, and pace of Mexico's reforms are remarkable. Between 1982 and 1990, import license coverage declined from 100 percent to 14 percent, the number of tariff categories dropped from sixteen to five, the maximum tariff rate fell from 100 percent to 20 percent, and the average tariff rate went from 27 percent to about 10 percent. Official import price coverage, a measure of the proportion of goods affected by an official pricing mechanism that artificially raised the prices of imports, was eliminated by 1988 after having exceeded 25 percent in 1985 (see Table 1.1). Under NAFTA, remaining barriers on imports from the U.S. and Canada are being eliminated over varying phase-in periods.

Extant explanations for these changes typically focus either on the overwhelming influence of international forces or on the decisive role played by technocratic government elites and state institutions. But Mexico's reforms far exceeded the requirements posed by international forces. Statist analyses typically emphasize the strength of the Mexican presidency and the state's autonomy from opposing social forces, rather than the creation of new sources of policy support (see Heredia 1996, Pastor and Wise 1994 for useful discussions). The critical role of business actors in this transformation, especially in its consolidation and extension since the late 1980s, has been neglected. As the Mexican political system becomes more competitive, the role of social actors, particularly the business community, in economic policy coalitions will continue to grow in importance.

How can we better account for the rapid and deep transformation of Mexico's trade policy regime? In terms of domestic politics, Mexico's lib-

---

1 One of the most notable attempts to liberalize trade was López Portillo's negotiation of a protocol of accession to the GATT in 1979. But the President rejected GATT membership in 1980 due to negative public opinion, divisions in his cabinet, and the discovery of large oil deposits that enabled the government to cover growing foreign exchange deficits (see Story 1982). A series of earlier reforms was also subsequently reversed.

Table 1.1. *Measures of Trade Barriers in Mexico, 1982–1990*

	1982	1983	1984	1985	1986	1987	1988	1989	1990
Import license coverage[a]	100.0	100.0	83.0	35.1	27.0	27.0	21.2	18.4	14.0
Number of tariff categories	16	—	10	—	11	—	5	—	5
Maximum tariff	100.0	—	—	100.0	45.0	40.0	20.0	20.0	20.0
Average tariff[b]	27.0	27.0	23.3	22.6	22.6	11.8	13.1	12.1	10.4
Official import price coverage[a]	—	—	—	25.4	18.7	0.6	0.0	0.0	—

(—) Data not available.
Source: Aspe (1992a), Ros (1992a), Ten Kate (1992), Vega Cánovas (1991a).
[a] As a percentage of domestic production value.
[b] Percentage, weighted by import value.

eralization is puzzling. The nature and strength of entrenched political and economic interests at the time suggest that such changes would face fierce domestic political resistance from many sides. Within the state itself, multiple generations of policy makers had risen to power through the structures and institutions of Mexico's traditional protectionist trade regime. They were educated and trained in a school of thought that espoused the benefits of industrial development via import substitution. Their careers were wedded to this model of development, and their professional advancement depended on its successful implementation. Simple bureaucratic inertia would be expected to obstruct meaningful trade reform.[2]

Equally intractable was the weight of protectionist interests within society, particularly in the business community. After more than forty years of protection, a large and strong import-competing sector had developed. This sector had been central to the "Mexican miracle" of earlier decades, when the economy grew at an average annual rate of 3.3 percent per capita between 1955 and 1972, while inflation averaged 5 percent per year between 1955 and 1973 (Dornbusch 1990, 314). Economic theory suggests that this sector, which produces almost exclusively for the domestic market, will pay the lion's share of the costs of adjustment to liberalization, with the gains accruing largely to exporters and consumers. Most import-competing firms, characterized by outdated technology, inefficient production, and inward-looking business strategies, were ill-prepared to compete in an open market. They were born and raised under state tutelage and protection, and they owed their political loyalty to the ruling Institutional Revolutionary Party (Partido Revolucionario Institucional, PRI) and to their bureaucratic allies within the state. Along with labor, this sector was a key member of the postrevolutionary alliance that has helped the PRI maintain power since 1929 (Davis 1992).[3]

The fact that Mexico embraced policies that ran directly counter to the material interests of powerful entrenched protectionist forces cutting across both state and society suggests that a static, domestic interest-based explanation is deficient. How were these domestic political obstacles to trade reform circumvented? Or were there other factors that simply overwhelmed them? Where else might we look to explain the policy reversal?

The most common general approach to explain these changes has been to focus on the constraining role of the external environment. A diverse

2 See Smith (1979), Camp (1980, 1995a, b) and Centeno (1997) for useful analyses of bureaucratic and political career paths in Mexico.
3 The PRI was originally founded as the National Revolutionary Party in 1929. Its name was changed to the Mexican Revolutionary Party in 1938, and finally to the Institutional Revolutionary Party in 1946.

collection of schools, ranging from neoclassical economists to neo-Marxian dependency theorists, posits that pressures from external economic and/or political elements pushed the changes through over domestic resistance. In one way or another, the functioning of the international economy required Mexico to overcome its domestic difficulties and undertake a program of trade liberalization, along with several other macroeconomic reforms. These types of arguments break down into two basic categories. The first is often associated with neoclassical economists, but also includes some mainstream political analyses as well. The argument is essentially that reform was necessitated by the failure of the ISI development strategy, which came to a head when the external economic shocks of collapsing international oil prices and the debt crisis hit Mexico in the early 1980s (see Lustig 1998). The large oil revenues and foreign borrowing that had fueled economic growth in the 1970s evaporated and the Mexican economy plunged into what would become a decade of economic stagnation as policy makers struggled to control hyperinflation and growing balance of payments deficits. Given the potential gains in efficiency and growth from free trade, the measures undertaken by Mexico would appear to have been inevitable. In other words, reform was simply an acknowledgment of the utter failure of the errant policies of the past (cf. Baer 1991, Buffie 1989, Dornbusch 1990, Weintraub 1990).

Others have argued convincingly that this argument does not succeed even on its own narrowly economic terms, for a country facing severe macroeconomic instability normally would not be expected to open its borders to free trade. This instability interferes with the reallocation of resources into more productive activities according to shifts in relative prices, and worsens the already onerous effects of adjustment to free trade. "High and variable inflation serves to confound price signals by making it difficult to disentangle relative price changes from movements in the price level. The slowdown in domestic activity renders structural change more painful by exacerbating transitional unemployment" (Rodrik 1992a, 89). A country facing the conditions under which Mexico and the other large debtor nations were operating in the 1980s may actually be the least likely candidate for lowering its trade barriers based on purely technical criteria of efficiency (Pastor and Wise 1994, 463).

A second variant of the external argument focuses on the political leverage of external actors, including foreign governments and multilateral organizations like the International Monetary Fund (IMF) and the World Bank. When oil revenues and private lending fell sharply in the 1980s, these organizations, the IMF in particular, became "lenders of last resort" for the developing world. These institutions would require the debtor nations to implement a series of orthodox policy measures, which typically included trade liberalization, in exchange for short-term balance of payments assistance (Rodrik 1992a). Their influence was magnified by the fact that a G-7-sanctioned lending agreement between the IMF or World Bank and a debtor nation often served as a "stamp of approval," without which the private banks would not resume lending. This view implies that trade liberalization was imposed from abroad and was accepted only to secure the necessary finance to survive the debt crisis.[4]

One might expect this to result in a tentative and unstable reform program, to be abandoned shortly after the release of conditional funds. "The trade policy recommendations of the World Bank were adopted by cash-starved governments frequently with little conviction of their ultimate benefits. This accounts for the high incidence of wobbling and reversal on the trade front" (Rodrik 1992a, 89). But in the Mexican case, the government not only sustained trade reform; it went far beyond the liberalization targets set by such organizations as the General Agreement on Tariffs and Trade (GATT) and the World Bank.[5] The Mexican case demonstrates the limited utility of this kind of approach. If foreign pressures are the only reason a country is lowering its trade barriers, why go so much further than those external forces demand?

These types of arguments are appealingly simple and straightforward. If the domestic situation discussed above seems to discourage trade reform, then it makes sense to assume that the causal explanation lies in the external environment. International factors are indeed a necessary component of any comprehensive account of trade reform. The role of external shocks, for example, has been well documented (see Grindle and Thomas 1991, Tornell 1995). The severe political and economic crises that often result from these shocks can open up the political space to undertake economic reforms "that would have been unthinkable in calmer times" (Rodrik 1992a, 89). But the experiences of the developing nations in the last two decades have demonstrated that even the strong influence of external shocks and actors is not *sufficient* to induce a deep, long-term policy reorientation such as that which Mexico has undertaken (and that has survived subsequent crises, such as the

4 See George (1990). See also Pastor (1987) and Sidell (1988) on the impact of the IMF on debtor nations. See Williamson (1983), Killick (1984, 1995), and Bird (1995), for a general treatment of IMF conditionality.

5 Mexico's 1986 protocol of accession to the GATT called for a reduction of tariffs to a maximum of 50% (Olea Sisniega 1990). They were lowered to a maximum level of 20% by 1988 (see Table 1.1). In addition, Mexico met (and in most cases exceeded) the targets set forth in the World Bank's Trade Policy Loans of July 1986 and October 1987 ahead of schedule, against the advice of even some Bank officials (see Rodrik 1992b, 30).

Table 1.2. *A Comparison of Trade Opening in Latin America, 1991–1992*

Country	Average protection of tariffs and paratariffs (percentage)[a]
Early reformers	
Chile	11.0
Bolivia	8.0
Mexico	4.0
Second-phase reformers	
Costa Rica	16.0
Uruguay	12.0
Third-phase reformers	
Brazil	21.1
Guatemala	19.0
Venezuela	17.0
Paraguay	16.0
Argentina	15.0
Peru	15.0
Colombia	6.7
Nonreformers	
Ecuador	18.0

Source: Edwards (1995).
[a] Unweighted.

1994–95 peso crisis). If that were the case, we would expect other similarly situated countries (vis-à-vis the international economy) to have experienced the same degree of policy reform in the 1980s. While economic adjustment was attempted across Latin America and the rest of the developing world during the debt crisis, nowhere was the policy conversion more profound or were the reforms implemented more thoroughly than in the Mexican case, especially with respect to trade liberalization. Table 1.2 compares a simple measure of trade protection, the average coverage of tariff and paratariff barriers, across several Latin American countries. Of the earliest reformers, Mexico went further than either Chile or Bolivia in lowering its trade barriers down to an average level of 4.0 percent on this indicator. Of the remaining cases, only Colombia, at 6.7 percent, came close to the Mexican standard.

Perhaps the most apt comparison with Mexico is the case of Brazil, which for many years had pursued an ISI development strategy similar in many respects to Mexico's and which had accumulated a roughly equivalent level of foreign debt during the 1970s and early 1980s. This suggests that Mexico and Brazil would be subject to

7

similar external balance of payments and trade policy constraints in the 1980s.[6] But Mexican and Brazilian trade policies diverged sharply in the 1980s. While Mexico was one of the first to initiate significant structural reform in 1985, Brazil remained closed to most imports and did not begin to open its trade regime until the early 1990s. Still today, Brazil's liberalization has not been as complete or as thorough as Mexico's, despite Brazil's leadership in the formation of the Common Market of the South (Mercosur). Table 1.2 shows that Brazil's average rate of protection of tariffs and paratariffs was seven times higher than Mexico's in 1991–92. Furthermore, Edwards's (1995) data show that Brazil's maximum import tariff was more than three times higher than Mexico's (65% vs. 20%) in 1994 after having been roughly equal in the mid-1980s (105% for Brazil in 1987 vs. 100% for Mexico in 1985) (126). When many developing countries faced roughly similar (though not identical) international constraints after 1982, why did their patterns of trade liberalization vary significantly? Why did Mexico open its borders so much faster, so much more dramatically?

International-level approaches often suffer from two central short-comings. One is that they frequently misconstrue external factors as exclusively constraining the options of policy makers. The other is that they are rarely incorporated into an interactive approach that traces the external and internal factors that together shape the policy-making process in complex ways. The developing countries may have faced similar circumstances since the early 1980s, but their policy outcomes depend ultimately on the manner in which these forces are transmitted through the domestic political system and policy-making arena (see Frieden 1995). Furthermore, external factors can also provide certain opportunities and political resources that can be mobilized, under certain conditions, to reshape and reconstruct the domestic political arena in which policy reform must always take place. In Mexico, for example, significant financial support from the United States and multilateral institutions such as the IMF and World Bank has gone beyond a mere constraining influence.[7] While constraining policy options through con-

---

6 See Villareal (1990) for an insightful comparison.
7 It can been argued, for example, that Mexico faces unique international conditions because it receives "special attention" from the United States. Offhand, it is not clear why such a relationship should necessarily lead to greater pressures for liberalization on Mexico, as an exclusive focus on the constraining influence of international factors might suggest. This kind of relationship could lead just as easily to more lenient treatment toward Mexico. If the U.S. government felt, for example, that Mexican trade liberalization would cause high levels of transitional unemployment and disaffection that could lead to political instability and high levels of illegal migration from Mexico to the United States, we might expect it to push against liberalization, or at least for a slower pace of liberalization. In fact, several

ditionality, such support can also provide important resources that can be mobilized politically to help facilitate the construction of the political coalitions necessary to carry out, implement, and sustain trade reform.

I take the role of such international factors as a starting point in an effort to analyze the trade policy coalition-building process. Exclusively international-level explanations of changes in trade policy are inadequate by themselves because they say very little about the actual mechanisms through which multiple external forces are translated into policy and are therefore unable to account for much of the variation in the responses of different countries to either similar or differing external conditions. External factors, therefore, may help provoke *some* sort of adjustment, but they do not necessarily dictate what it will look like, how thoroughly it will be implemented, or how successfully it will be sustained. These differences are better captured by supplementing the international-level variables with a focus on the dynamic, domestic-level factors that shape each country's individual response to external forces and with which such forces may interact to produce varying outcomes across a number of cases. These policy shifts require a deep social, economic, and political transformation that creates a winning coalition for liberalization.

If existing entrenched domestic interests weighed against reform, and if international forces cannot explain policy change, the question then becomes: How was a new domestic coalition of political support for free trade forged within this context? I identify the international and domestic politico-economic conditions under which certain types of political coalitions will (1) be constructed and (2) win. My approach focuses primarily on the impact of the interactive relationship between business and the state on trade policy coalition politics. This relationship, which has received little scholarly attention, has been central to the success of Mexico's trade reforms, especially in the implementation and consolidation phases. I apply this framework to the case of Mexican trade reform from the early 1980s to the early 1990s, placing special emphasis on the NAFTA negotiations of 1991–92. Over this relatively short period of time, a strong free trade coalition coupling public and private sector elites managed to take and consolidate control over the apex of the trade policy-making apparatus, guiding Mexico into the new world of North

international organization and U.S.-based economists did feel that Mexico proceeded too rapidly in liberalizing its trade regime in the mid- to late 1980s. Furthermore, external pressure on developing countries more generally is not always liberalizing. In the 1940s and 1950s, for example, certain U.S. big business interests sought to invest behind high tariff walls to serve domestic developing country markets and pushed their own government to support relatively mild forms of ISI in the developing world (Maxfield and Nolt 1990).

American free trade. A theoretically guided examination of these dynamics can also illuminate both the successes and failures of reform initiatives in a variety of other countries and issue areas.

THE STRUCTURE AND METHODOLOGY OF THIS BOOK

Chapter 2 puts forth the central argument on trade policy coalition building and delineates the essential causal relationships between international forces, domestic politics, coalitions, and trade policy outcomes. It then traces in greater detail the specific factors that explain the formation and relative strength of competing coalitions, focusing explicitly on the role played by business and state actors in different international contexts.

Chapter 3 examines the unique structural power relationship between business and the Mexican state. Because of its control over large amounts of investment resources, the business community has a distinct (from other social actors) set of relations with government policy makers, but one that varies over time and under different conditions. This chapter traces the evolution of these relations from the early 1970s to the early 1990s.

Chapter 4 addresses the early phases of trade policy reform in Mexico, from the aborted attempt to join the GATT in 1979–80, through the initiation of reforms in 1985, to the acceleration of liberalization in the 1987–88 Economic Solidarity Pact stabilization program. It charts the balance of power between competing trade policy coalitions and traces the initial weakness and later the greater strength of a nascent free trade coalition between young, foreign-educated state technocrats and a new class of business elites. This group would lay much of the groundwork for the NAFTA negotiations.

Chapter 5 examines the NAFTA negotiating teams in detail from the perspective of business-state coalition politics. The negotiations helped to consolidate the power of the free trade coalition within both the public and private sectors. Within the state, free traders took over several remaining bastions of traditional opposition to free trade, including the Ministry of Trade and Industrial Development, which coordinated Mexico's NAFTA negotiating teams. The business community organized itself institutionally to consult formally with the government during the negotiations; this process accentuated other tendencies that favored the largest, most internationally integrated firms.

Chapter 6 assesses the role of the private sector's different elements during the negotiations themselves. The establishment of a formal alliance between big business and the state helped consolidate the power of the free trade coalition and enabled it to assert control over the negotiations as well as a wider range of macroeconomic policy issue areas. A case study of the automotive industry highlights these trends.

Chapter 7 reconsiders the utility of the book's theoretical approach in light of the evidence presented in the previous chapters. More specifically, it charts the evolution of the influence of various causal factors over time, and assesses their relative degrees of explanatory power. It also conducts a brief comparison with Argentina, Brazil, and Chile, three other important Latin American countries with varying experiences with trade reform, in order to provide greater empirical leverage with which to assess the Mexican case and the importance of coalition politics. The chapter and book conclude with an assessment of the practical impact of trade policy coalition politics in Mexico and prospects for future economic and political opening.

This study's methodology is eclectic. The overall approach is a qualitative one that relies on several different Mexican and non-Mexican data sources, including public and private sector statistics, press reports, business and government documents and publications, and approximately fifty interviews, mostly with Mexican government and business leaders.[8] The purposes of this multifaceted methodology are, first, to use the most appropriate method for each specific task; and second, to test the argument with as many different types of data as possible in order to provide a more thorough examination of the process of trade opening in Mexico and of my argument's ability to explain that opening.

CONCLUSION

International factors alone cannot explain Mexico's move toward free trade that has been formalized in NAFTA. Along with domestic-level variables, however, they can help us understand how and why the balance of interests within the policy-making apparatus shifts to favor certain kinds of trade policies. Historically, vested interests within both the public and private sectors in Mexico had successfully opposed trade opening. But partly as a result of changes in international and domestic political and economic conditions, the relationship between the business sector and the state in Mexico changed in the 1980s and 1990s in such a way that free trade became not just a possibility, but a political and economic reality.

---

8 To promote maximum candor, all interviewees were granted anonymity. All interview responses are therefore cited in the text in a manner that is meant to provide information on the respondent but also to protect his or her identity. All respondents were told that their names would appear in a list of interviewees, which appears in the Appendix.

2

Coalition Politics and Free Trade

INTRODUCTION

Political coalitions make policy, and state and social actors form coalitions within a given international context. Coalition politics links economic policy to state institutions, society, and the international system. The relations among each of these aspects of contemporary political economy are interactive and dynamic, constantly shaping and reshaping one another over time. I place coalition politics at the center of this web, as the political mechanism through which the international system, the state, and society help determine trade policy outcomes. Of course, these and other variables also exert their own, independent influence outside of their role in coalition politics. But focusing on their interactive impact helps sort out many of the complex causal paths linking various political economy factors to trade policy that have yet to be untangled, both conceptually and empirically (see Hall 1995). One goal of this book is therefore to explore the critical role played by political coalitions in economic policy making, and to delineate the most important factors that determine the patterns of formation and relative strength of competing coalitions and the causal relations among these factors.

Figure 2.1 presents a schematic portrayal of this conceptual mosaic. Coalitions are a critical intervening variable, both cause and effect. As effect, they result from the influence of international developments, social structures, and state institutions. Shifts in these indicators strengthen one or another coalition competing for power. As cause, coalitions control the actual process through which policy is made. The different interests and relative power balance between competing coalitions determine which policies will be implemented and successfully sustained. Finally, feedback loops exist between economic policy and the outlying variables over time. For example, trade opening or closure at one moment in

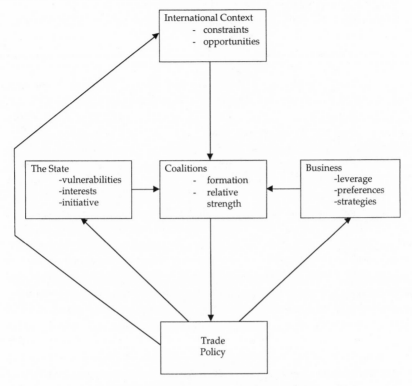

Figure 2.1. Trade policy coalition politics.

time can alter a country's social bases, state institutions, and place-ment within the international system (e.g., through international commitments, such as NAFTA or the GATT). These changes then induce realignments in the balance between competing coalitions, which in turn assert varying degrees of influence and control over future reforms. In sum, political coalitions represent a critical causal nexus between policy outcomes and the political economy forces that influence the reform process.

BUSINESS-STATE TRADE POLICY COALITIONS

Business and the State

Previous research has addressed many of the questions raised by this study, but has not yet answered them adequately. The process of Mexican trade liberalization has been covered,[1] but much of this literature tends to focus on either the international system or state actors and institutions as the principal impetus to trade opening. The role of business, and especially its relationship with the state, is seen primarily as an obstacle to reform, rather than an integral part of the process. Research on NAFTA has been abundant, but most works tend to analyze the U.S. perspective or to be more policy-oriented and issue-specific.[2]

Existing work on coalitions, trade policy, and business-state relations helps inform the Mexican case and raises interesting theoretical questions. Traditional economic theory and more contemporary political economy analyses trace the adoption of protectionist or open trade policies to the interests of competing producer groups,[3] but they typically focus on the direct influence of societal groups rather than on the interaction between those groups and different factions within the government. More general approaches to economic policy making pay more explicit attention to these relationships, but typically place greater emphasis on the influence of a given constellation of social actors on policy, rather than on the initial determinants of coalition behavior and change that subsequently guide policy.[4] Frieden (1991a), for example, examines the role of political lobbying of policy makers by business actors, especially those whose assets are relatively fixed and not easily liquidated in the face of deleterious economic policies or broader downturns in an economy.

Winters (1996, chap. 1) addresses many of Frieden's considerations of asset mobility, but does so from a more state-centric perspective that

1 See Kaufman (1988, 1989), Cronin (1994), and B. Heredia (1994, 1996) for good examples.
2 Just a few of the numerous examples include Baer (1991), Hufbauer and Schott (1992, 1993), and Baer and Weintraub (1994). Vega Cánovas (1991a, b, 1993), Davis (1992), Rey Romay (1992), Arriola (1994b), Blanco Mendoza (1994), Bulmer-Thomas, Craske, and Serrano (1994), C. Heredia (1994), Kessel (1994), Pastor and Wise (1994), Poitras and Robinson (1994), del Castillo (1996), Dávila Villers (1996), von Bertrab (1997), and Wise (1998) offer complementary analyses from the Mexican perspective.
3 Magee, Brock, and Young (1989) test competing economic theories of trade policy interests, while Rogowski (1989) examines the impact of trade liberalization on the political activities of different groups. Milner (1988) traces liberalism in France and the United States to the domestic political influence of internationally integrated firms.
4 See Gourevitch (1986) for an application of this approach to Europe and the United States, and Frieden (1991a) for a similar treatment of Latin America. Much like Milner (1988), Frieden's approach is a pluralist, demand-side one that discounts the role of the state: "My argument is that government actions are the response of policy makers to sociopolitical pressures brought to bear upon them by interest groups" (5–6). I address both the demand and supply sides of coalition building and policy making.

examines the varied preferences and political incentives of the government policy makers who face not only intense lobbying but also the possibility of destabilizing capital flight.[5] Maxfield (1990) adopts a similar approach to link shifts in Mexican macroeconomic policy making to the economy's reliance on capital inflows and susceptibility to capital outflows. These kinds of approaches to monetary and financial policies help fill in many of the gaps left by the pluralists, but their central insights provide more questions than answers about the politics of trade policy making.

These varied strands of literature suggest several pertinent questions for research. When, with whom, and under what circumstances are policy makers likely to form coalitions? Conversely, when and why do different groups within the business community seek to participate in policy coalitions? Finally, what determines which coalitions will succeed or fail?

My approach to these questions rests on three analytical pillars: (1) the *international* context; (2) *business* leverage, preferences, and strategies; and (3) *state* vulnerabilities, interests, and initiative. Business plays a distinctly subordinate role in most previous analyses of Mexico's economic reforms in the 1980s and 1990s. Facing tremendous pressures during the debt crisis (especially after the 1985 fall in oil prices), President Miguel de la Madrid and a small team of advisors used their control over key state institutions and agencies to adopt radical new trade policies beginning in 1985. Mexico's presidentialist and corporatist political system facilitated the power of free market government technocrats, whose rapid rise through the political hierarchy coincided with the collapse of Mexico's inward-looking, oil- and lending-based development strategy. The role of business, according to this general view, was one of grudging compliance and ineffectual opposition. State policy makers did indeed provide the critical leadership in initiating Mexico's liberalization. But we know very little about the behavior of the private sector, which must adapt to these changes and will ultimately determine the success of Mexico's export-led growth strategy. Furthermore, as Mexico's political system has opened up, the technocrats' monopoly over the economic policy-making process has begun to erode. The apparent continuation

---

5 Mahon (1996) and Schneider (1997) address similar issues in Latin America. See Lindblom (1977, 1982), Bates and Lien (1985), Frieden (1988, 1991b), Przeworski and Wallerstein (1988), Garrett and Lange (1991), Goodman and Pauly (1993), Silva (1993, 1996a) Andrews (1994), Garrett (1995), Cohen (1996), Frieden and Rogowski (1996), Haggard and Maxfield (1996), Keohane and Milner (1996), Pauly (1997), Schneider (1997), and Schneider and Maxfield (1997) for useful examples of this rich literature that provide general treatments and applications to other countries and regions.

and proliferation of democratic reform in Mexico will make it imperative that we better understand the political role of this critical, yet under-
researched actor.

The broader theoretical rationale for the focus on business is based on
that sector's potential political power derived from its unique position
in a capitalist economy. Because the business sector controls important
investment resources, it possesses capabilities unmatched by other societal actors (Lindblom 1977). Albert Hirschman's pioneering use of the
concept of exit, which he defines as "withdrawal from a relationship with
a person or organization" (Hirschman 1986, 78), captures many of these
notions.[6] Bates and Lien (1985) adapted these insights to demonstrate
the historical dependence of the state on the private sector as a source
of state revenue and an important component of the engine of economic
growth at the time of the formation of representative political institutions in Europe. They argue that nation-states were forced to grant broad
concessions to the owners of the most liquid assets in order to secure
their compliance with state taxation, lest they move those assets to a
lower-tax jurisdiction.[7] And as Winters (1996) and others have noted,
businesspeople can express their dissatisfaction with government policy
by exiting the economic system (e.g., by engaging in capital flight or disinvestment). This sends a clear message to government policy makers,
who may then respond by reforming policy.

The concept that the state is structurally dependent upon private capital
as the engine of investment, production, employment, and economic
growth is not new, nor does it respect rigid disciplinary boundaries.[8] This
dependence is structural because it is a characteristic of the capitalist
system itself, "not of the occupants of governmental positions nor of the
winners of elections" (Przeworski and Wallerstein 1988, 11). It results
directly from self-interested, atomistic private investment decisions. Collectively, these individual choices have tremendous public consequences in

6 See Hirschman (1970) for the original treatment.
7 This relates back to an interesting debate on Hirschman's (1970) original discussion of exit and voice, or political protest. Hirschman suggests that those actors
   with fewer exit alternatives are more likely to exercise the voice option in response
   to a decline in quality, which puts pressure on the firm (or organization, or state)
   providing the good to improve quality. This is consistent with Frieden's (1991a)
   assumption that government policy reflects the interests of the most effective lob-
   byists, who tend to hold fixed and concentrated assets. Bates and Lien (1985) argue
   that the controllers of mobile assets have less incentive to exercise voice but are
   much more likely to have their wishes respected by the tax-dependent state. The
   silent maneuverings of mobile asset controllers may be more forceful than the
   impassioned screams of fixed-asset holders, who have nowhere else to turn if their
   cries are ignored by the state.
8 Przeworksi and Wallerstein (1988) note these ideas are central to both Marxism
   and neoclassical political theory.

a capitalist economy (Lindblom 1982). Capitalists provide signals to policy makers by increasing or decreasing investment in response to government policy. If rates of investment fall, then production slows, employment decreases, and economic growth tapers off. These forces pressure governments to adopt policies that protect the interests of mobile investors. Authoritarian and democratic capitalist regimes alike are subject to this "investment imperative," as each regime's stability hinges on the continued growth of the capitalist economy (Winters 1996).

Winters (1996) presents a theory of structural power that centers on the related concepts of capital mobility and multiple jurisdictions. Investors unhappy with current policy have two options. First, they can engage in "simple withdrawal" of their investment resources, also sometimes referred to as a capital "strike" or "boycott," until a favorable change in policy is achieved. This strategy can entail high costs to the capital controller for the duration of the withdrawal.[9] It would be the only exit option in a single-jurisdiction world. Second, investors can employ a strategy of "relocation," where they redeploy their investment assets to other political jurisdictions. This option also imposes costs on investors, but profits in the new location can mitigate them (ibid., 22). Relocation also tends to be more permanent and therefore imposes greater hardship on the deprived jurisdiction. When more than one jurisdiction (such as a nation-state) exists *and* when capital can move relatively freely between them, the power of capital controllers within and across those jurisdictions rises. In a world of multiple jurisdictions, "greater mobility translates into greater power" (ibid., 17).

In contrast, labor does not enjoy the same degree of intrinsic power that business does (Milner and Keohane 1996). First, labor is generally not as internationally mobile as capital because of cultural and family ties that can be difficult to sever and the legal restrictions placed by many countries on labor immigration, especially from poorer nations. Although air travel makes labor migration easier, it is still much more time-consuming and costly than most capital transactions, many of which can be consummated at the press of a few computer keys. Second, any ability that labor might have to deprive the state of economic resources (through such measures as a general strike) is widely dispersed and subject to stubborn collective action problems. Whereas capital controllers undertake strategies of exit and disinvestment because it is in their individual – not necessarily collective – self-interest, a general labor strike would require the cooperation of a country's heterogeneous and numerous labor force (Lindblom 1977).

---

9 Winters uses the term "capital controllers" because those who control capital (e.g., mutual fund managers) do not necessarily own it.

In the Mexican context, the formal political organization and relative influence of the labor sector over economic policy have decayed in recent years (see Samstad and Collier 1995, Teichman 1996). Davis (1992) traces Mexico's trade opening to the restructuring of its corporatist political system and the relative decline of labor within the governing PRI and of the PRI itself (relative to the President). Pastor and Wise (1994) explain Mexico's free trade policy by adopting Rodrik's (1992b) notion of a "political cost-benefit ratio," the level of which was influenced in the Mexican case by institutional exclusion, the fight against inflation, asymmetric information flows, and policy makers' ideology. In particular, the potential opponents of free trade, including labor, were institutionally distanced from the decision. These developments helped lower the political cost of opening to the government enough to make it a viable alternative. At the same time, business, especially the managers of large, outward-oriented national and multinational firms, became much more active in economic policy making (Luna 1995, Valdés Ugalde 1996, Schneider 1997, Thacker 1999b). The exclusion of labor, which had been a subordinate political actor in the hierarchical corporatist political system even in the best of times, cannot adequately explain Mexico's dramatic turn toward free trade.[10] It is therefore necessary to look to other social actors, especially business, and their relations with the state to understand this opening more fully. For these reasons, and because the political exclusion of free trade's losing factions has been well covered elsewhere,[11] I focus my attention on the process of incorporation of the potential business winners from free trade into the policy-making apparatus.

Policy makers across the globe have been keen on shaping trade policies to attract increasingly mobile investment resources, and on publicly signaling their intent to do so. Mexican government officials have frequently used precisely this sort of rationale to explain the move to free

---

10 Labor's opposition to free trade is puzzling. The Stolper-Samuelson theorem predicts that the relatively abundant factor of production (labor) will support opening and oppose closure, while the opposite is true for the relatively scarce factor (capital). The lack of unanimous labor support might be better explained by the Ricardo-Viner-Cairnes model, which predicts a division within labor (and capital) according to whether it works in the import-competing or exporting sector (see Magee, Brock, and Young 1989). More explicit attention to the political dynamics of Mexican corporatism would be necessary to understand labor's broader opposition (albeit stifled) to liberalization (see Middlebrook 1995). A nuanced political economy approach, such as the one proposed here, is necessary to understand business's participation in trade policy.

11 In addition to the above-cited sources, see Kaufman, Bazdresch and Heredia (1994) and Heredia (1996). Shadlen (1997) offers a very useful analysis of the political exclusion of the small and medium firms, another important group of potential losers, from the economic reform process.

trade and especially the negotiation of internationally binding commitments such as the GATT and regional free trade accords. Academics lag far behind the politicians on these issues. Some economists, most notably Dani Rodrik (1989, 1991), have emphasized the critical role that policy credibility and commitment play in the private investment decisions that drive economic growth. Among others, Maxfield (1990), Mahon (1996), Winters (1996), and Schneider (1997) address the political impact of such decisions on development and macroeconomic and financial policy making. But the impact of these decisions on trade policy has not been carefully examined, despite the ready clues provided by high-ranking politicians in Mexico and elsewhere, and the common perception that such pressures exist.[12] Several studies have used international trade openness or closure as an indicator of globalization to explain other economic policy outcomes (see Garrett 1995), yet few have attempted to relate trade politics to trends in international capital markets and the reaction of domestic polities to them. Could the need to attract investment encourage policy makers to adopt trade policies that the owners of internationally mobile capital assets might favor? Exactly what kinds of trade policies might such actors prefer? How would politicians and businesspeople go about building the kinds of political coalitions necessary to effect policy change to reflect such interests? The Mexican case suggests that strong international pressures and state institutions can substitute for such coalitions in the initial stages of reform, but that coalitions play a crucial role in the subsequent sustainability and success of the new policies.

Existing research offers only limited guidance here. In particular, structure alone cannot take us very far. Because of its inherently atomistic nature, it is very difficult to see structure actually at work in any given policy-making episode. I therefore seek the connection between structure and outcomes in the more explicitly political processes of coalition building and policy making. Structure can help define interests and relative capabilities, but not necessarily how those interests and capabilities translate into effective political action that influences policy. Furthermore, as discussed below, a purely structural explanation of trade policy changes (i.e., one that required *no* actual political activity) would leave several questions unanswered and, if interpreted strictly, false predictions about the participation of business in trade policy coalitions. I incorporate a modified conceptualization of structure into a more broadly based framework of business-state trade policy coalition building and strength that addresses some of the limitations of this body of research.

12 One possible reason for this gap in the literature is the lack of a convincing structural theory of the trade policy preferences of different segments of the business community. I take up this problem in the section on business preferences and in Thacker (1997a).

Big Business, the State, and Free Trade

Trade Policy Coalitions

Following Katzenstein (1978) and Maxfield (1990), I adopt the term "trade policy coalitions" to denote the competing business-state alliances that join together leaders from the public and private sectors with similar interests to promote or oppose certain trade policies. Katzenstein employs the concept of a "policy network spanning both the public and the private sector" to help explain the variation between the economic policies of advanced industrial states (308). Meanwhile, the central players in Maxfield's story are the "Bankers' alliance" and the "Cárdenas coalition," two groups that link elements of the private sector to their allies within the state to compete for the direction of macroeconomic policy in postrevolutionary Mexico. Maxfield's (1990) general definition serves as a useful starting point: "Policy currents or alliances are defined as loose coalitions of public and private sector actors brought together by the desire to push for or against a particular policy" (29). I adapt these ideas to define trade policy coalitions as formal or informal alliances of public and private sector actors joined together by shared interests to support or oppose certain kinds of trade policies. Though trade interests are typically diverse and sometimes malleable, for simplicity's sake I define two principal competing alliances in trade policy: the "protectionist coalition" and the "free trade coalition." I hypothesize that trade policy reflects the character and relative strength of these competing policy coalitions that cut across and bring together different segments of the private sector and the state. When the protectionist coalition is stronger, trade policy is expected to be more restrictive. On the other hand, when the free trade coalition is more powerful, trade policy should be more open.

The obvious next tasks, to which this book devotes most of its attention, are to explain conceptually the formation, character, relative strength, and shifts of these two competing trade policy coalitions, and to trace their evolution over time in the Mexican case. Why do these groups form? Who are their members, and what do they want? Why and under what circumstances are some groups stronger than others? How can existing coalitions be torn apart and reconstructed to provide the kind of political support necessary to sustain effective trade policy reform like that which Mexico has undertaken?

THE INTERNATIONAL CONTEXT

International actors, such as the IMF, World Bank, and foreign creditor governments, can impose heavy constraints on policy options through the use of conditionality in their lending practices, the application of their technical expertise, and the imposition of economic sanctions. Such pressures can alter policy makers' political calculations of the relative benefits of different policies and even effectively exclude some from consideration. Much less commonly recognized in studies that emphasize the influence of international forces are the potential opportunities that the international context presents. General market conditions, the openness of the international economy, and the financial support offered through lending packages and capital flows can also offer the recipient governments politico-economic resources that can be used, under the right domestic circumstances, to help construct political coalitions to carry out policy reform. The relative weights of international constraints and opportunities depend on a country's location in the international system and the ability of domestic actors to capture and channel international forces.

International Constraints

A context of deep economic crisis like the developing countries experienced in the 1980s enhances the power of foreign creditors. Faced with burdensome balance of payments deficits and no private source for financing those deficits, a debtor government is often forced to turn to multilateral agencies and foreign governments for short-term balance of payments support. In turn, these actors typically condition their loans on the attainment of certain economic policy objectives by the recipient government. This conditionality constrains the choices of developing country policy makers. Desperate for external financing in a context of economic crisis and unfavorable private international credit markets, these governments would appear to have little choice but to adopt the market-oriented reforms requested by these international actors.[13]

These kinds of forces have clearly operated across the developing world since the 1980s, and in the Mexican case in particular. Mexico received several short-term adjustment and stabilization loans from the IMF, as well as a pair of Trade Policy Loans from the World Bank in 1986 and 1987. These kinds of loans typically specify certain policy goals that the borrower must attain before the next tranche of credit is released. If a borrower did not reach these goals, it would be cut off from both official and private sources of international credit after losing the "seal of approval" of the international financial institutions (IFIs). Foreign governments, especially the United States, often play a key role here. In the Mexican bailout of 1982-83, for example, the U.S. govern-

---

13 Some of the most useful examples of works that consider the constraining influence of external factors include Kahler (1989, 1992) and Stallings (1992).

ment negotiated a package with the IMF, the Mexican government, and Mexico's private creditors in which those creditors would agree to provide additional funds to Mexico in exchange for the IMF's participation in the program and its certification of the Mexican government's policy reform efforts. While such factors can certainly be exaggerated (see Kahler 1992), and while there are significant conceptual and empirical problems with some of these arguments (see Chapter 1), the influence of these forces is widely considered to constrain severely the options of economic policy makers across the developing world.

International Opportunities

Not all international level factors constrain uniquely. Funding from IFIs and foreign governments and the position of a state in the international system can also provide opportunities and resources that policy makers can mobilize in support of the process of trade reform. In addition to the constraining impact of policy conditionality, the lending programs of the multilateral agencies and foreign governments provide crucial financing that can ease the redistributive pain of policy reform, help court winners, and appease losers. In the case of the World Bank's 1986 and 1987 Trade Policy Loans, for example, the Bank gave credit to the Mexican state to facilitate the difficult process of structural adjustment, the conversion of nontariff barriers into tariffs, and the overall lowering of tariffs across the board. This enabled the government to accelerate the 1985 liberalization program with greater financial resources at its disposal. In conjunction with a sharp devaluation of the Mexican peso, these resources helped undercut some of the political opposition to trade opening (see Lustig 1998).

The relative position of a state in the international system explains some of the cross-national differences in trade policy reform at the international level. In the case of Mexico, its unique position as a large debtor nation abutting the United States comes into play here. When Mexico first entered into crisis in 1982, its status as one of the two (along with Brazil) most heavily indebted developing countries in the world, and its special relationship to the United States led the U.S. government to coordinate a special package of debt support in tandem with the IMF and Mexico's private creditors (Kraft 1985). In subsequent instances of debt restructuring or reduction (e.g., the Brady Plan), Mexico was often the first country to receive a package. Mexico was also the World Bank's second-largest client and the U.S. Export-Import Bank's largest (Williamson and Haggard 1994, 566). There is no better example of this "special relationship" than the events that unfolded in the aftermath of the Mexican peso crisis of December 1994. In response to the free fall of the value of the peso, President Bill Clinton pushed through a multi-billion-dollar aid package to support the Mexican currency in early 1995, drawing the ire of the new Republican majority in Congress for his discretionary and unprecedented use of the Treasury Department's Exchange Stabilization Fund to support a foreign currency (see Roett 1996). These packages each posed stringent policy conditions on the Mexican government, but they also provided it with relatively greater resources than other countries.

Another aspect of a country's international position is geographic: its proximity to large export markets. Easy access to foreign markets can provide incentives for export-based platforms. Because it shares a 2,000-mile border with the United States, Mexico faces relatively lower transportation costs to export to the world's single largest market than do other developing countries. The potential payoff for a transformation to an export-oriented model of development was therefore relatively greater in the Mexican case. Of course, Mexico's geographical position has not changed in recent years. This geographical constant alone cannot explain Mexico's shift. This opportunity was always there; why did Mexico wait until now to take advantage of it?

The role of economic crises can help answer these questions. Apart from helping to open the political space necessary to carry out trade reform, crises can also encourage certain activities and discourage others. In a context of domestic recession, the greatest opportunities lie not in the domestic but in foreign markets. Mexico needed an open trade regime to make the transformation away from the domestic and toward the more promising and consumption-driven foreign markets, especially that of the United States. An increasingly more export-friendly international context in which the barriers to the entry of most imported goods in the developed countries were relatively low also encouraged reform.[14] In sum, Mexico faced a relatively more open international trade regime, bleak prospects of significant growth in a closed domestic market, and special access to the largest national market in the world.

In contrast to the 1970s, when Mexican policy makers allied with loose-credit international bankers during the petrodollars lending boom, in the 1980s context of economic crisis and loan conditionality Mexico's economic policy makers shifted their international alliances toward the representatives of the IMF, World Bank, and U.S. government. While a certain portion of this shift can be attributed to the external constraints generated by the debt crisis and the global economic recession, part of it can also be traced to the international opportunities that Mexico

---

14 Certain sectors, such as agriculture and textiles, continued to be exceptions to this rule.

enjoyed in the areas of external support for structural adjustment, position in the international system, and the relatively greater economic returns to export activities during this time.

International context helps us account for some of the variation in policy responses between certain countries. But it is domestic political factors that determine policy makers' reaction to international constraints and their ability to mobilize the resources provided by international opportunities to form winning coalitions for reform. The impact of international forces depends on the nature and strength of domestic political institutions and the organization and political capacities of different societal groups. In the Mexican case, certain international actors associated with the IMF and World Bank served as important allies to a small group of technocrats within the Bank of Mexico (central bank) to sponsor and initiate the process of trade reform in 1985. But a solid coalition of support was still needed to help solidify the reforms and make them politically viable. The role of business in forming such coalitions is critical.

THE BUSINESS SECTOR

The business side of Mexico's trade story has received little analysis compared with its international and statist aspects. This case suggests that state policy makers, in conjunction with international pressure and allies, can undertake dramatic reform in the short term without a significant base of political support (see Chapter 4). I argue, however, that after the initial adoption of reforms, their implementation and consolidation requires the creation of a strong coalition of support amongst the new policies' potential winners. The economic and political factors that promoted the creation of such a coalition, which ultimately led to the successful consolidation of Mexico's free trade policies, have received scant scholarly attention. My approach differs from international and statist accounts less in its interpretation of the original instigation of reform efforts than in its emphasis on the importance of the construction of a strong alliance between state and business leaders to carry the reforms through the late 1980s and early 1990s.

The business sector represents a vital source of potential coalition partners to state policy makers. In the Mexican case, existing business-state coalitions at the beginning of the 1980s did not favor free trade. I argue that both internationally and domestically induced changes within the business sector alter the landscape of potential allies available to state policy makers and encourage certain types of coalitions over others. A complete analysis will require a parallel consideration of the state, which I undertake in the next section. In addition to the state's own autonomous role, government policy helps redraw the distributional map of the business community to favor certain potential coalition partners over others. But first I address the following questions: Which segments of the business community offer the greatest potential influence to state policy makers as possible coalition partners? Which groups within the private sector would be expected to participate most actively in different coalitions? What tools do different groups within business have at their disposal for pressuring the state to adopt favored policies? Which are more effective?

I divide the business community's participation in trade policy coalitions into three related aspects. The first is the private sector's overall structural leverage vis-à-vis the state. This touches on one half of the equation of the structural power relations between business and the state (the other half taking up the state's susceptibility to business pressures). Using Hirschman's (1970) language, what influences the effectiveness of the exit strategy? When, why, and under what conditions is the threat of business exit successful or unsuccessful in extracting concessions from the state?

Second, business participation in trade policy coalitions depends on the internal balance of forces within the private sector. We can measure this balance along several dimensions. For the purposes of this study, the most relevant distinctions relate to the size, sector, and asset mobility of different groups within the private sector, and shifts in the relative weight of each group within the overall business community. I hypothesize that those groups within the private sector whose relative weight in the economy grows over time tend to make more attractive and influential alliance partners than those whose influence is on the wane. The participation of the "winners" of this internal rebalancing in a given coalition increases its relative power.

Third, business participation is also related to the political and economic strategies that the private sector engages in to attempt to influence policy and participate in its formulation and implementation. Some of these strategies are structural in nature and correspond roughly to the notion of exit. Others are more purely political and fall under the general category of voice, which Hirschman defines as "any attempt at all to change, rather than to escape from, an objectionable state of affairs ... known sometimes also as 'interest articulation'" (1970, 30). Still other strategies combine both exit and voice, a possibility not acknowledged in Hirschman's original framework. Such strategies are partially related to the first two factors mentioned above (the leverage and internal makeup of the private sector) in that those groups that tend to be favored by the first two factors often tend to possess more effective pressure strategies as well. But there are also other, more analytically autonomous pressure strategies that affect the process of trade policy coalition building.

Business Leverage

The structural leverage of mobile capital controllers vis-à-vis state policy makers varies according to the international mobility of capital that a given country faces. It is important to note that not all countries face the same levels of international capital mobility (Cohen 1996), as some of the talk surrounding the globalization debate would seem to imply (cf. Rodrik 1997). Countries' locations in the international economy, their domestic asset bases, and their macroeconomic policies contribute to a fairly wide differentiation among the levels of international capital mobility they face. Leverage should also not be confused with power. Leverage refers to the tools or means at one's disposal, while power is the ability to shape others' behavior. I define leverage as the ability of one actor to exert pressure on another. The structural leverage of business is the capacity to exert pressure that derives from the private sector's control over investment resources. Power, or the ability to control policy outcomes, is a relational concept that takes into account the state's vulnerability to other actors' leverage. For an actor to have potential power, the state must be susceptible to its pressure strategies. This vulnerability, which I treat below, can be structural, electoral, or both.

In general, higher levels of international capital mobility facing a country give greater leverage to the business sector, primarily to the holders of the greatest number of mobile capital assets (Milner and Keohane 1996). Any strategy of exit necessarily imposes costs on the user. These initial costs can be prohibitive, even if the venture promises to be profitable in the future. Anything that might lower these costs makes the prospect of engaging in such a strategy more attractive to investors. Increases in the international mobility of capital lower the costs of exit and make asset relocation more lucrative. This makes exit a more effective strategy *even if it is not used*, because the threat of exit becomes more credible.[15] Thus, policy makers should pay greater attention to the interests of the controllers of mobile capital assets when the level of international capital mobility facing the country rises. These investors should also become more attractive as coalition partners.

The logic of this argument is straightforward, but it appears to contradict a basic insight of economic theory. The opening of international

---

15 One of the most important characteristics of structural power is that it need not be exercised to have an effect. The corollary to this is that it is also often difficult to measure, which is one of its limitations as an explanatory variable.

capital markets would actually be expected to *lower* the bargaining power of capital versus the state in capital-scarce countries, all else being equal. The initial returns to capital should be higher in capital-scarce countries than in countries where capital is relatively abundant. Capital market opening should then increase the bargaining leverage of the capital-scarce country's government as potential investors compete for access to the higher returns now available in those countries. This competition should diminish the structural leverage and relative attractiveness of existing mobile asset holders as coalition partners.

Despite the weight of economic theory (e.g., the factor-price equalization theorem) backing it, this is not a commonly held view. I argue that in this case common wisdom is correct, but for largely unrecognized reasons having to do with the dynamics of investor perceptions and behavior. We can reconcile the intuitive capital mobility argument and traditional economic theory by broadening the definition of the preferences of investors and policy makers. Most crucially, the expected returns to capital in a given country should be discounted by a figure that captures the effects of political risk inherent to a given country, as well as a general risk aversion factor for investors (see also Alesina and Perotti 1993). Such a relationship might be expressed in equation form as

$$R_k^e = pr R_k \qquad (2.1)$$

where for any single country the left side of the equation represents the expected risk-adjusted returns to capital. On the right side, p is a decimal between zero and one that captures investors' perceptions of the probability of the maintenance of a favorable investment climate, which depends on such factors as political stability and the policy responsiveness of government officials. r is a decimal between zero and one that captures the innate willingness of investors to accept risk. R_k represents the "objective" returns to capital, political risk notwithstanding (e.g., real interest rates). Expected returns to capital, and therefore the relative bargaining position of mobile asset holders with the state, are a partial function of the political and policy environments of a given country, as well as the willingness of investors to take on that risk.

Lower levels of p and r lower expected returns to capital, which can undermine a theoretical gain in bargaining power for the state. This discussion sheds light on a long-standing puzzle in international economics. As international barriers to capital movements fall, objective returns to capital should converge. Despite growing levels of international financial integration and flows in recent decades (see Chapter 3), such factor-price convergence has not occurred (Osler 1991). I argue that one reason for this anomaly is the effect of political risk on investor perceptions and capital flows.[16] At the nominally low levels typical of a capital-scarce developing country like Mexico, p and r could conceivably lower expected returns to capital below that of a relatively capital abundant – but politically stable – country. The only way for a government to counter this tendency would be to alter p and R_k, since r is a characteristic of the investors themselves. State policy makers could undertake measures such as interest rate hikes in an attempt to raise R_k directly to compensate for the downward pull of p and r. Conversely, they could make efforts to raise p, either by increasing political stability (a rather difficult short-term option), or by crafting compensatory policy measures in other realms, such as fiscal, exchange rate, and trade policies, that improve the overall policy environment and make investing more lucrative.

A good part of political risk relates to the stability and content of basic macro- and microeconomic policies. Reforming the policy environment can thus alter the value of p and therefore of Equation 2.1 and make it relatively more (or less) attractive for mobile capital holders to channel their investment resources toward that country. At the same time, the state is competing against other similarly endowed countries that may have more or less stable political and policy environments and that are likely to undertake similar efforts to attract increasingly mobile investment. In the end, any possible increase in bargaining power for the state in a capital-scarce country is often mitigated by policy instability. The increase in the international mobility of capital and the resulting increased competition between states for investment could be expected to lead, contrary to mainstream economic logic, to an increase in the bargaining power of mobile capital controllers vis-à-vis the capital-scarce and politically unstable state that may now feel compelled to provide a more favorable policy environment.[17] In other words, states often have to undertake specific policy concessions in order to raise the risk-adjusted expected rate of return to capital above that of other countries and attract internationally mobile investment resources.

Returning to the question of business leverage, the level of international capital mobility facing a country depends on both international and domestic factors. The global level of international financial integra-

16 If we had a reliable measure of R_k^e trends toward factor-price convergence might be more apparent.
17 Following this logic, the biggest winners should be the governments of those countries that measure high in both country variables on the right side of Equation 2.1: politically stable, capital-scarce countries. This is a very rare and often fleeting case. Recent possible examples might include South Korea and Taiwan until the late 1990s and Chile in the early to mid-1990s. A developed country, *ceteris paribus*, would be expected to have a higher p, but a lower R_k, since it usually relatively capital-abundant.

tion affects the ability of all investors to move capital resources across national boundaries. Patterns of international financial integration are related in part to changes in technology and to the evolution of the international monetary regime. Technological advances in transportation and communications have dramatically lowered the transaction costs of moving capital. For example, financial capital can be transferred virtually instantaneously via satellite from Mexico City to Tokyo, from Bangkok to New York. In the international monetary system, the Bretton Woods principle of free convertibility of currencies, along with flexible exchange rates and decreases in exchange controls and financial regulation across the globe since the end of Bretton Woods in the 1970s, have also served to integrate international financial markets (cf. Maxfield 1990, Winters 1996). According to Frieden, international financial integration should enhance the economic and political leverage of investors generally:

The 1980s may have indeed seen a secular shift in response to increased capital mobility, in which governments all over the world were forced to provide more attractive conditions for capitalists. . . . Inasmuch as this effect holds, increased financial integration implies an across-the-board, lasting increase in the social and political power of capital (Frieden 1991b, 434).

But these effects are not identical in every country, for the nature of capital itself and of local capital markets also influences its mobility (Cohen 1996). If these effects were indeed uniform, we would expect to see similar levels of business structural leverage everywhere. But the structural capacities of investors to pressure the state also depend on the mobility of their actual assets and on the development of the domestic capital markets through which they may be traded. Frieden (1991b) differentiates between three broad categories of capital, in descending order of mobility: financial capital, equity capital, and firm- or sector-specific capital. Following Frieden, Winters (1996) distinguishes between two general types of capital: liquid (finance and portfolio capital) and fixed (direct investment). The most liquid assets are financial capital, defined as money and money-like assets. These assets are by definition liquid, and, barring exchange controls and high transactions costs, mobile.[18] Next are portfolio assets, which I define as assets invested in equities and bonds. Portfolio assets can help to make a firm's overall assets relatively more liquid as the securitized assets of a firm's less liquid underlying "hard" assets can be much more easily traded, *if* there are well-

18 Liquidity and mobility are not coterminous. Liquidity allows one to shift assets from one activity or unit to another, while mobility refers to the ability to move assets from one political jurisdiction to another. Mobility usually requires liquidity, but liquidity does not necessarily confer mobility.

developed markets for such assets. For example, an investor who owns a controlling share of a company can liquidate her assets much more readily if they are securitized and there is a strong portfolio capital market. By contrast, an investor whose assets are tied up in a specific firm that is not publicly traded and whose assets are relatively more "fixed" has less flexibility. There is generally less of a market for such assets, so they are normally much less liquid than either financial or portfolio assets.

In a context of a permissive international environment (i.e., a financially integrated one), policy makers in a country rich in liquid capital assets would on average be expected to feel more pressure to ally with mobile capital controllers than would their counterparts in a country with relatively greater fixed assets because liquid assets can be more easily transferred into more internationally mobile forms of capital. Much of the mobility of a country's capital assets has to do with the extent of its exchange controls and the nature and level of development of its capital markets. First, unless the relatively free conversion of national currency is permitted, even the holders of liquid assets will have difficulty converting them into other currencies in order to relocate them abroad. In other words, in the face of strict exchange controls those liquid assets will not be internationally mobile. Second, a country with thin, poorly developed financial and portfolio capital markets is likely to have a relatively less internationally mobile capital asset base than a country with strong markets. For example, an investor holding stock in a Mexican company can sell shares on the open market and then transfer the assets to other activities or to other countries only if there exists a strong portfolio capital market.

The Internal Makeup of the Business Sector

Among the many divisions that exist within the business community two are especially relevant to trade policy coalition politics. The first has to do with the relative attractiveness of different segments of the private sector as coalition partners, and the second is rooted in the trade policy interests of different private sector groups. The relative attractiveness of different segments within business is closely related to the structural leverage of the private sector and the different groups within it, while the focus on trade policy interests touches on a wider array of issues.

The attractiveness of a given private sector actor as a potential coalition partner depends on her relative degree of structural leverage. When barriers to capital movement fall, political and economic influence accrues to the holders of the largest amounts of the most mobile assets. Segments of the business community will see their leverage increase as a result of changes in capital mobility, while others may suffer, at least in relative terms. For example, the holders of liquid capital assets are best situated to take advantage of the benefits of international capital mobility because their assets are more easily transferred or relocated. All else being equal, the more mobile capital assets that one possesses, the more attractive one should be as a potential trade policy coalition partner.

The primary consideration in determining trade policy interests is a sectoral one: Is production import-competing or exporting? What is the overall balance between these two sectors (see Shafer 1994, 1997)? The sectoral distribution of an economy is difficult to measure. Fortunately, Mexico's economic geography provides a reasonable proxy. Businesses in the northern part of the country tend to be both much more oriented toward the United States and international economies (in terms of both inputs and outputs) and relatively independent of state protection, control, and patronage. Firms in the center of the country near the Mexico City metropolitan area have historically depended more heavily on the domestic market and state protection. Developments that favor businesses in one region over another also often shift the overall balance of forces within business toward one type of activity or another. This causes the relative strength of each trade policy coalition's constituency to shift.

Traditional economic theory makes no predictions about the influence of size and mobility on a firm's trade policy interests. I argue that these considerations can also affect the internal distribution of trade policy interests within the business community. (This implies an interactive relationship between trade policy interests and structural leverage.) The controllers of large, mobile capital assets on average may be relatively more likely to favor free trade and therefore to sympathize with the free trade coalition. Generally speaking, the holders of the largest and most mobile assets should be better able to adjust to trade liberalization. Size itself can generally make liberalization easier to swallow because the costs of adjustment often weigh relatively less heavily on large firms than on small ones (Winters 1996). But inferring policy preferences strictly based on size alone can be difficult. Most scholars support the notion that the larger industries should be more adaptable to economic opening (see, for example, Maxfield 1989a), but Luis Rubio claims that in Mexico the "small and medium-sized firms, in spite of their declarations to the contrary, are actually much better at adapting to and surviving in a competitive environment" (Rubio 1988, 39). Certainly, there are many protectionist large firms in Mexico. However, the most important exporters (and importers) are almost exclusively large firms, as evidenced by the annual lists of the most important exporters and importers published by the magazine *Expansión*. In other words, not all of the large firms are pro-free trade, but nearly all of the most important exporters and importers are large firms. By contrast, the smaller firms tend to rely more heavily on state protection and to produce for the domestic market. Very few of them have extensive ties to the international economy.

These notions are consistent with and build upon some of trade theories associated with the "new international economics" (Krugman 1986), which attempt to go beyond the logic of comparative advantage associated with a Ricardian, Stolper-Samuelson, Heckscher-Ohlin vision of the world to explain trade patterns and make policy recommendations. A purely comparative advantage theory of trade policy interests would make no predictions about the policy preferences of large versus small business. Stolper-Samuelson, for example, would predict that all capitalists, regardless of size or sector, would be expected to oppose free trade. Their production would be expected to decline as the economy specializes in the labor-intensive products in which it has a comparative advantage and imports displace the capital-intensive sector. The Ricardo-Viner-Cairnes model would instead classify different business concerns into either the import-competing or exporting sector, again without regard for size or mobility (Magee, Brock, and Young 1989).[19] I adapt some of the concepts associated with new international trade theory that attempt to explain some of the anomalies not accounted for by the theory of comparative advantage (e.g., intraindustry and intrafirm trade, and trade between similarly endowed countries). Such theories borrow from the field of industrial organization and focus on several other factors affecting international trade, including the role of oligopolies, learning curves, and increasing returns to scale (Gilpin 1987). Many of these arguments can be extended to explain the trade policy interests of large versus small producers. They allow us to make unambiguous predictions about the trade policy preferences of firms according to their size by linking the competitiveness of a particular business concern to such issues as economies of scale. According to these theories, the larger the scale of a firm's production, the lower its marginal costs will be and the more internationally competitive its product will be. Because they enjoy greater benefits of increasing returns and economies of scale, larger business enterprises should on average tend to favor free trade, while smaller firms should be more likely to favor protection because they face higher per unit costs.

Differences between types of capital assets also affect trade policy interests. The holders of liquid assets should be better situated to respond to the new market signals that result from a trade opening by liquidat-

19 See Thacker (1997a) for a more detailed discussion of these issues.

ing and redeploying their capital assets from a losing to a winning sector (again, assuming effective markets exist). A large portfolio investor, for example, would find it much easier and less costly to move assets from the import-competing to the export sector simply by trading equity shares on the stock exchange than would a small, single-shop industrialist, who must attempt the more difficult task of either competing with foreign competition or trying to liquidate what are likely relatively fixed assets. The holders of large, mobile capital assets therefore may enjoy competitive advantages under free trade and should thus be more likely to become members of the free trade coalition. Furthermore, large mobile asset holders tend to have more well-diversified asset portfolios, thereby lessening any potentially negative impact of a trade liberalization in a given sector or sectors on their overall position. Conversely, small, fixed asset holders located in the import-competing sector should be more likely to sympathize with the protectionist coalition because they tend to be less capable of adjusting to the new market signals associated with free trade. Factors that favor each of these groups also then favor the coalition to which they belong.

It should be noted that if capital were perfectly mobile, its holders could be expected to be fairly ambivalent with respect to trade policy. Capital should move wherever returns are highest, and there should be little incentive for its controllers to invest the time and energy to attempt to influence policy one way or the other. Despite recent trends, capital is of course still not perfectly mobile, but any increase in the international mobility of capital could still lessen the intensity of any mobile asset holders' policy preferences. This view neglects the constraining and opportunity-creating role of contextual variables. In other words, it does not take into account the basic underlying determinants of the relative returns to exporting versus import-competing activities. Conceivably, if returns were sufficiently high, the controllers of mobile capital assets could favor a policy of protection. In fact, it can be argued that this was the case in Mexico in the early postwar period, when multinational corporations invested large amounts of liquid capital resources in the Mexican economy to operate behind Mexico's high tariff walls and serve the domestic market (Maxfield and Nolt 1990). This kind of strategy worked well in the 1940s and 1950s, when several developing economies like Mexico's began to grow rapidly and offer rising levels of domestic demand for the products of multinational corporations, and when the external environment for export opportunities from a country like Mexico was unfavorable due to relatively high levels of global protection. By the 1980s, however, the Mexican economy was deep in crisis, and domestic demand offered little in terms of a potential market for the owners of internationally mobile capital assets. Meanwhile, global trade

Trade Policy Interests

		Protectionist	Free Trade
	Low	Weak member of Protectionist Coalition	Weak member of Free Trade Coalition
Leverage			
	High	Influential member of Protectionist Coalition	Influential member of Free Trade Coalition

Figure 2.2. Cross-cutting private sector cleavages and coalition membership.

barriers were a good bit lower after the Kennedy and Tokyo Rounds of the GATT and the opening of the Uruguay Round in 1986. The trade policy interests of mobile capital controllers in the 1980s and 1990s should therefore favor free trade because export activities offered the highest potential returns during this time.

In sum, an actor's structural leverage determines his attractiveness to the state as a coalition partner. The intensity of his trade policy preferences (related to his sector, size, and the mobility of his assets) determines his incentives to participate in trade policy coalitions. The direction of those interests (toward protectionism or free trade) determines in which coalition he will seek to participate. When an actor possesses high scores on both structural leverage and free trade interests, he is most likely to be included in a free trade coalition. By contrast, an actor who possesses significant structural leverage but whose interests favor protection is most likely to be incorporated into a protectionist coalition.[20] Actors with little structural leverage but clear trade policy interests will be members of each respective coalition, but not particularly influential ones. Figure 2.2 outlines four possible combinations

20 Note that because of the dual impact of asset mobility in helping to determine both structural leverage and trade policy interests, this scenario is somewhat less likely than the first, though not necessarily improbable. As noted above, the international context can modify the effect of asset mobility on trade policy interests.

along these two continua. Those actors who fall in the southeast quadrant should be the most influential members of the private sector in a free trade coalition, while those who fall in the southwest quadrant should become influential members in the protectionist coalition. Those who fall in the northeast and northwest quadrants will be relatively weak members of the free trade and protectionist coalitions, respectively. Those who fall in the very middle of the diagram will be moderately attractive as trade policy allies but will have ambivalent trade policy interests. Taken together, these considerations help explain both the shifting *identities* and relative *strength* of competing policy coalitions from the business perspective. But how does business attempt to secure a place in trade policy coalitions and influence policy?

Business Strategies

Business as a political and economic actor has multiple methods at its disposal for participating in trade policy making. As originally conceived by Hirschman (1970), the strategies of exit (silent withdrawal) and voice (political activation) are mutually exclusive. One either withdraws from an unfavorable situation by exiting, or remains engaged but exercises voice in an attempt to improve the situation. In Hirschman's view, exit is dominant because it is less costly than voice. If it is possible and feasible to exit, an actor will not normally need to activate voice. Anything that makes exit easier or more effective should undermine the use of voice by those who can exit. In other words, mobile asset holders should have less incentive to invest in changing political outcomes as mobility rises. Similarly, this structural leverage should lead, rather automatically, to favorable policy outcomes (see Mahon 1996). But in the Mexican case, the active participation of large mobile investors in policy making increased *along with* their structural power. Investors engaged in simultaneous strategies of exit and voice, of structural and political attempts to influence policy outcomes. Several observers have noted these patterns, but none have resolved their implicit logical contradictions.[21]

One reason for mobile asset holders to engage in direct participation (or voice) in the policy-making process relates to the role of communication and information. The policy response to investor decisions may not be completely automatic. At any given moment, government policy makers may be pursuing a wide range of economic policies that affect the controllers of mobile capital resources. It may often not be possible

---

21 For example, Schneider and Maxfield (1997, 20) argue that business "votes twice," once with its voice and again with its investment decisions, but they do not explore in detail the theoretical incentives to engage in both strategies simultaneously.

to discern the precise reason for business exit or relocation without direct communication between policy makers and business. Direct political participation that facilitated such communication would be complementary to a structural strategy if it clarified investor intentions and interests and made it easier for state policy makers to respond accurately to them.

Active participation in the policy-making process can also help mobile capital controllers capitalize on their greater structural leverage at any given moment over a longer time horizon. If capital controllers secure an active role in policy making when their ability to exert structural leverage is high, they may be able to extend some of that influence to periods when their leverage is weaker. Furthermore, the exertion of structural power may not always be less costly than direct participation in the policy process. Referring back to Equation 2.1, investors could increase the expected returns on their investments (or potential investments) by participating more actively in policy making to raise the level of policy responsiveness (or p). The ability to move elsewhere does not preclude mobile asset holders from seeking to increase their expected returns in individual countries. Firms may derive benefits from direct participation in the policy process that they cannot secure as easily through exclusively structural means.

The role of investor confidence and trust in the state also come into play in a trigger capacity (see Maxfield and Schneider 1997). As long as the expectations of private mobile capital controllers and state policy makers are reasonably congruent and stable, a structural logic of business participation may yield satisfactory results (as it did for much of the postwar period – see Maxfield 1989). If these kinds of asset holders remain reasonably confident that policy makers will not stray too far from a basic policy consensus, they may forgo a direct role in policy making and punish minor policy deviations with disinvestment and capital flight. As later chapters demonstrate, this was the pattern for much of the postwar period in Mexico, when business served as a more or less "silent partner" to the state. After the 1982 bank nationalization, however, many businesspeople felt that they could no longer trust the government to abide by this basic operating agreement, and during the 1980s and 1990s many of them began to seek out a more direct role in politics and economic policy making. This event triggered the political activation of many segments of the business community, which would now combine its exit and voice strategies to exert double-barreled pressure on the state.

Triggered in this manner, the effectiveness of voice and the participation of different factions of the private sector in trade policy coalitions depend on a series of factors. First, collective action issues favor the private sector's larger segments, who have more at stake and who are fewer in number (cf. Olson 1971, 1982). Thus, those groups whose structural leverage tends to be higher also often face fewer collective action problems in participating directly in trade policy coalitions. This condition can give them double sources of influence in the policy process. In contrast, those groups whose structural leverage tends to be lower – small firms with fixed assets – are normally more scattered and varied. They find it much harder to achieve the collective action necessary to participate in trade policy coalitions.

Similarly, organizational and institutional variables related to the size of firms condition their participation in policy coalitions. Smaller firms in general face greater logistical problems, or "transactions costs," in participating directly. Large firms, which often have specialists or even entire departments devoted to governmental relations and policy issues, can devote the time and resources necessary to participate in trade policy coalitions. Owners of small firms likely cannot afford to take time off from running the everyday operations of the business nor pay to hire someone to participate on their behalf because such costs would consume a much greater proportion of a firm's total revenues. These firms must therefore often depend on indirect representation, through the institutional channels of business chambers and associations, for example. Business organizations often represent a wide variety of interests, which undermines their ability to advocate zealously on behalf of any single firm or group of firms. Sectors and firms with more effective institutional representation can counteract these effects to a certain degree, but they are not likely to attain the kind of active, direct participation that is possible for the larger firms.

THE STATE

One hypothesis of this study is that policy makers are more likely to form coalitions with those private groups whose structural leverage is greatest, who gain the most in the internal rebalancing of the private sector, and whose pressure strategies are most effective. But the state itself is a key actor in the policy reform process. By no means should it be considered a passive receptor of international and societal pressures (cf. Evans, Rueschemeyer, and Skocpol 1985). Policy reform formally takes place within the confines of the state. Even the most forceful international and societal pressures must pass through the state, where they may be modified, circumvented, or manipulated. State policy makers exert direct impact on the process of policy reform, and the participation of different factions within the state in competing policy coalitions is crucial to their relative strength and success. Furthermore, state-centered actors can interact with business, intentionally or unintentionally reshaping the distribution and relative influence of potential private sector coalition partners in the process.

I divide the participation of the state in trade policy coalitions into three related spheres, organized parallel to the discussion of the business sector. First, the vulnerability of the state to pressures exerted by societal actors affects the manner in which it forms alliances with those actors. This vulnerability can be structural or electoral. Structurally, state leaders rely to varying degrees on mobile private investment as they seek to maintain power through the promotion of economic growth and employment. Electoral pressures and party competition can also threaten the position of established state leaders. The vulnerability of state leaders to these pressures influences the manner in which they build political alliances.

Second, the structure and balance of power of state institutions exerts a direct effect on policy and on the formation of policy coalitions. In addition, the political interests and institutional affiliation of different actors within the state help determine their policy preferences and coalition-building patterns. Actors within the state whose political influence is on the rise (often as a result of changes in the international context) tend to make more attractive coalition partners for the business sector.

Third, state actions affect the societal groups. The measures enacted by policy makers at one point in time affect the interests and relative strength of different groups within the private sector in the future. This alters the panorama of business preferences and capabilities available for future recruitment by state leaders as trade policy coalition allies. This relationship between business and the state is interactive and reciprocal. Business leverage, makeup, and strategies affect the identity and relative strength of the state's trade policy coalition partners, while state policies in turn modify some of those very same variables.

State Vulnerabilities

I start from a basic assumption that fundamental considerations of political power underlie the participation of the state and different factions within it in constructing coalitions with the private sector. I assume that state leaders want to maintain political power, which they can do through a variety of means. Likewise, threats to politicians come from various sources. One way in which state leaders respond to different challenges to their authority is by constructing coalitions with social actors. The susceptibility of the state to such pressures helps explain when, why, and with whom state leaders will seek to form alliances.

38

State vulnerabilities to societal pressures have both structural and non-structural elements. The structural vulnerability of the state is linked to the state's dependence on the private sector for investment. This variable captures the degree to which state policy makers are susceptible to the structural leverage exerted by the private sector. The state can also be vulnerable to electoral pressures and the dynamics of party competition. Even in a quasi-democratic political system such as Mexico's in the 1980s and early 1990s, these forces can threaten incumbent rule. The effects of structural and electoral variables can also either exacerbate or ameliorate each other, depending on their respective values, to increase or decrease the state's vulnerability. For example, structural factors can amplify electoral pressures through the effects of capital flight and disinvestment on economic growth and employment. A slow economy can weaken the electoral position of incumbent politicians. I argue that a more complete explanation of state vulnerabilities should combine both structural and nonstructural variables that take into account the political process through which coalitions are built. Much of the literature on structural power relations links structure directly to outcomes, paying little attention to the political mechanisms linking them. Studies that address both structure and process rarely link the two causally. Schneider (1997) argues that Mexico's faster pace of reform resulted from the fact that it had a deeper investment crisis and stronger social concertation mechanisms than Brazil. In addition to the independent effects of political institutions, I posit that the Mexican state's structural vulnerability is an important reason that it formally incorporated business into the concertation process of stabilization and reform in the late 1980s and early 1990s.

If business leverage is one side of the coin in business-state structural power relations, the state's structural vulnerability is the other. Examining the capability of business to exert structural leverage on the state does not by itself tell us how the state will react to such pressure. When and why will the state be more susceptible to the structural leverage of mobile capital controllers? When might policy makers be better able to resist it? International financial integration and capital mobility have been increasing over a period of many years. Why are policy makers more constrained by business interests in certain periods than in others? Even differences in the degree of mobility that different countries face cannot fully explain cross-national differences in responses to structural leverage. When and why is the state more or less *structurally dependent* on mobile capital controllers?

Politicians depend on a certain amount of societal support to retain power. This can occur through elections in a democratic system or through social quiescence in a more authoritarian system (provided that high levels of repression of social discontent are not a viable long-term option). One of the most important factors affecting mass societal support for a political regime is the overall level of economic well-being, which can be measured by the levels of economic growth, real wages, and employment. As growth rates fall, the state becomes more dependent on infusions of new investment to drive the economy. Another way of putting this is to say that *the marginal social utility of investment increases as the rate of economic growth declines.*[22]

Holding the level of economic growth constant for the moment, the principal determinant of the state's vulnerability to business pressures is its access to alternative investment resources (Winters 1996, 36). Put differently, the state's vulnerability to structural pressures depends on how well it can cope without business support, or with private disinvestment and capital flight. When the state has ample access to alternative sources of capital that it can use to foment employment and economic growth, it can pay less attention to the interests of private capital controllers. On the other hand, when a state finds itself in a financial squeeze with few options outside of the private sector, it becomes more vulnerable to the structural leverage of mobile capital controllers because the entire society's economic well-being depends more heavily on private investment.

Several factors affect a state's access to alternative investment resources. A country might possess specific attributes that afford policy makers control over alternative sources of investment capital and thus make it easier to resist the demands of private investors. In particular, policy makers can channel resources derived from valuable commodities, foreign lending, and nonconditional aid toward a variety of economic activities that may appease political opponents and solidify political support. Specific commodities, particularly oil, can provide this type of resource, if it is the state that administers them. In addition to Mexico, access to oil has altered the structural adjustment programs of Venezuela, Nigeria, Ecuador, and Indonesia (Haggard and Kaufman 1989). Inflows of private foreign lending can provide similar resources to the state, as

22 Note that the marginal *private* utility of investment (that is, to the investor) demonstrates the reverse relationship. As the overall level of economic activity slows, the returns to a new investment project typically fall due to decreased domestic demand. (I am grateful to John Sheahan for pointing this out.) This accentuates the power shift already under way, as the state becomes more dependent on private investment at precisely the moment when investors become less willing to invest. Investors producing for export, who would benefit from the lower labor costs that result from domestic recession and who produce for a much larger international market, face a different calculus. The relatively greater willingness of export-oriented interests to invest in the liberalizing economy also helps explain their greater attractiveness as coalition partners.

occurred in several middle-income developing countries in the 1970s. During such times, the private sector may actually become dependent on the state for credit allocation. Military and strategic considerations can also generate large amounts of bilateral aid for strategically located countries like India, Pakistan, and Egypt, which received almost $2 billion in military aid and grants following the Camp David accord in 1979 (Haggard 1985, 182–83). Mexico's special relationship with the United States has conferred similar benefits upon Mexico. Though it did carry conditionality, the most recent example of this was the 1995 peso bailout package that provided $20 billion in U.S. credits and an additional $27.8 billion in IMF and Bank for International Settlements (BIS) funds (Roett 1996, 39).

Second, external and domestic economic conditions also affect the state's access to different types of investment resources. International commodity prices have profound effects on countries whose exports are concentrated in a small number of commodities. During periods of high prices, the position of the party that controls those resources improves, while the inverse applies during periods of low prices. In the Mexican case, the oil price increases of the 1970s lowered the vulnerability of the state to pressures from private capital controllers,[23] while the collapse of oil prices in the mid-1980s had the opposite effect. Similarly, favorable external macroeconomic conditions, such as international interest rates, trends in global economic growth, and patterns of foreign lending can lower the state's vulnerability. Conversely, negative international conditions and external shocks would make a state more susceptible to the structural leverage of private mobile capital controllers.[24]

A good summary measure of national economic conditions is the status of public finances. When a government's fiscal burden is high, its ability to substitute its own resources for private ones is curtailed. The revenue side of the fiscal account can further compound these problems. In addition to oil revenues and foreign lending, if the tax base is not growing fast enough or if there are inadequate tax collection mecha-

---

23 The discovery of large oil reserves in a world of high petroleum prices was one of the principal factors behind López Portillo's rejection of GATT membership in 1980 (see Chapter 4).

24 Note that the terms capital controllers, business, the private sector, the business community, or any similar references in this study refer to both national *and* foreign investors. Any important differences between the interests and behavior of national and foreign firms are captured by the other variables. As far as the state is concerned, except for balance of payments considerations it seems to make little difference whether capital comes in from abroad or is of domestic origin. Apart from the use of foreign investment flows (or, for that matter, the repatriation of flight capital) to finance current account deficits, the primary advantage of foreign investment is that the pool of potential foreign investment is much larger.

nisms, the state will be less capable of taking up the slack for any short-falls in private investment. This problem can be especially severe in liberalizing developing countries, where tax collection mechanisms are often weak and ineffectual. In this institutional context, tariffs often provide an important source of fiscal revenue to the state. The lowering of tariffs in trade liberalization can exacerbate the fiscal vulnerability of the state.

Political pressures arising from party competition and electoral challenges can also make politicians more vulnerable to societal pressures and encourage them reconstruct their political coalitions of support to remain in power. Electoral challenges to politicians' political authority can in and of themselves inspire a coalition shift that may in turn encourage policy makers to enact changes in economic policy that better reflect the strength and identity of their new bases of support. I hypothesize that ideological affinity between government policy makers and opposition groups and practical power-sharing considerations shape politicians' reactions to these kinds of pressures.

In Mexico, growing political pressures resulting from the incremental gains made by the business-oriented National Action Party (PAN) over the course of the 1980s and the rapid strides made by the left-leaning National Democratic Front (FDN) in the 1988 elections jeopardized the PRI's sixty-year hold on power. PRI officials responded by forming an unofficial alliance with PAN leadership in which a greater number of PAN electoral victories would be recognized by the government in exchange for PAN support for constitutional reforms central to the Salinas government's broader political agenda. Meanwhile, the FDN and its successor, the Democratic Revolutionary Party (PRD), continued to complain about PRI-sponsored electoral fraud. Though the biggest electoral threat came from the left, the PRI shifted its electoral alliance to the right. This was largely because PRI and PAN leadership shared similar ideas about market-oriented reform, and because it allowed the PRI to make fewer political concessions to maintain power than if it had tried to appease the left.

The structural concerns highlighted previously also mediate the choice of electoral alliance partners. An important consequence of the government's response to these electoral challenges was to help foster the creation of a new alliance between state policy makers and those within the private sector who supported the PAN's calls for less state intervention in the economy. This new coalition provided political backing for the trade liberalization process already under way in Mexico and helped accelerate and deepen free trade policies in the late 1980s and early 1990s. In this sense, changes in trade policy are both cause and consequence of the dynamics of coalition formation and reconstruction.

Coalition Politics and Free Trade

State Institutions and Interests

The characteristics of state institutions and leaders exert relatively straightforward, direct effects on trade policy coalitions. The most important factors here are the balance of power among state agencies, the identity and interests of key policy makers, the degree of independence of the executive branch from judicial and legislative oversight, and the effectiveness of the state's organizational control over societal groups.

The balance between protectionist and market-oriented state agencies and the interests of their leaders guide state participation in trade policy coalitions. If protectionist agencies and bureaucrats control the key policy-making institutions, the state's contingent in trade policy coalitions will favor protectionism. Conversely, changes that empower free-market agencies and technocrats will strengthen the free trade coalition. In Mexico, a fundamental power shift from inward-looking developmentalist to free market financial-planning agencies in the 1980s helped break the hold of the protectionist coalition and created support within the state for the formation of a free trade coalition.

The role of political and economic ideas in economic policy making has received much attention.[25] Much has been made of the spread of neoliberal economic ideas across the globe, fostered by the influence of IMF and World Bank technocrats and the cross-fertilization resulting from the education of developing country policy makers in industrialized country universities. While the economic impact of ideas is an important part of the story of trade reform in the developing world, I assume that ideas do not possess any independent political power of their own. They must be captured and sponsored by politically influential people or organizations, in the domestic or international spheres (Schneider 1998). Economic ideas play a role, but only to the degree to which they find political representation in the policy-making process. The neoliberal ideas of trade reform in Mexico found political expression only once politico-economic conditions shifted so as to empower their sponsors in the Bank of Mexico, IMF, and World Bank. Furthermore, I argue that simple political sponsorship is not sufficient to sustain these ideas in policy. A minimum coalition of support must also be constructed around them.

The perspective of state institutions and leaders gains even more importance in the absence of effective judicial and legislative review of executive-led policy measures. An independent executive can grant policy makers great leeway in crafting reforms, especially in the initial phases

---

25 See Hall (1989), Sikkink (1991), Goldstein (1993), Goldstein and Keohane (1993), Domínguez (1997), Centeno and Silva (1998), and Golob (1999).

when the new policies have not yet generated sufficient interest group support. Corporatist control of societal groups can also enable policy makers to isolate a policy's losers and organize its winners. In the Mexican case, executive dominance insulated policy makers from sources of potential opposition from other branches of government. PRI control of the official union movement helped quell labor unrest. Mexico's business chambers law, which makes association with the relevant business chamber obligatory for all firms, served to contain the potential opposition of import-competing firms, particularly small and medium business.

State Initiative

The initiative of state policy makers in forming coalitions with different private actors, and the factors that determine the motivation for such alliances, are subtle but crucial ingredients in the formation and shifting of policy coalitions. The state often plays a less direct but potentially active role in promoting new socio-political alignments and forging coalitions with societal actors. For example, state policies can alter the internal makeup and balance of forces within business. This in turn changes the relative strength and availability of the state's potential private sector coalition partners down the road and the types of pressures that such actors can exert. In some cases, state policy can even *create* new organized constituencies with which it can later construct coalitions that eventually may carry out reform (Bates and Krueger 1993, 466).

These issues assume a prominent role in this account of Mexican trade opening. Partially as a result of state policies adopted in the 1980s, the internal makeup of the business sector began to shift in favor of its more outward-looking, big-business elements. In addition, early rounds of trade opening created a positive feedback loop that helped build greater support for subsequent reforms. These processes laid the foundations for the creation of a new coalition of support for free trade that had not existed previously. This new coalition expanded and fortified the political base upon which liberalization rested from a narrow group of political sponsors within the state to a more solid base of support that spanned across both the public and private sectors.

The most politically and economically successful and effective state policy makers tend to be those who align themselves with the more powerful elements of the business community, including those whose strength grows as a result of state policy. "Reform results when political movements secure sufficient backing from the reform-minded interests that they capture power and use their control over the government to impose reform programs" (Bates and Krueger 1993, 465). The ability of groups within the state to recognize opportunity and construct a strong free trade coalition with key members of the private sector is thus a critical ingredient in a successful transformation to free trade. Several factors affect the ability of state policy makers to forge these kinds of coalitions with powerful private actors. The institutional factors discussed above are especially important. For example, powerful state agencies and leaders are more likely to attract the support of private actors who want to cast their lot with a winning team. This is especially true in a patronage-based, hierarchical political system like Mexico's.

SOME CAVEATS

The approach outlined in this chapter is intended to take a first step in the formulation of a theoretically sound, generalizable, and convincing explanation of trade coalition politics. I do not, however, pretend to tell the entire story. I necessarily leave out a number of interesting variables and neglect many compelling arguments. For example, I say relatively little about the independent role of ideas and the international osmosis of neoclassical economic theory that has seemingly spread the doctrine of free trade from the classrooms of Harvard, MIT, and the University of Chicago to far corners of the world. Neither do I place great emphasis on the independent effects of political institutional variables on policy (apart from their role in coalition formation), or on the strategic impact of the formation of regional trade blocs across the globe. These and many other important issues have been dealt with elsewhere.[26] Although they are relevant to the problem at hand to one degree or another and will pop up at various points throughout the story, to include them all within the confines of the central analytical framework would undermine any theoretical cohesion it might possess and dilute the explanatory power of its central propositions. What I do attempt is to explain Mexico's free trade policy by incorporating international and domestic level variables into an analytical framework organized around business-state coalition politics. The answer to the question of how well such an approach actually performs is in the data.

CONCLUSION

Trade policy is formulated and implemented by trade policy coalitions that join together key members of the public and private sectors. Trade

---

26 For a discussion of the role of political institutions in Mexico, see B. Heredia (1994, 1996), and on the effect of the development of regional free trade areas, see Baer (1991).

policy itself reflects the relative power of the two competing trade policy coalitions. When the protectionist coalition is stronger, trade policy should be more closed; when the free trade coalition predominates, trade policy would be expected to be more liberal. The nature and relative strength of the two opposing coalitions is determined by the power dynamics associated with the participation of their various business and state constituent elements in varying international contexts. These dynamics are in turn a function of the relationship between business and the state and the formation of alliances between and across different groups within each. The international context offers both constraints and opportunities for trade policy reform, while changes in business's leverage, internal balance of forces, and pressure strategies modify the layout of the playing field where the game of coalition construction and reconstruction is played. At the same time, the state's structural and political vulnerabilities, institutional makeup, and initiative in helping to redesign the internal landscape of the business community determine the state's role in the formation of business-state trade policy coalitions.

Empirically, the protectionist and free trade coalitions in Mexico have reversed their fortunes in recent years. Historically, the protectionist coalition had long been the stronger of the two. Its predominance in the policy process kept Mexico closed to most imports for several decades, and any free traders, within both the state and the private sector, were exiled from any positions of real power in the trade policy making apparatus. (This is one reason why Mexico's turn to free trade was so initially surprising in terms of domestic politics.) Recently, however, circumstances in the international context and on both the business and state sides of the trade policy coalition equation have strengthened the free trade coalition and weakened the protectionist coalition. This, I argue in the following chapters, explains much of the success of Mexico's turn toward free trade since the 1980s.

3

Structural Power Relations Between Business and the Mexican State

INTRODUCTION

The structural power relations between business and the Mexican state shifted in favor of business in the 1980s and 1990s. Both business's structural leverage and the state's dependence on private investment rose noticeably. These shifts, in turn, affected the incentives and capacities of both business and state leaders to construct policy coalitions. While the approach of this study goes well beyond a purely structural one, it is useful to separate out the structural components of the analytical framework in order to trace them empirically. The next section of this chapter deals with the issue of business leverage, and the third takes up the state's vulnerability to that leverage. The fourth assesses the combined effect of these changes on the overall structural power relationship between business and the state from the early 1970s to the early 1990s.

BUSINESS LEVERAGE

The structural power of business is a positive function of business leverage and state dependence. This section addresses the issue of business leverage, which is closely related to patterns of international capital mobility facing a country. The level of capital mobility faced by asset holders for a given country can be traced to two different sets of factors, one of which operates at the international level and the other at the domestic level. The first concerns the impact of international financial integration, while the second deals with the nature and characteristics of capital assets and markets present in the given country.

International Financial Integration

The external context faced by capital asset holders is an important variable affecting their ability to transfer investment resources across juris-

47

dictional boundaries, which in this case are national boundaries. The principal measure of this external context used in this study is the degree of international financial integration. More highly integrated international financial markets suggest a world of relatively free capital movement where investors can shift their resources from one country to another easily and inexpensively, while less integrated markets indicate higher external barriers to such transfers. With higher barriers, we would expect to see generally fewer international capital flows, while lower barriers would be expected to make greater international capital flows possible.

International Financial Transactions. The degree of international financial integration facing the world's investors has increased steadily and rapidly since the early 1970s. Partly because of technological advances in computers and satellite communications that have lowered transportation and transaction costs, it is now much easier and simpler to transfer liquid capital assets across the globe than it was twenty-five years ago. External policy barriers to capital movements have also fallen in the past several decades. These developments have produced a tremendous increase in the volume of international financial transactions. Though precise measures of international financial integration per se do not exist, several specific indicators of international financial capital *flows* and a general qualitative consensus indicate that the world's financial systems have become much more highly integrated in recent years. Measures of international bank transactions, foreign exchange trading, and Eurocurrency transactions each show large increases in the levels of international financial transactions, which have grown at a much faster rate than world trade. Maxfield (1990, 6) points to disproportionate increases in Eurocurrency transactions, the number of foreign bank branches, and total bank profits derived from international transactions since the mid-1960s. Frieden (1991b) and Goodman and Pauly (1993) cite BIS data on international bank and bond lending that show exponential increases in international capital flows between the late 1970s and early 1990s. One result of this growth is that by early 1989, "foreign exchange trading in the world's financial centers averaged about $650 billion *a day*, equivalent to nearly $500 million a minute and to forty times the amount of world trade a day" (Frieden 1991b, 428, emphasis in original).

A useful summary measure of international financial transactions are BIS estimates of net financing in international markets, which include data on international bank credit, Euro-note placements, and international bond financing. Figures 3.1 and 3.2 highlight the overall trends in annual flows and in total net stocks. Net annual new international

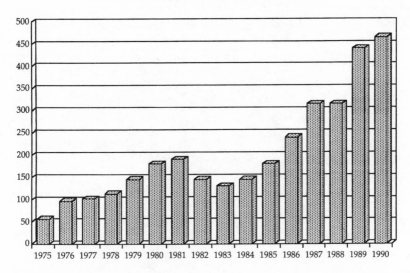

Figure 3.1. Net annual new international financing, 1975–1990 (U.S. $ billion). *Source*: Bank for International Settlements (various years).

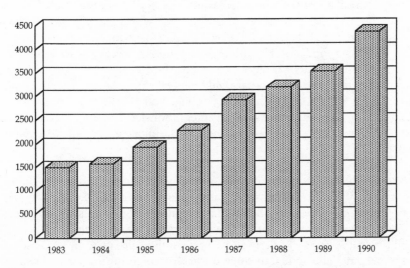

Figure 3.2. Net international financial stocks, end of year, 1983–1990 (U.S. $ billion). *Source*: Bank for International Settlements (various years).

Table 3.1. *Global Patterns of Direct and Portfolio Investment, 1976–1991 (U.S. $ billion, annual averages)*

	1976–80	1981–85	1986–90	1990	1991
Total outflows of DFI from industrial countries	39.2	42.1	157.4	213.0	171.1
DFI inflows to developing countries	6.6	17.6	23.0	29.8	41.5
Total outflows of portfolio capital from industrial countries	15.0	60.6	185.0	152.8	274.0

Source: Bank for International Settlements (1993).

financing rose steadily throughout the 1970s before slowing down briefly in the early 1980s and finally rising more sharply from 1983 to 1990. Overall, net annual new international financing grew by more than 700 percent from 1975 to 1990, increasing from $57 billion to $465 billion (see Fig. 3.1). By way of comparison, total world trade in goods and services grew 348 percent from 1975 to 1989 (Bank for International Settlements 1990, 63). The number of total net stocks shows a similar pattern in the 1980s. From 1983 (the earliest year for which data are available) to 1990, net international financial stocks nearly tripled, going from $1.5 trillion to $4.4 trillion (see Fig. 3.2). These data suggest that patterns of international financial integration led to sharp increases in international flows of financial capital, the most mobile of all capital assets.

International Direct and Portfolio Investment Flows. BIS data on global patterns of direct and portfolio investment reflect similar tendencies, as shown in Table 3.1. The annual average of total outflows of direct foreign investment (DFI) from the industrial countries went from $39.2 billion in the 1976–80 period to $171.1 billion in 1991, an increase of 336 percent. The annual average of direct foreign investment inflows to the developing nations logged even more impressive growth, increasing by 529 percent from $6.6 billion in 1976–80 to $41.5 billion in 1991. But the most spectacular growth in international investment flows has taken place in portfolio investment, an indication that portfolio capital markets around the world have become more closely integrated. The annual average of total outflows of portfolio capital from the industrial countries increased from $15.0 billion in the 1976–80 period to $274 billion in 1991, for a total growth of *1,727 percent*.[1] These figures suggest that international financial integration has led to greater international investment flows across the board since the 1970s, but that a disproportionate share of this growth has taken place in the more mobile portfolio capital sector.

These patterns of rapidly increasing international capital flows provide strong, albeit indirect, indications of greater levels of international capital mobility on a global scale. This mobility should favor the holders of the most mobile capital assets, who are the most well positioned to take advantage of the lower barriers to international capital flows that international financial integration entails. All else being equal, this favorable international context should give investors greater policy leverage vis-à-vis a given state in the international financial system (see Chapter 2). But all else is *not* equal. The actual degree of mobility of capital assets for a given country, and therefore the structural leverage of asset holders vis-à-vis that country's government, also depends on factors specific to the country in question.

Country-Specific Factors

The nature of capital assets and markets at the national level is an important determinant of the inward and outward mobility of capital and its impact on business leverage for a given country. In fact, it is these kinds of factors that best help us explain the differences in business leverage among different countries that face a similar external environment of international financial integration. Many countries face similar external conditions, yet the ability of investors to relocate their assets into or out of any country still varies widely cross-nationally. International context is necessary, but not sufficient to explain changes in business leverage.

A lack of liquidity impedes mobility. A country with weak financial and portfolio capital markets is likely to face less international capital mobility than a country that has well-developed markets. Financial, equity, and bond markets make it easier for investors to liquidate their assets so that they can more readily relocate them to other jurisdictions. Similarly, a country that is relatively rich or "abundant" in liquid (finance and portfolio) capital assets on average will be characterized by greater inward and outward capital mobility than a country that is relatively abundant in fixed (direct investment, or firm- and sector-specific) capital assets. Changes in the relative "endowments" of these two broad cate-

1 The proportion of these assets that went to developing countries cannot be determined because the BIS does not break down these figures by destination.

gories of assets signal shifts in the level of capital mobility facing a country. Increases (decreases) in the relative share of liquid versus fixed assets in the domestic economy therefore increase (decrease) the structural capability of business to pressure the state through a strategy of exit or relocation of investment resources.

Mexico's financial, stock, and bond markets underwent dramatic changes from the 1970s to the 1990s, especially during the 1980s. The development of these markets has spawned high growth of the assets traded on them, especially in comparison with the fixed assets sector. Liquid capital markets, particularly in the financial sector, have existed in Mexico for decades (see Maxfield 1990). For example, wealthy Mexicans have long held U.S. dollar-denominated bank accounts as a hedge against inflation and devaluation. But the menu of choices in the financial, equity, and bond markets offered a much wider and more varied selection to investors in 1992 than it did in 1972. This has resulted in a fundamental transformation of Mexico's domestic asset base.

Financial Markets. Mexico experienced a series of rather severe pendular movements in its financial markets from the early 1980s to the early 1990s. During this time, the Mexican financial system evolved through the following four basic stages: (1) a predominantly privately run system until 1982; (2) a brief period of total state control from September to December 1982, followed by slightly looser state command until the mid-1980s; (3) dual public and private control from the mid-1980s to the early 1990s; and (4) private sector predominance since the early 1990s. Facing rapid capital flight and mushrooming balance of payments deficits and debt service obligations, President José López Portillo issued an executive decree nationalizing Mexico's private banks on September 1, 1982. At the same time, he also imposed strict exchange controls. His rationale for making these moves was to stem the flow of capital leaving the country and to give the government greater control over the nation's financial system (Maxfield 1990). The impact of these measures was felt immediately, though not exactly in the way that López Portillo had intended. Although exchange controls did slow capital flight (Lustig 1998), the principal result of the nationalization was massive unrest in the private sector, which felt that its property rights had been violated. This fear undermined confidence in the government, not just in private financial circles, but also in other sectors of the business community. If the government could take over the banks by simple executive decree, it could conceivably (and constitutionally) intrude into virtually any other realm of enterprise without notice.

The bank nationalization policy of the de la Madrid administration was designed to ameliorate business fears of government infringement on property rights and to restore the confidence of the private sector. Despite his earlier claim that the bank nationalization was "irreversible," de la Madrid came into office just three months after the nationalization and began almost immediately to reverse the measure: "Even before de la Madrid accepted the presidential sash from López Portillo, the PRI began trying to undo the damage" of the nationalization (Maxfield 1989, 223). The two main concessions granted to ex-bankers were indemnification and a path back into the financial system (ibid.). Indemnification was fairly substantial. The ex-bankers were paid 93 billion pesos, which was 36 percent higher (in real terms) than the government's estimated value of the banks at the time of expropriation (Hernández Rodríguez 1986, 252).[2] Perhaps more important, the government allowed the exbankers to reenter the financial system by auctioning off 34 percent of the bank stocks to the highest national bidder on December 29, 1982, just four weeks after de la Madrid took office. He later sold off all of the banks' nonbank financial operations and institutions, selling 341 businesses back to the private sector in March 1984 (Hernández Rodríguez 1986, 251, 252). These initial reprivatization measures were complete by 1985–86 (Davis 1992, 26).

The most important effect of these policies was the development of a parallel private sector financial market not subject to direct government control and that operated side-by-side with the state-controlled banking system. The government auction of the nonbank financial operations that had been nationalized included stock brokerage houses, exchange houses, insurance companies, guarantee companies, and mortgage companies: "That is to say, a group of institutions that, along with the banks, constitute the national financial system" (Hernández Rodríguez 1986, 252). This parallel market grew rapidly and increased the financial power of the larger financial conglomerates, at the expense of the banks and small industrialists. For example, the portion of savings captured by the commercial banks dropped from 90 percent in 1982 to 67 percent in 1987, when the private stock brokerages accounted for the other 33 percent. "In real terms, between 1982 and 1987, the financial savings channeled to the banks fell 49 percent, while the portion going to stock brokerages rose 169 percent" (Maxfield 1989, 225). Many regulations of the private financial markets were also reduced or eliminated during this time. These actions helped create a parallel private sector financial market more independent of state control and regulation. The bank nationalization and exchange controls had temporarily succeeded in stemming the flow of capital flight out of Mexico, but few of these

---

2 The bankers complained that this settlement underestimated the true value of their former holdings (Hernández Rodríguez 1986).

resources were channeled into productive investments. The new parallel financial market captured much of this money in highly speculative short-term investments. Meanwhile, the fixed-asset sector languished, as bank credit became scarce and costly. Maxfield (1989) estimates that credit was up to 20 percent less expensive to obtain in the parallel financial system than in the banking system, but access to the parallel market was limited to the 200 corporations on the Mexican stock exchange.

Between May 1990 and June 1992 the banks were reprivatized, returning control of most of the last remaining area of the financial sector subject to state ownership to the private sector.[3] In addition, several new banks began operations and the Ministry of Finance approved a number of others. This process led to the emergence of a new class of private bankers linked to the previously separate parallel market. These new financiers were generally not the same people who had owned the banks before the nationalization. As President Carlos Salinas de Gortari (1988–94) himself described the process, the bank reprivatization has opened the "doors to a new generation of Mexican businessmen" (cited in Elizondo 1993, 15). Rather than grant special preference to the previous owners, the government sold the banks to the highest bidders, most of whom had made their fortunes in the private parallel financial market during the turbulent and speculative 1980s (Baker 1991). Some of the ex-bankers were active in this bidding, and a few were successful in purchasing one of the reprivatized banks (though not necessarily the same one they had owned before). But in general their profile was fairly low, and most of the new bankers had not owned a bank before the nationalization (Elizondo 1993, 16). The owners of brokerage houses, among the biggest winners from the 1980s, were especially active in the reprivatization. For example, Banamex, Mexico's largest bank, went to Accival, a relatively small brokerage house before the nationalization that had become Mexico's largest by 1991 (Elizondo 1993). The banks and the nonbank operations that had been separate entities for the better part of a decade had now been brought back together to form a new, dynamic private financial sector.

Portfolio Markets. The Mexican stock and bond markets also experienced tremendous growth and development from the 1970s to the 1990s. While the types of assets traded on these markets are not as supremely liquid as financial capital, they are much more so than the fixed assets involved in direct investment. Assuming a permissive international context and no exchange controls, growth in these markets usually

---

3 The only banks remaining in the hands of the state were the development banks (e.g., Nafinsa, Bancomext). See Elizondo (1993, 20).

signals growth in the mobile capital asset sector as they capture a growing proportion of a country's total capital assets.

If enough investors responded to any particular change (or even reports of a change) in government trade policy by exiting the Mexican stock market, this would send a clear signal to policy makers that they are dissatisfied. It would also put strong, though somewhat indirect, structural pressure on the state to reform policy. The first effect of this kind of exit would be to cause share prices in the Mexican portfolio capital markets to go down as domestic and foreign investors liquidated their Mexican assets. Although there is no a priori theoretical reason for a simple drop in share prices in and of itself to have any direct effects on the real (as opposed to the financial) economy, spillover effects via exchange rates and currency markets can affect economic growth, inflation, and interest rates. This logic works as follows: Investors, unhappy with government policy, sell off their peso-denominated holdings in the Mexican stock market. They immediately convert those pesos into another currency, say, U.S. dollars, which they can hold as a hedge against inflation or relocate to other international markets. Back in Mexico, this decrease in demand for the peso causes it to depreciate, which puts upward pressure on inflation due to the increase in the peso price of dollar-denominated imports. To avoid a total collapse of the peso, the Mexican government essentially has two choices. First, it can intervene in international currency markets by buying pesos in sufficient quantities to drive their price back up. This is limited by the amount of foreign reserves in the central bank. Second, the government can raise interest rates in the hopes of attracting or retaining portfolio investment in Mexico by raising the nominal rate of return. The second strategy is where the effects on the real economy are felt most strongly. Increases in interest rates make credit more expensive, thereby lowering aggregate demand as producers and consumers borrow less. This in turn causes gross domestic product (GDP) growth to fall and unemployment to rise.

This is essentially what happened in 1994 in Mexico. In response to growing political instability and negative policy signals (especially current account deficits approaching 8% of GDP), investors began to pull out of the Mexican market in early 1994. The government responded by spending its foreign reserves to shore up the value of the peso in international currency markets until those reserves were virtually depleted in December (Edwards 1995). The December 20, 1994, devaluation caused remaining investors to liquidate their peso-denominated assets and convert them into dollars before they lost even more (in dollar terms) than they already had. This pushed the peso even lower, and the Mexican government was forced to let the peso float and implement sharp increases in interest rates, which approached nominal annual levels of 100 percent in the first half of 1995. Inflation picked up after having dropped to single-digit levels in 1993 and 1994, and the economy contracted by 6.5 percent in 1995 (see Thacker 1999b). In trade policy, it is easy to imagine a similar scenario occurring if the NAFTA negotiations had failed. In fact, several people interviewed for this project indicated that they believed a collapse of the negotiations would have triggered tremendous capital flight from Mexico (see Chapter 5).[4]

Mexican stock and bond markets were very underdeveloped before the 1980s. As of the mid-1970s, most investment was direct, as opposed to the more liquid portfolio investment. Mexico simply did not possess markets adequate to sustain a high volume of equity and money market trading (Solórzano 1993). But the Mexican stock and bond markets experienced a series of significant changes after the 1970s that allowed them to flourish and grow at a fast pace in the 1980s and early 1990s. For example, between 1980 and 1992, the end-of-year Price and Quotation Index of the stock market went from 1.43 to 1,759.44 (INEGI 1994). This growth was particularly impressive after the mid-1980s. From 1987 to 1992, the index increased in real terms by 432 percent and capitalization by 602 percent. Average daily trading volume nearly tripled, going from 33 million shares in 1988 to 95 million in 1992. Total share trading volume expressed in U.S. dollars increased by 558 percent from 1988 to 1992 (Bolsa Mexicana de Valores 1993).

The origins of this growth lie in institutional changes in the Mexican stock and bond markets.[5] Before 1975, asset holders (especially foreign) who wanted to invest in Mexico had few options outside of direct investment. But in that year the Securities Market Law was passed, giving operational autonomy to the stock exchange for the first time. This law also promoted the opening of stock brokerage houses to act as intermediaries. In 1976, the name of the exchange was changed to the Mexican Stock Exchange (Bolsa Mexicana de Valores S.A. de C.V.). Some of the more important developments since the initial changes in 1975 include the first issues in 1978 of Treasury Bills (*Cetes*), which became far and away the most frequently traded money market instrument. In 1980, the first commercial paper was issued in Mexico, and the Mexican Association of Brokerage Houses (AMCB), which has been a central actor in Mexican finance since the bank nationalization, was founded. The year 1989 was another big one for these markets, as the government first issued U.S.

4 The main fear in the Mexican press in the fall of 1993 was that a defeat for NAFTA in the U.S. House of Representatives would lead to the kind of economic meltdown that eventually occurred in 1994–95.
5 See Bolsa Mexicana de Valores (1993), Fernández Aldecua (1993), and Solórzano (1993) for useful accounts of these and related developments.

dollar-indexed Federal Treasury Bonds (*Tesobonos*) and Adjustable Federal Government Bonds (*Ajustabonos*), both of which eventually became frequently traded issues. That same year also witnessed the passing of the Law to Promote Mexican Investment and Regulate Foreign Investment, which opened up many areas of the Mexican economy to private Mexican and foreign investment that had previously been limited to only national private and/or state capital participation. (See Table 3.2 for additional details on the evolution of the Mexican stock market since 1975.)

Foreign Investment. The attraction of foreign investment into the domestic economy has been one of the principal goals of the Mexican government since the 1980s (see the 1989–94 National Development Plan, reprinted in Arriola 1994a). Two of the main objectives of the Salinas administration were to balance national accounts and to promote economic growth while keeping a lid on inflation. The best way to do that, policy makers reasoned, was to attract foreign capital into the Mexican economy. Growing current account deficits needed to be offset by surpluses in the capital account, and domestic capital was viewed as insufficient to sustain any reasonable level of economic growth, especially in light of the contractionary, anti-inflationary measures pursued by the government. The opening of domestic portfolio capital markets to foreign participation thus became a central tenet of this program. Before 1989, foreign participation in Mexican portfolio markets was tightly restricted by law in both size and scope, and also by bureaucratic obstacles. To attract more foreign portfolio capital into the country, the government had to make several adjustments in Mexico's existing foreign investment laws. The May 1989 Law to Promote Mexican Investment and Regulate Foreign Investment (hereafter referred to as the 1989 Foreign Investment Law) was the vehicle used to achieve these goals.

The 1989 Foreign Investment Law opened up many previously restricted or prohibited areas of the Mexican economy to foreign participation. The law liberalized DFI in many sectors, but some of its most important consequences were felt in the portfolio capital markets. Table 3.3 summarizes some of the more important provisions of the 1989 Foreign Investment Law as they affected the stock market. These changes were generally intended to allow greater foreign participation in Mexican stocks, to expand the range of stocks available to foreigners, and to make it bureaucratically simpler for foreigners to participate in the stock market. Several creative measures were adopted to circumvent some of the constitutional restrictions on foreign investment. Neutral Investment Regimes were set up to allow foreign participation in stocks where it was otherwise not allowed or limited. Foreign investors could purchase an

Table 3.2. *Key Developments in the Mexican Stock Market since 1975*

Date	Event(s)
1975	Publication of the Securities Market Law, which gave operational autonomy to the stock exchange and fostered the emergence of brokerage houses as mechanisms for intermediation.
3 Feb. 1976	Name of stock exchange changed to Bolsa Mexicana de Valores S.A. de C.V. Beginning of period of institutional transformation and development of the stock market.
1977	Oil Bonds and Note-of-Hand Debentures issued.
1978	Treasury bills (*Cetes*) issued and Securities Deposit Institute founded.
1979	Mexican Stock Exchange Law Academy founded.
1980	First commercial paper issued. Mexican Association of Brokerage Houses (AMCB), Mexican Capital Markets Institute (IMMEC), and Investors' Protection Contingency Fund founded.
1981	Bank acceptances entered into circulation. First shares of Mexico Fund issued in New York City.
1983	Following September 1982's bank nationalization, Bank Indemnization Bonds (BIBs) issued.
1984	Investment companies appeared in Mexico.
1985	Bank Development Bonds came out. Federal Treasury Promissory Notes (PAGAFES) and Urban Renovation Bonds (BORES) introduced.
1987	Capital Investment Companies (SINCAS), Equity Investment Certificates (CAPS), Subordinate Convertible Obligations, Real Estate Share Certificates, Federal Government Development Bonds, and Silver Certificates (CEPLATA) created.
1988	Promissory notes with redeemable yield at maturity and new versions of commercial papers introduced.
1989	Federal Treasury Bonds (*Tesobonos*) and Adjustable Federal Government Bonds (*Ajustabonos*) created.
16 May 1989	Publication of the Law to Promote Mexican Investment and Regulate Foreign Investment.

Source: Bolsa Mexicana de Valores (1993).

Table 3.3. *Key Aspects Affecting Foreign Participation in the Mexican Stock Exchange of the 1989 Foreign Investment Law*

Mechanism	Effect
General principles	Allow greater (>49%) foreign participation in Mexican stocks and participation in some previously excluded areas through alternative investment mechanisms. Streamline bureaucratic processes to register companies with foreign investments.
Neutral Investment Regime	Allows foreign participation in stocks where foreign investment is restricted or not permitted through the purchase from a bank-managed trust of an Ordinary Participation Certificate (CPO), which grants the investor all financial but no voting rights to the stock.
Automatic Authorization Regime	Eliminates the requirement for previous authorization from the National Commission of Foreign Investments for foreign participation in a new or existing company, except for certain specified activities.
Temporary Investment Regime	Allows foreign investors to participate via temporary investment trusts in activities from which their participation was previously excluded or limited.

Source: Bolsa Mexicana de Valores (1993).

Ordinary Participation Certificate (CPO) from a development bank (such as Nafinsa) and receive all the financial rights but none of the voting rights to a stock. Another way that foreigners could sidestep restrictions was through the Temporary Investment Regime, which employed temporary investment trusts to foster indirect foreign participation. Finally, the Automatic Authorization Regime was designed to cut down on the red tape and paperwork associated with the National Commission of Foreign Investments' authorization process by eliminating this requirement for most investments.

Table 3.4 summarizes some other ways in which foreigners could participate in Mexican portfolio markets. If foreign participation in a stock did not exceed 49 percent, foreigners could purchase stocks directly on the stock exchange (otherwise they had to employ the Neutral Investment Regime's CPOs). Foreigners could also purchase up to 49 percent of a given stock mutual fund on the Mexican market, as well as shares

Table 3.4. *Methods of Foreign Participation in Mexican Portfolio Capital Markets*

Method	Guidelines
Direct purchase of stocks	Foreign investment in most stocks is allowed up to 49%.
Mexican stock mutual funds	Foreigners may own up to 49% of a stock mutual fund, with no single investor holding more than 10%.
Offshore mutual funds	Funds listed outside of Mexico (e.g., NYSE, London, Luxembourg).
ADRs traded in the U.S.	As of 1993, there were 31 Mexican companies with ADRs traded in the United States.
Treasury Bills	As of November 1990, nonresident foreigners allowed to participate in Mexican treasury bills (*Cetes*).

Source: Bolsa Mexicana de Valores (1993).

in Mexican stock mutual funds listed offshore. In addition, several Mexican companies' stocks are traded in the United States. And as of late 1990, nonresident foreigners were allowed to purchase *Cetes*, or Mexican Treasury Bills, the most important Mexican money market instrument.

These changes in the rules governing foreign participation in Mexico's portfolio capital markets led to very large increases in foreign portfolio investment in Mexico. Both the stock and bond markets received increasingly large amounts of foreign capital in the late 1980s and especially the early 1990s leading up to and during the NAFTA negotiations. The growth of foreign investment flows into Mexico during this time was truly remarkable. By the end of 1992, Mexico had already surpassed its foreign investment goals for the entire 1989–94 period (Bolsa Mexicana de Valores 1993). As the Bank of Mexico's balance of payments data presented in Table 3.5 show, the U.S. dollar value of total foreign investment annual flows grew by 557 percent between 1988 and 1992. Over the same time period, direct foreign investment increased by only 86 percent. The difference is made up by the portfolio sector, in which foreign investment increased by 2,647 percent between 1989, the first year this figure was included in the Banco de México's data, and 1992. Breaking down portfolio investment into stock and money markets, we see that foreign participation in the stock market grew by 870 percent

Table 3.5. *Foreign Investment Flows into Mexico, 1988–1992 (U.S. $ millions)[a]*

	1988	1989	1990	1991	1992[b]	Increase, 1988–92[c] (%)
Total	2,880.0	3,668.8	4,627.7	14,631.8	18,918.9	557
Direct investment	2,880.0	3,175.5	2,633.2	4,761.5	5,365.7	86
Portfolio investment	—	493.3	1,994.5	9,870.3	13,553.2	2,647
Stock market	—	493.3	1,994.5	6,332.0	4,783.1	870
Money market	—	0.0	0.0	3,538.3	8,770.1	148

Source: Banco de México (1993).
[a] Figures derived from balance of payments data.
[b] Preliminary.
[c] Figures for portfolio investment and stock market measure the increase from 1989 to 1992. Figure for money market measures the increase from 1991 to 1992.

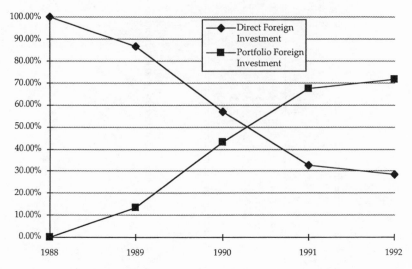

Figure 3.3. Direct and portfolio foreign investment as a percentage of total foreign investment, 1988–1992. *Source*: Banco de México (1993).

during the same period. Meanwhile, foreign investment in the money market, which did not officially begin until foreign Treasury Bill purchases were permitted at the end of 1990, more than doubled in its first two years. By 1992 it had established itself as the predominant mode of foreign investment in Mexico, easily outdistancing foreign participation in the stock market and total direct foreign investment. Overall, the proportion of total foreign investment accounted for by portfolio investment surpassed that of direct investment in 1991, and in 1992 portfolio foreign investment accounted for 72 percent of all foreign investment (see Fig. 3.3). These data suggest two general conclusions about foreign capital in Mexico. First, foreign capital, which has always played an important role, became relatively more weighty in the Mexican economy in the late 1980s and early 1990s. Second, the growth of foreign investment was disproportionately concentrated in portfolio capital markets, as opposed to the more traditional (and less liquid) direct investment sector.

The development of Mexico's liquid capital markets and the disproportionate growth of its liquid capital assets (of both domestic and foreign origin) suggest that the relative inward and outward mobility of Mexico's capital assets increased substantially in the 1980s and early 1990s. It became much easier and less costly for investors to move their capital assets into or out of the Mexican economy quickly via the financial and portfolio capital markets, which captured a relatively greater proportion of Mexico's total investment resources. In a context of international financial integration, these patterns imply that the ability of business to exert structural leverage over the state increased substantially after the 1970s. If investors contemplated exit in response to perceived policy inadequacies, they now faced fewer barriers to capital movements than ever before.[6]

THE STRUCTURAL DEPENDENCE OF THE STATE

At any given level of business leverage, the susceptibility of state policy makers to business pressure can vary significantly. This vulnerability is a function of the state's structural dependence on private investment. The factors that determine the degree of this structural dependence fall into two basic categories. First, a country may possess specific attributes that provide it with alternative investment resources. Second, a country's position in its national and international accounts can affect its demand for private capital. In both instances, an examination of Mexico shows that the structural dependence of the Mexican state on the business sector passed through two waves from the 1970s to the early 1990s. Initially, the state's dependence on private capital went down in the late 1970s and very early 1980s as the state was able to deploy several different types of assets as substitutes for private capital. After 1982, state dependence took a sharp turn upward as the state became even more reliant on private capital than it had been before the downturn in the late 1970s.

Country Attributes

In the Mexican case, the principal country attribute that has contributed nonconditional resources comes from a single commodity: oil. Mexico has been an oil-producing country for several decades, but it was only after several large petroleum deposits were discovered and tapped in the 1970s that this resource assumed a dominant position in the Mexican economy. Until the 1970s, Mexican oil output increased steadily and gradually, but not remarkably. Total crude oil production went from 320 thousand barrels per day in 1961 to 550 thousand barrels per day in 1973, a total increase of 72 percent over twelve years (Jenkins 1989,

---

6 Similarly, the same factors enhance business's ability to reward the state for policies it favors by investing in the domestic economy. In this sense, mobile capital inflows and outflows are opposite sides of the same coin. Mobility encourages the state to adopt policies that promote capital inflows and discourages it from following policies that trigger capital outflows.

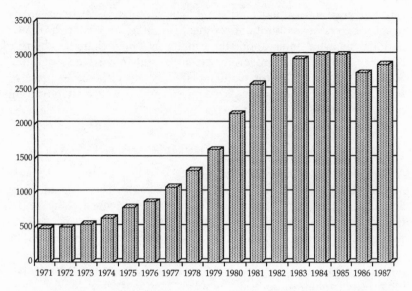

Figure 3.4. Mexican crude oil production, 1971–1987 (thousand barrels/day). *Source*: Jenkins (1989).

121). Beginning in 1973, and especially from the latter part of the decade until about 1982, Mexican crude oil production grew much faster. It topped 3 million barrels per day in 1982 for a total rate of growth of 446 percent for the 1973–82 period (see Fig. 3.4). By the turn of the decade, oil was providing the Mexican state, which has controlled the country's petroleum industry since its 1938 nationalization, with valuable alternative sources of investment capital that it could and did use to substitute for private capital. After 1982, however, crude oil production in Mexico leveled off, even declining very slightly from 1982 to 1987. The lack of growth of the production of this valuable nonconditional resource limited the Mexican state's access to one of its most important alternative sources of investment capital.

National and International Accounts

Three general categories of variables capture the effects of a state's position in the national and international economies on its access to alternative forms of investment resources. The first concerns the international prices that a country receives for its exports, especially of state-controlled commodities. The second looks at the availability of foreign lending and

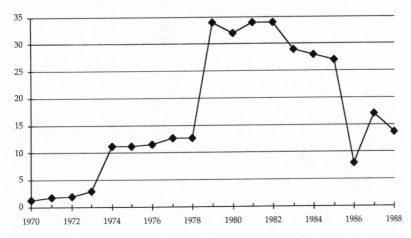

Figure 3.5. The international price of crude oil, 1970–1988 (US $ per barrel). *Source*: Jenkins (1989).

the burden of external debt repayment. Finally, the third takes into account the status of public finances.

International Commodity Prices. A country's foreign exchange earnings are closely tied to the international prices for its major exports. This issue becomes particularly relevant to the question of state dependence when the exports under consideration are controlled by the state. As prices of these goods go up, the state's access to alternative sources of investment capital increases. As prices go down, the state must depend more heavily on the private sector to provide the investment resources to spur economic growth and employment. The most important state-controlled export product in Mexico is oil.

International oil prices have been critical to the health of the Mexican economy since at least the late 1970s, when recently discovered petroleum deposits were first exploited. Figure 3.5 illustrates the pattern of international crude oil prices from 1970 to 1988. The first international oil shock in 1973 helped oil revenues, but Mexican crude oil production was still relatively low at that time (see Fig. 3.4). The 1979 shock, however, created a huge windfall of foreign exchange earnings for the Mexican state. These earnings are reflected in the relative proportion of Mexico's export revenues accounted for by the mining sector, which includes petroleum. After averaging just 18.3 percent of total export revenues from 1960 to 1969, and 27.2 percent from 1970 to 1979 (Weintraub 1990), the proportion of Mexican exports accounted for

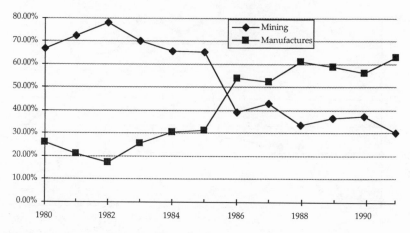

Figure 3.6. Mining (including petroleum) and manufactures as percentage of total exports, 1980–1991. *Source*: INEGI (1994).

by the mining sector topped 60 percent in 1980 and reached nearly 80 percent in 1982 before beginning to drop off. Most of this growth came at the expense of the export share of manufactured goods (see Fig. 3.6). These new oil revenues conferred upon the state a prolific source of capital resources that could be used to substitute for private capital, lessening the structural vulnerability of the state to business pressures. This situation remained fairly stable until 1982, when international crude oil prices leveled off in the $30–35 per barrel range. After 1982 they entered into a brief period of slow decline before falling quite sharply in 1986. In that same year the share of mining exports dipped back below 50 percent of total exports to begin a downward trend that continued fairly consistently into the early 1990s, while the share of manufactured goods overtook the mining sector, exceeding 60 percent of total exports in 1991. After the 1986 crash in oil prices, the Mexican state could no longer count on oil revenues as a consistent and plentiful source of investment resources, and the state became more dependent on the private sector to provide them.

Mexico's overall terms of trade follow fairly closely the patterns of international crude oil prices, which is not surprising considering the relative weight of the petroleum sector in Mexico's exports during this time. Mexico's terms of trade rose sharply in the 1973 and 1979–80, reaching 125 percent of the 1971 levels in 1980. They then fell dramatically before leveling off between 1986 and 1992 at about 65 to 70 percent of their 1971 levels (see Fig. 3.7). Although specific data on the terms of

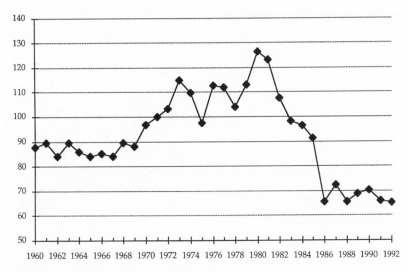

Figure 3.7. Mexico's terms of trade, 1960–1992 (1971 = 100). *Source*: Banco de México (1993).

trade of exclusively state controlled goods and services are not available, those trends are likely very similar. These figures suggest that the Mexican state's export revenues fell rather sharply from the early 1980s to the early 1990s.

Foreign Lending. Foreign lending can provide a similar, though perhaps even more volatile, source of investment resources that can lower the degree to which the state must depend on private capital. Much international bank lending has traditionally been made to governments rather than to private individuals and firms. High levels of foreign lending to the state can insulate it from business pressures by providing policy makers with access to capital. Conversely, when credit is tight and when the burden of repayment of previous loans becomes onerous, the state becomes more dependent on private capital.

Mexico was one of the most active developing nations in the international credit market in the 1970s, when petrodollar recycling helped lead to much higher levels of lending on the part of private northern banks to developing countries. Beginning in the middle part of the decade, Mexico began to borrow heavily from the transnational private banks. Annual long-term loan disbursements to Mexico climbed steadily throughout this period, starting at less than $2 billion in 1972 and reaching their high point of $17 billion in loans disbursed in 1981

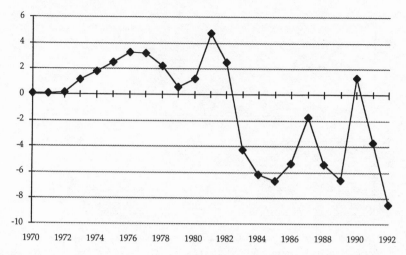

Figure 3.8. Net transfers on public and publicly guaranteed debt, 1970–1992 (US $ billion). *Source*: World Bank (various years).

alone (World Bank 1989). Even having to repay previous loans, the government was able to secure enough new credit to more than cover those payments, as net transfers remained positive through 1982 (see Fig. 3.8). The public sector received the lion's share of these disbursements. When combined with the increased oil revenues, these disbursements made the late 1970s and very early 1980s a time of loose money with few restrictions on the Mexican state. This period was a low point in the state's dependence on private capital in the postwar period. The state could ignore many business demands, withstand relatively high levels of capital flight, and still keep things running smoothly, at least in the short run.

When the debt crisis hit following the López Portillo administration's August 1982 announcement that Mexico could no longer meet its debt service obligations, Mexico's international credit dried up virtually overnight.[7] At the same time, increases in international interest rates had raised the burden of repayment on past debt, much of which had been contracted at adjustable interest rates in the 1970s, when rates were much lower. As a result, net transfers (disbursements minus total debt

7 Just a few useful examples from the extensive literature on the debt crisis include Williamson (1983), Kahler (1986), Remmer (1986, 1990), Pastor (1987), Frieden (1988, 1991a), Kaufman (1988), Handelman and Baer (1989), Sachs (1989), Stallings and Kaufman (1989), Nelson (1990), and Haggard and Kaufman (1992).

service payments) quickly turned negative, dropping to –$6.6 billion in 1985 before recovering briefly in 1987 and 1990, only to bottom out again at –$8.5 billion in 1992 (see Fig. 3.8). Debt service consumed the few new loans made, as well as a large number of other public resources that might have otherwise been channeled to the domestic economy. For a short time, the state could count on oil revenues to compensate partially for some of these losses. But when oil prices fell from 1985 to 1986, the Mexican state was left with very little support from its two most important alternative sources of investment resources. This became a huge net drain on government assets. After that point in time, the state became heavily dependent on private capital.[8]

Public Finances. The status of government accounts provides a useful summary measure of the ability of state policy makers to substitute government resources for those of the private sector. Higher government deficits make it more difficult for the state to withstand the withdrawal of private investment resources from the national economy. On the other hand, public sector surpluses would be expected to give the state a somewhat freer hand in dealing with the private sector, at least for as long as the surplus lasts.

Mexican public finances took a sharp turn for the worse in the 1980s. Mexican government deficits expressed as a percentage of GDP nearly quintupled between 1980 and 1982, when they exceeded 14 percent of GDP. On the revenue side of the fiscal equation, the government's tax revenues declined during the de la Madrid administration as a result of tax evasion, loopholes in the tax laws, and the effects of economic crisis (slow growth, high inflation) on the tax base (Elizondo 1994). Although they improved somewhat in the mid-1980s, by the latter part of the decade government deficits again exceeded 10 percent of GDP, despite cutbacks in government spending. Only in 1990 did the Mexican government actually run a surplus (see Fig. 3.9). This was largely due to the Salinas administration's tax reforms lowering tax rates while increasing enforcement (ibid.), and to a privatization program that had begun to generate substantial one-time revenues from the sale of state-owned companies. Given Mexico's poor position with respect to oil revenues and foreign lending, the status of government finances did not offer any easing of the burden in the 1980s. These deficits further limited the state's ability to substitute for private investment.

8 The period in the early 1970s before the oil and lending booms was also a period of relatively high state dependence, though not as high as Mexico experienced in the 1980s and 1990s. In the early 1970s, Mexico had not yet become so heavily reliant on petroleum exports, and it also faced a lower debt service burden. Additionally, the private sector's structural leverage was relatively lower then.

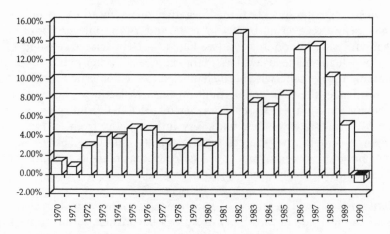

Figure 3.9. Government deficits as a percentage of GDP, 1970–1990. *Source*: International Monetary Fund (1994).

THE STRUCTURAL POWER OF BUSINESS
AND INVESTMENT CRISES

Structural power relations between business and the state shifted noticeably in favor of business beginning in the 1980s. In the 1970s, the leverage of business was just beginning to increase as capital became slightly more mobile internationally. The integration of international financial markets was still in its infancy. International capital flows were increasing, but remained relatively low, especially when compared with the growth of the 1980s. Mexico's domestic capital markets were still very underdeveloped in the 1970s. The private financial sector, concentrated primarily within the private banks, had only a few instruments with which to carry out financial transactions. The Mexican stock market offered portfolio investors limited opportunities, and effective bond markets did not really emerge until the 1980s and 1990s. The balance of Mexico's capital assets between liquid and fixed holdings roughly paralleled the development of domestic liquid capital markets, favoring fixed over liquid assets. The arsenal of tools available to the private sector to exert structural leverage in the 1970s was still limited.

At the same time, the structural dependence of the state on the private sector decreased demonstrably in the 1970s. The discovery and exploitation of large petroleum deposits, access to cheap and plentiful foreign lending, and rises in international oil prices all provided the Mexican state with greater access to alternative investment resources and lowered its dependence on private investors. This lessened dependence translated into lower structural vulnerability to business pressure. Combined with the still rather limited leverage of business, lower state dependence on private investment shifted structural power relations in Mexico in favor of the state in the late 1970s.

In the 1980s the two components of this structural power relationship both moved in favor of business. Business's structural leverage increased sharply. International financial integration created a more favorable external environment for the holders of mobile capital assets, especially from the mid-1980s on, and the development of domestic private capital markets and liquid assets made for a stronger internationally mobile capital assets sector. The nationalization and eventual reprivatization of the banks served in the end to foster the emergence of a more vibrant private financial sector comprised of the banks and the now stronger nonbank operations. The explosion of the portfolio capital markets, especially in terms of foreign investment in the stock and bond markets, brought a large number of national and foreign mobile capital assets into the Mexican economy, at the expense of fixed assets. This greater international capital mobility facing Mexico offered investors greater and easier opportunities to move their capital in or out of the country.

The vulnerability of the Mexican state to the private sector's structural leverage reversed course in the 1980s, increasing more or less in conjunction with business leverage. The Mexican state suffered through difficult times after 1982, both in its country-specific attributes and its position with respect to the national and international economies. Oil production continued but leveled off after reaching its peak in 1982. Meanwhile, the collapse of international oil prices in the mid-1980s cut deeply into the state's petroleum revenues. Simultaneously, Mexico was cut off from international lending, and international interest rate hikes made the repayment of previous loans more burdensome. Finally, growing government deficits further tied the hands of policy makers. By the middle part of the decade, the state's position was such that it had few options outside of the private sector for attracting the investment resources necessary to bring the economy out of crisis. All told, the 1980s and early 1990s witnessed a significant increase in the structural power of business vis-à-vis the state.

Investment Crises

The degree to which structural power is actually exercised is more difficult to measure. Indirect indicators of the status of the structural relationship between business and the state can be derived from data on investment in the domestic economy. The investment question touches on both sides of the equation: Business relocates its investments if it is

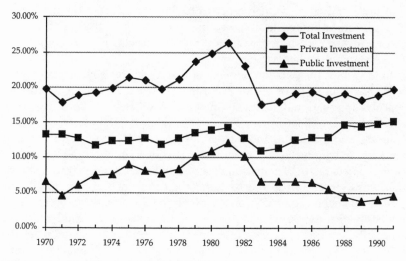

Figure 3.10. Total, private, and public investment as percentage of GDP, 1970–1991. *Source*: Pfeffermann and Madarassy (1992).

unhappy with policy and it is capable of doing so, while the state's degree of structural dependence on the private sector depends on its ability to substitute its own resources for private investment. Patterns of investment in Mexico closely parallel the more general argument regarding the evolution of business leverage and state structural dependence in Mexico since the 1970s.

From 1970 to 1981, total investment as a percentage of GDP increased from 19.8 percent to 26.4 percent. Public investment, which grew from 6.6 percent to 12.1 percent of GDP, accounted for most of this increase. Much of this growth came from the additional resources supplied by oil revenues and the government's foreign borrowing. Private investment's share of GDP increased only from 13.2 percent to 14.3 percent over the same period (see Fig. 3.10). The net result of these changes was that the share of private investment in total investment declined from 66.7 percent to 54.2 percent between 1970 and 1981, while public investment increased from 33.3 percent to 45.8 percent (see Fig. 3.11). The Mexican state fueled investment and economic growth in the 1970s not by courting greater private investment, but by increasing public investment. It is was able to do this because it had access to rich alternative sources of investment resources.

After 1981, these patterns reversed themselves. Total investment fell off sharply to 17.6 percent of GDP in 1983. Private investment also fell

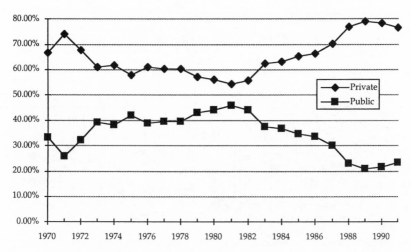

Figure 3.11. Public and private investment as percentage of total, 1970–1991.
Source: Pfeffermann and Madarassy (1992).

(to 11 percent of GDP), but not nearly as fast as public investment, which dropped back to its 1970 level of 6.6 percent. Total investment eventually began to recover somewhat, but only as a result of increases in private investment, which rebounded to 15.1 percent of GDP in 1991. Public investment continued to decline, hitting a low of 3.8 percent of GDP in 1989 (see Fig. 3.10). As a consequence, the Mexican state became much more reliant on the private sector to provide investment resources over the course of the 1980s. The share of total investment accounted for by the private sector increased to a high of almost 80 percent of total investment in 1989, with the public sector's share accounting for the remaining 20 percent (see Fig. 3.11).

Although these problems were not unique to Mexico, they were more severe there than in most other developing nations. For all of the developing countries included in Pfeffermann and Madarassy's (1992) study, the private sector's share of total investment increased from 56.4 percent in 1981 to 63.2 percent in 1991. In contrast, Mexico counted on the private sector for 76.6 percent of its total investment in 1991 (see Fig. 3.12).

Table 3.6 shows the real net changes that took place in private, public, and total investment in Mexico between 1981 and 1991. Taken together, these figures suggest that the Mexican economy suffered through an acute investment crisis during the 1980s.[9] Only private sector investment

9 I follow Schneider's (1994, 1997) use of the term "investment crisis."

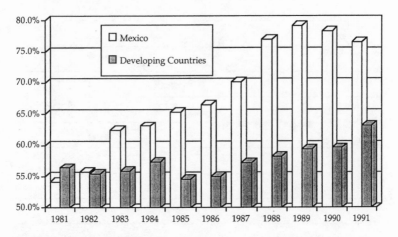

Figure 3.12. Private investment as a percentage of total investment in Mexico and the developing countries, 1981–1991. *Source*: Pfeffermann and Madarassy (1992).

Table 3.6. *Indicators of Investment Crisis in Mexico, 1981–1991*

Indicator	Real net change, 1981–91 (%)
Public investment	−57.3
Private investment	18.6
Total investment	−16.2

Source: Pfeffermann and Madarassy (1992), International Monetary Fund (1994).

rose during this time, and this increase was not nearly enough to offset a 57 percent drop in public investment. Furthermore, this problem was more serious in Mexico than elsewhere. Using slightly different measures than my Table 3.6, Schneider (1994) compares the decreases in total investment in Mexico and Brazil from 1981 to 1987. Both countries experienced severe drop-offs early on, with Mexican investment falling by 47 percent and Brazilian by 39 percent from 1981 to 1984. But investment in the Brazilian economy recovered much faster, rising by 35 percent between 1984 and 1987, compared with only 2 percent in Mexico. In addition, Brazil's public investment fell much less precipitously and recovered more strongly than Mexico's (Schneider 1997).

Business-State Structural Power Relations

The pressures associated with the investment crisis were powerful. Capital flight, always a problem for Mexico, was rampant in the 1980s. Although precise measures are difficult to calculate, Dornbusch (1990) estimated Mexico's total accumulated flight capital at $60 to $100 billion. The increased dependence of the Mexican state on private investment in the 1980s made it more vulnerable to business exit. This vulnerability was especially severe during a period of low growth like the 1980s. At the same time, it was getting easier for business to engage in such tactics. The low levels of investment and the related problems with capital flight, in combination with the low growth, high unemployment, and high inflation that persisted in the Mexican economy throughout most of the 1980s, put an economic and political squeeze on the Mexican state. Since the structural power relationship now favored the holders of mobile capital assets, the state needed to find a way to attract greater amounts of mobile investment capital into the economy. One conceivable – and underexplored – way to do this would be to reform trade policy.

Trade Policy

The actual process and content of trade policy making and coalition building are subjects of the next three chapters, but an admittedly incomplete, initial cut based on the arguments and data presented thus far is instructive. Large mobile capital asset holders would on the whole be expected to favor free trade because of their ability to take advantage of increasing returns to scale, their greater relative ability to adjust, and the diversity and breadth of their holdings (see Chapter 2). When they experience relatively low levels of structural power, trade policy would not be expected to open up. When the structural power of large mobile capital controllers is higher, trade policy should become more liberal. In general, Mexican trade policy follows the pattern of structural power relations between business and the state fairly closely. When the overall balance of structural power favored the state in the late 1970s and very early 1980s, trade policy remained closed. When the balance shifted in favor of the controllers of mobile capital assets from the mid-1980s through the early 1990s, trade policy was reformed in a series of liberalizations that culminated in the signing of NAFTA.

While this correlation is plausible, it falls well short of a full explanation. Simply because certain powerful forces may favor free trade does not necessarily mean that it will come to fruition. Much of this literature emphasizes the negative power that structure connotes (Schneider 1997, 213). Business, and interest groups more generally, are seen as more successful in vetoing policies than in promoting them (cf. Bates and

75

Krueger 1993). Political coalitions, which link interest groups and policy makers to promote their shared interests, are necessary for effective policy adoption and sustainability. Structure is but one important part of the coalition-building process.

4

Trade Policy Coalitions in the 1980s

INTRODUCTION

Coalitions provide the critical link between structure, politics, process, and policy outcomes. Trade policy coalitions are cross-cutting state-society alliances that band together to promote or obstruct certain trade policies. The level of the state's trade policy coalition members varies, from the rank of Secretary or cabinet member down to middle-level bureaucrats. Private sector participation ranges from business organization leaders, to sectoral representatives, to directors or employees of individual companies. Maxfield's (1990) general definition serves as a useful starting point: "Policy currents or alliances are defined as loose coalitions of public and private sector actors brought together by the desire to push for or against a particular policy" (29). I adapt these ideas to define trade policy coalitions as formal or informal alliances of public and private sector actors joined together by shared interests to support or oppose certain kinds of trade policies.

This chapter identifies two competing business-state trade policy coalitions: the protectionist coalition and the free trade coalition. Adopting such a definition risks oversimplifying trade preferences. Most actors' policy interests are more complex than such a simple dichotomy would seem to permit. Interests can change over time, and a certain amount of gray area lies between the ideal types of complete protection and pure free trade. A concerned industrialist, for example, might support a limited liberalization of some products, but not of others. To cite an extreme case, a garment manufacturer might prefer to have textiles and fabrics (his inputs) liberalized, while apparel (his output) is protected, thereby conferring upon him high rents. Overall, however, most trade policy interests can be sufficiently differentiated and categorized in very broad terms as either protectionist or free trade. Furthermore, in actual policy debates the issue usually comes down to a juxtaposition of two opposing coalitions exhibiting similar patterns: one that favors opening versus one that prefers closure; one that pushes for a rapid opening versus one that holds out for a slower opening; or one that favors a gradual opening versus one that wants additional protection. Typically, one group leans in the direction of protectionism, the other toward free trade.

This chapter traces the evolution and relative strength of the protectionist and free trade coalitions in Mexico from the late 1970s to the early 1990s, a period that witnessed a major overhaul of the Mexican foreign trade regime. Trade policy is directly related to the character and relative strength of these competing business-state alliances. As the relative strength of each coalition shifts, policy should change to reflect the new power dynamics. The relationship between business and the state in Mexico changed a great deal during the 1980s, and these changes had important effects on trade policy. After years of serving as a more or less "silent partner" to the government, business began to modify its approach in the 1980s, seeking a more direct role in the policy-making process. At the same time, it also found a more receptive audience within key state ministries, where a new generation of young, mostly foreign-educated free traders was rising quickly through the ranks of power in the administrations of Miguel de la Madrid (1982–88) and Carlos Salinas de Gortari (1988–94). This convergence led to the incorporation of big business as an "active partner" in Mexico's new policy of free trade. Certain powerful segments of the private sector, primarily big business, allied with newly strengthened actors within the state to create a powerful free trade coalition that, by the early 1990s, came to control most of the trade policy-making apparatus in Mexico.

The next section of this chapter briefly examines the roles played by the two competing trade policy coalitions and their members in the 1980s episodes of trade reform. It pays less attention to the specific details of these reforms because others have discussed them extensively.[1] This section charts out the basic sequences of events, and provides an initial treatment of the participation of different segments of business and the state and the relative strength of the free trade and protectionist coalitions from which the more detailed analyses of later sections flow. The story begins with Mexico's decision not to enter the GATT in 1979–80, continues through the unilateral liberalization program of the 1985–86 period (which included Mexico's eventual entry into the GATT in 1986), and concludes with a discussion of the series of economic stabilization and structural adjustment pacts negotiated between Mexican government, business, and labor leaders beginning in late 1987.

---

1 Just a few examples include Kaufman (1988, 1989), Cronin (1994), B. Heredia (1994, 1996), and Kaufman, Bazdresch, and Heredia (1994).

The remaining two sections of the chapter trace the private and public sector members' participation in trade policy coalitions. The following section examines the remaining business side of the story. It discusses the changing profile of Mexican business since the 1970s, and analyzes the private sector's evolving economic and political strategies that influenced its participation in trade policy coalitions. The final section addresses the state's participation in Mexican trade policy coalitions. It examines changes in the state's institutional, bureaucratic, and ideological makeup that altered the state's overall perspective on trade issues, and explores the state's initiative in forming trade policy coalitions with the private sector.

TRADE POLICY COALITIONS IN THE 1980S

The reformulation and redefinition of business-state coalitions figured prominently in the politically difficult process of opening the Mexican trade regime to foreign competition in the 1980s. At the outset of the decade, big business remained a silent partner in its relationship with the government. Direct participation by big business in policy making was constrained by mutual consent (cf. Amparo Casar 1992, Mizrahi 1992). As prominent businessman José María Basagoiti, who would call for private sector political participation in the mid-1980s, once said, "those who don't know think we aspire to political power. A businessman should dedicate himself to what he does, to producing, and the government to governing" (quoted in Puga 1993a, 51). The minimal private sector participation that did occur generally went through the official business organizations, which faced tight constraints from laws that prohibited political activity by business organizations. This, coupled with the relative prominence of ISI-era elites within the state, helped make for a winning protectionist coalition until the mid-1980s.

Over the course of the 1980s, however, the overall level of business participation in trade policy making gradually increased, becoming more important with each passing policy episode. Members of a newly powerful finance-banking and planning elite within the state were gaining control of the state's policy bureaucracy and initiated the first round of trade reforms. They also began to solicit selectively the participation of their big business constituencies in the policy-making process. As outward-oriented state elites and big business each became more influential and more actively involved in the policy-making process, the relative power of the free trade coalition grew. By the time the NAFTA negotiations began in 1991, both sides of the free trade coalition were poised to fortify and consolidate their positions in the trade policy-making arena.

79

Big Business, the State, and Free Trade

The 1979–1980 GATT Debate

In the first three years of the his presidency, López Portillo undertook a series of very moderate steps toward trade opening as part of a broader scheme to reorient the economy toward the exterior and to win back some of the business support that had been undermined during the Echeverría administration. To this end, the government negotiated a very favorable protocol of accession to the GATT early in 1979.[2] In November, López Portillo called for an unprecedented public debate (*consulta pública*) on the relative merits of GATT membership. Representatives from different government agencies, social groups, business organizations, and intellectual concerns each had their say in public hearings. After hearing arguments from several interested parties, López Portillo, who reportedly initially favored GATT entry – why else would he have proposed it in the first place? – appeared to have a change of heart. On March 18, 1980, he declared that Mexico would not join the GATT (Story 1982).[3]

Existing explanations of the President's reversal vary in the importance they ascribe to different aspects of the event. Helms (1985) discusses the decision within the context of societal pressures on the authoritarian Mexican state, and Story (1986) argues that "the domestic detractors of the GATT were the principal constraining forces that prevented [López Portillo] from taking Mexico into that international body" (140). Mares (1985) adopts a more state-centric approach, claiming that the President called for the debate merely to generate opposition for a policy that he had already decided he did not want to pursue.

Private sector participation in the GATT decision was carefully controlled and limited to the forum of the public consultation, and within the state the ISI-oriented agencies held the strongest positions. Before the public consultation, business's participation in the negotiation of the protocol of accession was basically nonexistent (interview with business organization official). During the consultation, the business community was organized according to the structure of its formal organizations, which were divided over GATT entry. The private sector organizational proponents of GATT entry included the Employers Federation of the Mexican Republic (COPARMEX) and the National Association of Importers and Exporters (ANIERM), while more ambivalent, but generally favorable toward entry were the National Chamber of Commerce (CONCANACO) and the National Federation of Chambers of Industry (CONCAMIN). The business opponents who participated in the debate

2 The protocol recognized Mexico as a developing country and gave it substantial leeway in matters concerning national economic development (Story 1982, 773).
3 This date is an important symbol of Mexican nationalism: It is the anniversary of the nationalization of the petroleum industry in 1938.

were concentrated within the National Chamber of Industries (CANAC-INTRA), which lobbied hard against the measure for fear that its members would be forced out of business by fierce foreign competition. The state was also divided over the issue, with the Ministries of Industry, Foreign Relations, Finance, Agriculture, and Labor opposed, and Commerce, Interior, Programming and Budget, and the Bank of Mexico (the central bank) in favor. Also in favor, at least initially, was López Portillo. An influential group of intellectuals, the National College of Economists, joined the opposition (Story 1982, Helms 1985, Escobar Toledo 1987, Luna, Tirado, and Valdés 1987).

The outcome of the Mexican GATT decision reflects the relatively greater power of the protectionist coalition within both business and the state. Structural factors explain part of these dynamics. As discussed in Chapter 3, the structural leverage of mobile asset holders had not yet started to peak, and the large business groups were less capable of exerting pressure on the state. In the same year that Mexico was negotiating GATT entry, international oil prices shot up, Mexican crude oil production increased, and foreign lending continued to arrive in growing quantities. These conditions provided large amounts of alternative investment resources that collectively lowered the state's structural vulnerability to business pressures and weakened the hand of the financial and planning ministries that would normally push for orthodox policies and open trade markets. Taken together, this meant that the large, mobile asset holders and their free trade counterparts within the state did not make the most attractive or influential alliance partners in late 1979 and early 1980. The policy outcome reflected the fairly weak position and limited participation of the free trade coalition.

The 1985–1986 Liberalizations

The years 1985 and 1986 represent a period of transition, from a protectionist trading system to a more liberal one, and from the general exclusion to the initial opening to big business elites in the trade policy process. This period also witnessed the weakening of the protectionist coalition and the initial steps toward the formation of the free trade coalition. In the very early years of the de la Madrid administration, it appeared that trade policy would stay the course set by López Portillo in 1980. Upon assuming office in December 1982, de la Madrid declared that the official policy of his government was that Mexico would not join the GATT, and in May 1983 he repeated his conviction to not enter (Story 1986, 145). But some tentative first steps toward opening were carried out in 1983, and in July 1985 de la Madrid announced a sharp reduction in Mexico's trade protection. Import licenses on about 3,600 tariff lines were eliminated, leaving just 908 under control. Tariff levels were raised slightly to ease the sting and make the system more transparent, but the net effect was to lower barriers to imports (Ten Kate 1992; see also my Chapter 1, Table 1.1). In November 1985 the government announced that it was going to reapply for GATT membership. In August 1986, after a limited public debate, Mexico acceded to the GATT on less favorable terms than it had negotiated in 1979 (Vega Cánovas 1991a, Blanco Mendoza 1994).[4] In 1986 and 1987 the official reference pricing system was phased out, and within a short time Mexico would meet or exceed most of the liberalization requirements of the GATT (Ten Kate 1992).

In neither business nor the state had there been great enthusiasm for opening before 1985–86. Within the private sector, most actors were hesitant to support an opening of the trade regime in the early 1980s. Potential supporters were fewer in number and still reluctant to come out strongly in favor of lowering barriers after López Portillo's reversal, and the more numerous opponents remained steadfastly opposed. Most of the earliest liberalizations were thus made over the objections of much of the business community, rather than with their active support. By 1985–86, however, the opening had begun to gain *some* initial support within business.[5] Francisco Gil Díaz and Manuel Zepeda, two of the Bank of Mexico's leading architects of the liberalization program, note that the "private sector was generally opposed to, or skeptical of, the opening. However, as the opening progressed, many industrialists became aware that they had a competitive advantage that had been obscured by their inability to purchase inputs at world prices" (Gil Díaz and Zepeda Payeras 1991, 12). These kinds of firms included many multinationals, as well as selected categories of potentially competitive national firms (ibid., 13–14). By the time of the new GATT negotiations and debates in 1985 and 1986, business supporters were much better organized and more strongly supportive of the measure than they had been in 1980. The open support of ANIERM, COPARMEX, CONCANACO, and CONCAMIN leadership countered

---

4 See Olea Sisniega (1990) for a summary of the 1986 protocol. See Trejo Reyes and Vega Cánovas (1987) for a contemporaneous analysis of Mexico's accession to the GATT.

5 A similar process occurred in the United States in the 1930s. After the failure of the Smoot-Hawley Act and the impact of the Great Depression, political opposition to liberalization weakened enough to permit the passing of the Reciprocal Trade Agreements Act in 1934. The dramatic trade opening that followed created economic opportunities for exporters, who became more powerful political actors and lobbied Congress successfully for further opening in later years (Bailey, Goldstein, and Weingast 1997). Milner (1988) presents a similar explanation of liberalism in France and the United States in the 1970s based on the political influence of internationally integrated firms.

the continued opposition of CANACINTRA, whose president claimed in November 1985 that GATT membership threatened the survival of Mexico's small and medium businesses (Puga 1993a, 196–97). As their preference for free trade and the state's ideological commitment to liberalization crystallized, export interests gradually moved over to the free trade coalition. As this rebalancing within business began to take shape, the state slowly began to incorporate limited business interests into the policy-making process. As one longtime observer who has participated in the opening of Mexican trade from within both the state and the private sector noted, select, ad hoc business participation in the 1985–86 GATT negotiations was substantially greater than it had been in 1979–80. Certain firms and groups hired advisors and consultants to meet with government representatives to try to protect their interests and keep abreast of the negotiations (interview with business official). By the time of the public debate, there was little open business opposition to GATT entry. Vega Cánovas (1991a) even goes so far as to state that "the terms of the debate in 1986 were mainly technical" (61), and Luna, Tirado, and Valdés (1987) wrote at the time that a "new neoliberal philosophy predominates in business discourse, especially among the sector's most powerful faction" (14).

Sharp divisions over trade policy existed within the state in the early 1980s. The de la Madrid administration initially indicated that it would make only minor adjustments to the basic trade regime inherited from the ISI era. It did not appear initially that the constraining influence of the 1982 crisis and external forces would inspire a radical shift in Mexican trade policy. The negotiation of a short-term stabilization package with the IMF in 1983 targeted mostly the severe macroeconomic imbalances in the Mexican economy and incorporated only very limited trade liberalization measures. Within the state, the only real proponents of breaking with protectionism resided in the central Bank of Mexico. Bank of Mexico personnel began to undertake a series of initial dialogues with officials from the World Bank in 1983 and 1984 regarding Mexico's economic stabilization and eventual structural adjustment, including trade liberalization. At this point, the combination of external constraints and opportunities began to create incentives for undertaking an initial reform program. The World Bank made an export development loan to Mexico in 1983, and in 1984 it first proposed a wider-reaching structural adjustment loan that would condition loan releases on trade liberalization measures adopted by the Mexican government. The Mexican government rejected the structural adjustment loan, but discussions between Mexican and World Bank officials continued into 1984 (Cronin 1994).

Part of the reason for Mexico's rejection of trade liberalization in the early years of the de la Madrid *sexenio* was a lack of consensus within the administration.[6] Many of the battles within the government over the control of trade policy were fought in the Tariff Commission, a body made up of representatives from the assorted relevant government ministries and charged with implementing trade policy. In the early years of de la Madrid's administration, the main and perhaps sole institutional proponent of a rapid liberalization program was Miguel Mancera's Bank of Mexico, represented on the commission by Gil Díaz and Zepeda (various interviews with government officials). Facing off against the central bank was a collection of ministries with ties to protectionist groups, including Trade and Industry (SECOFI), Agriculture, Fisheries, Health, and Energy, Mines and Parastatals (SEMIP). Finance and Public Credit (SHCP) and Programming and Budget (SPP) occupied the middle ground between these two extremes (Cronin 1994). Trade Minister Héctor Hernández's Undersecretary for Foreign Trade, Luis Bravo Aguilera, led the group opposing a rapid trade opening (interviews with government officials).

Until mid-1985 this standoff impeded any significant progress in trade reform, but by then the Mexican economy had begun to deteriorate at a faster pace, with rising inflation and an increasingly untenable balance of payments position. In July of that year de la Madrid announced his trade reform program and the pieces began to fall into place within the Tariff Commission.[7] After the announcement, Pedro Aspe, an enthusiastic free trader with a Ph.D. in economics from MIT, was promoted from president of a relatively low-level agency, the National Institute of Statistics and Geography (INEGI), up to Undersecretary for Programming and Budget by SPP head Carlos Salinas de Gortari. Salinas also put Aspe on the SPP delegation on the Commission (Presidencia de la República 1992). Aspe's arrival helped push SPP over to the Bank of Mexico's side and turned the tide in favor of the free traders within the Tariff Commission, where de la Madrid's new trade policies would be carried out (Cronin 1994).

A useful distinction can be made between the notions of policy *sponsors* and policy *coalitions*. The first round of significant liberalizations in Mexico was politically sponsored by officials from the World Bank, IMF, Bank of Mexico, and SPP, along with President de la Madrid. This small group of sponsors got the reform process moving in response to a new set of international constraints and opportunities. As later developments would demonstrate, however, this sponsorship was not strong enough to solidify the position of these reforms or to deepen or extend them in the future. The construction of a somewhat more broadly based,

6 The term *sexenio* refers to the Mexican President's six-year term in office.

7 In the patronage-based, hierarchical Mexican political system the approval of the President carries a great deal of weight with his subordinates, whose chances for advancement depend heavily on their loyalty to the President.

cross-cutting business-state coalition was necessary to cement and extend these reforms, and to reap the potential economic and political benefits that they offered.

The 1985–86 period was seminal to the development of the new free trade coalition, especially within the state but also between the state and business. During this period, the structural power relations between the state and the private sector shifted in favor of the controllers of large mobile capital assets. International capital markets were becoming more integrated and international capital more mobile, and domestic capital markets and assets were developing in ways that favored liquid asset holders. Despite the drying up of most foreign sources of credit after 1982, until 1985 the Mexican state had been able to avoid a major restructuring of the economy by relying on short-term external financing and oil revenues to pay its debts. But when international oil prices tumbled in 1985–86, much of the state's remaining alternative source of capital resources disappeared. At the same time, the PRI government faced growing political and electoral challenges from certain business factions, which began to voice opposition to the government mostly through the opposition PAN. De la Madrid moved decisively to recapture business support and investment by initiating a program of economic stabilization and adjustment, which included trade opening. Though many in the private sector and the state still questioned liberalization, de la Madrid's reforms helped promote the construction of an alliance between the financial and planning sectors of the state, now led by Gil Díaz, Salinas, and Aspe, and a new big business elite, led by the controllers of multinational and national outward-oriented capital. This newly emerging coalition became crucial to the success of subsequent reforms.

The 1987–1988 Economic Solidarity Pact

The liberalization of trade included among the various stabilization and structural adjustment components of 1987's Economic Solidarity Pact (PSE) took the development of the free trade coalition and the inclusion of the big business elite into policy making an important step further, institutionalizing some of the patterns that had been loosely established in previous episodes of policy reform. The members of the protectionist coalition were largely excluded from the most important decision-making arenas, while for the first time key members of the free trade coalition were officially incorporated into the country's upper echelons of decision-making bodies to negotiate the reform package beginning in December 1987. The pact originally was to last for six months, but it was subsequently renewed several times (eventually under the name Pact for Economic Stabilization and Growth (PECE) after the Salinas administration attached the "solidarity" name to Pronasol, a social spending program). The pact involved peak-level negotiating among government policy makers, business leaders, and official labor movement representatives. Its primary goals were to stabilize prices, cut fiscal deficits, and accelerate trade liberalization. It had five original components mutually agreed upon by the participants: (1) a large one-time increase in prices and an accompanying reduction in fiscal deficits; (2) an adjustment of the official exchange rate to bring it in line with the market rate; (3) a one-time wage increase and the indexation of future wages to inflation; (4) a mutual agreement by business and labor to not raise prices and to not press for wage increases; and (5) an acceleration of trade opening. The pact reduced tariff levels beyond the levels originally specified in the 1985–87 reforms. The new tariff schedule resulted in a maximum tariff level of 20 percent ad valorem (Ten Kate 1992, 666), and a production-weighted average tariff of about 12 percent (see Chapter 1, Table 1.1).

The nature of business's participation in the pact negotiations reinforced the existing trend toward the inclusion of the largest segments of the private sector elite and the exclusion of the smaller and medium firms' representatives (cf. Hernández Rodríguez 1990). These negotiations took place at the highest levels, and on the private sector side they passed first through the peak Business Coordinating Council (CCE), in which the largest firms and groups predominate. The president of the CCE at the time was Agustín Legorreta, a member of the private sector financial elite. This aspect of the negotiations was critical "because it magnified the interests of large financial-industrial groups that were in a reasonably good position to absorb the costs of economic liberalization" (Kaufman, Bazdresch, and Heredia 1994, 391). Though much of the private sector, even some of the larger firms, still opposed the acceleration of trade liberalization, the organization of the negotiations discouraged this kind of dissent. The concerns of CANACINTRA, for example, were muted by the relative predominance of its parent big business organization CONCAMIN in the pact (ibid.). In addition, the linking of trade reform to the stabilization components of the package, especially its anti-inflationary measures, helped undercut much of the remaining private sector opposition to trade reform (see Rodrik 1992b). Even if they feared some of the potential foreign competition that would be expected from the accelerated liberalization, most big businesspeople viewed trade reform as a necessary and essential component of an overall reform package that would benefit the Mexican economy as a whole and their interests in particular (Kaufman, Bazdresch, and Heredia 1994).

Within the state, the previous decisions to open the trade regime by President de la Madrid further facilitated the power shift among state agencies that had begun to take shape earlier in the decade. Prominent once again on the side of liberalization were the Salinas group in SPP and the Bank of Mexico, and by now SHCP had come on board with the reforms as well. SECOFI hesitatingly went along with the changes supported by the more influential groups directing the negotiations. Furthermore, as Kaufman, Bazdresch, and Heredia (1994) point out, the linking of trade to financial and macroeconomic policy concerns in the pact legitimated the views of the ideologically unified financial and planning government agencies and permitted them to assert greater control over trade policy.

The PSE represented the final takeover of trade policy by the financial and planning interests in the state, and a first step toward the institutional incorporation of the big business elite in trade policy making. It witnessed the formation and takeover of the free trade coalition and dealt a hard blow to the protectionist coalition, whose constituency had now been severely weakened within both the state and private sector. Facing rising inflation, fiscal deficits, and the growing structural power of business, the de la Madrid government used the pact to formalize its ties to the private sector's largest, most dynamic elements. In the words of CCE president Legorreta, the pact was negotiated "by the president of a presidential country with a small, very comfortable group of 300 people who make the important economic decisions" (quoted in Valdés Ugalde 1997, 220). Legorreta claimed that the official overture to business was a direct result of the government's fear that hyperinflation could cause the PRI to lose the 1988 presidential elections (ibid.). For many business and government officials, the private sector's incorporation into the pact was a key turning point in improving their relations with the state that had deteriorated so badly during the Echeverría and López Portillo administrations (interviews). After that time, the growing trust, consultation, and confluence of policy goals brought big business and the state closer together. This new coalition would also be crucial to Mexico's negotiations with the United States and Canada for NAFTA. A consideration of the two main actors in trade policy coalitions sheds further light on the alliance transformations that produced these policy changes.

BUSINESS PARTICIPATION IN TRADE POLICY COALITIONS

The nature and degree of business participation in trade policy coalitions shifted noticeably from the 1970s to the 1990s. At various times different segments of the private sector grew more rapidly or more slowly, got stronger or weaker, became more active or more passive. Traditionally, overall business participation in trade policy coalitions was limited, and that which did occur was typically carried out under a system of fairly tight state control and by private sector groups that were closely tied to the state and the protectionist trade regime. Beginning in the 1980s, however, the participation of certain groups, especially those not so closely wedded to state protection, grew impressively both qualitatively and quantitatively. Several firms and groups, generally larger and more independent of state control and protection, saw their participation and influence rise. This section examines two aspects of business participation in trade policy coalitions. First, the internal balance of forces within the private sector in Mexico changed significantly during the 1980s. These changes affected the relative abilities of different groups to participate in TPCs and their relative attractiveness as coalition partners. Second, the various segments of the private sector employed different combinations of exit and voice strategies in an attempt to capitalize on or compensate for their changing capabilities and strengths.

The Shifting Balance of Forces within the Business Sector

Shifts in the internal balance of forces of the private sector in Mexico have had important consequences for business participation in trade policy coalitions, as groups favored by the rebalancing make more attractive and influential alliance partners and the coalitions to which they belong are strengthened. Shifts in this balance alter the potential bases of private sector TPC membership. Two of the most important dimensions along which these shifts have occurred are size and geographical distribution. We should expect the largest firms with access to the most mobile capital assets and markets to have been relatively favored in the 1980s and early 1990s. Evidence from Mexico's recent history suggests that the internal rebalancing of forces has indeed favored the larger, more outward-oriented firms. But these changes have not been evenly distributed in terms of Mexico's economic geography. Many of the winning firms are concentrated in the northern part of Mexico, most notably in and around the city of Monterrey. Finally, the result of these shifts has been the rapid development of a northern-oriented, large-firm corporate elite with close linkages to the financial sector and to external markets. This newly strengthened business elite would become a central base of support for the free trade coalition.

Size. One relevant dimension upon which the balance of forces within the private sector can be measured turns on the relative economic weight of different sized firms and the degree of firm concentration in the economy. The greater the relative economic weight of small or large business, the more attractive and effective each should be as a trade policy coalition partner. Conversely, if a certain class of firm becomes weakened over time, we would expect its leverage in TPCs to diminish. If smaller firms, which often rely heavily on state protection and the internal market, become relatively stronger over time, the protectionist coalition would have a healthier base from which to draw its membership. On the other hand, if large firms increase their relative economic weight, the free trade coalition should become stronger, since larger firms (at least certain types of them) tend favor freer trade, all else being equal. Lustig (1998), for example, cites research that demonstrates that larger firms experienced much greater gains in export performance in the 1980s because "they are able to reap the benefits from the change in trade regimes more quickly than smaller firms," especially where economies of scale are present (121). A November 1996 survey on the effects of NAFTA by the American Chamber of Commerce of Mexico found a strong correlation between company size and export performance (Riner and Sweeney 1998, 166). Some 76.1 percent of very large manufacturing firms surveyed reported increased exports under NAFTA. Figures for large, medium-sized, and small manufacturing firms were 52.1, 59.6, and 36 percent, respectively (ibid.).

Data on recent trends in the structure of Mexican business offer evidence of a sharp reversal of fortune that favored the largest firms at the expense of small and micro firms in the 1980s (see Table 4.1). In the late 1970s, the smaller firms gained some ground on the medium and large firms, each defined in terms of production value and income. In 1975, small businesses accounted for about 57 percent of all industrial establishments, but only 2 percent of total fixed investment. Meanwhile, large firms, with only about 4 percent of total establishments, took up almost two-thirds of total fixed investment. By 1980, however, the smaller firms found themselves in a somewhat better (though still not enviable) position, accounting for more than 97 percent of all industrial establishments and 27 percent of total fixed investment, a twelve-fold increase over 1975. Large firms saw their presence fall to approximately 0.3 percent of establishments and 39 percent of fixed investment.

Many of these trends took a 180-degree turn in the 1980s. By 1988, the portion of gross fixed capital formation captured by small firms was just over 3 percent, while their share of total establishments remained relatively high at about 82 percent. In addition, the investment share of medium business, which had been stable between 1975 and 1980, fell from about one-third of fixed investment in 1980 to less than 10 percent of gross fixed capital formation in 1988.[8] The small and medium firms'

8 The use of two different indicators for investment shares reflects the different variables used by the two data sources. In addition to gross fixed capital formation, several other alternative measures point (even more strongly) to the same conclusions (see below and Table 4.2). While each indicator provides a slightly different measure, they all portray the same basic tendencies.

Table 4.1. *Industrial Establishments and Investment by Size, 1975–1988*

Year	Size[a]	Percent of total establishments	Percent of total fixed investment[a]
1975	Small	57.4	2.1
	Medium	38.5	31.4
	Large	4.1	66.5
1980	Small	97.4	27.5
	Medium	2.3	33.3
	Large	0.3	39.1
1988[b]	Small	82.4	3.2
	Medium	14.4	9.5
	Large	3.2	87.3

Source: Hernández Rodríguez (1991), INEGI (1993).
[a] Size categories:
1975: Small: production value less than 500,000 pesos
   Medium: production value between 500,001 and 20 million pesos
   Large: production value greater than 20 million pesos
1980: Small: income less than 3 million pesos
   Medium: income between 3 million and 50 million pesos
   Large: income greater than 50 million pesos
1988: Small: production value less than 250 million pesos
   Medium: production value between 250 million and 5 billion pesos
   Large: production value greater than 5 billion pesos
[b] Figures for 1988 are for percent of total gross fixed capital formation. See Table 3.2 for a comparison of other similar measures that confirms the same trends. INEGI adjusts the values of their size breakdowns to compensate for inflation and to make them comparable over time. The categories were determined by collapsing the parallel strata of data for each year into three basic categories.

loss was the large businesses' gain: With just over 3 percent of total establishments, they took up more than 87 percent of gross fixed capital formation in 1988. Several other measures of the relative weight of small, medium, and large industry in 1988 tell a similar story: Big business

Table 4.2. *Size and Relative Economic Weight in Industry, 1988 (percent)*

Size[a]	Total gross fixed capital formation	Total fixed assets	Total value of gross industrial production	Total gross value added
Small	3.2	2.0	2.0	1.9
Medium	9.5	4.1	9.6	8.2
Large	87.3	93.9	88.4	89.9

Source: INEGI (1993).
[a] Size categories:
Small: production value less than 250 million pesos
Medium: production value between 250 million and 5 billion pesos
Large: production value greater than 5 billion pesos

held the lion's share of industry's economic resources, with almost 94 percent of total fixed assets, over 88 percent of the total value of gross industrial production, and nearly 90 percent of total gross value added, in addition to its preponderance in total gross fixed capital formation. Small firms' share ranged from less than 2 percent in gross value added to just over 3 percent in gross fixed capital formation, while medium-sized industry's did not reach the 10 percent mark in any category (see Table 4.2).

Many of these overall patterns of industrial concentration can be traced to a combination of both long- and short-term economic developments, which include patterns of international financial integration and international capital mobility. Over the long term, the large firms' generally closer ties to the international economy enabled them to take advantage of the integration of international financial markets that gathered momentum in the late 1970s and early 1980s. The largest firms in Mexico, mostly large Mexican conglomerates and multinational subsidiaries, had preferential access to mobile capital assets, especially foreign lending. These conglomerates normally link industrial concerns with, among others, the financial sector. The large firms' close ties to the international financial system gave them access to low-cost dollar financing, which the banks would reserve "for their privileged customers" (Maxfield 1989b, 80). This favoritism was especially prevalent between 1979 and 1982. "Uneven access to dollar financing created a dualism within the Mexican industrial sector, with small and medium-sized businesses excluded from the cheaper internationalized segment of the

Mexican financial market. This contributed to industrial concentration" (ibid.).

The post-1982 economic crisis and the government's policy response had a similar impact over the short term, accelerating and crystallizing the process of industrial concentration that had begun to develop during the first years of the decade in Mexico. Facing suppressed domestic demand, rising inflation, greater foreign competition, and higher credit costs, thousands of small firms went bankrupt in the 1980s (Maxfield 1989a, 1990, Vega Cánovas 1991a, Davis 1992). In addition, the government's stabilization and structural adjustment policies, particularly fiscal cutbacks, trade reform, and tight monetary policies, also helped undercut the position of small industry. Large differentials in the post-bank nationalization cost of credit on the private parallel and official state-controlled financial markets also led to a greater divergence between small and big business. The large firms' preferential access to the parallel market's cheaper credit in the 1980s again favored the financially connected conglomerates at the expense of the smaller independent firms.

Similar patterns of economic concentration can also be found at other levels and with different measures. Economic resources have always been highly concentrated in Mexico's developing economy, but this tendency became even more pronounced after the 1980s. The very top firms saw their relative weight in the national economy rise significantly, causing the gaps between sizes to become more pronounced even among the large firms. The magazine *Expansión* publishes an annual list of the top 500 firms in Mexico.[9] Analyzing these data, one author concluded that "a relative increase of the importance in sales of the top 500 firms with respect to the national economy is clearly observed" during the 1980s (Garrido 1992, 41). Between 1987 and 1992 alone, the ratio of the top 500 firms' sales to Mexico's GDP grew by more than 50 percent, from 0.20 to 0.31 (Garrido 1993, table 3). By 1992, the sales of the top 500 firms in the country accounted for nearly one-third of Mexico's GDP.[10]

The same trends can be observed, in an even smaller subset, within the uppermost echelons of the private sector. Excluding Pemex and all other state-owned companies, the data published by *Expansión* indicate

9 Because of some occasional problems with missing data and the fact that the data are self-reported, the *Expansión* data on firms and groups should be interpreted with caution. Less attention should be paid to slight differences from year to year than to the overall trends.

10 Because he excludes Pemex, the state-owned oil company, Garrido actually works with the top 499 firms. The fact that these figures exclude Pemex, the largest firm in Mexico, makes them all the more striking.

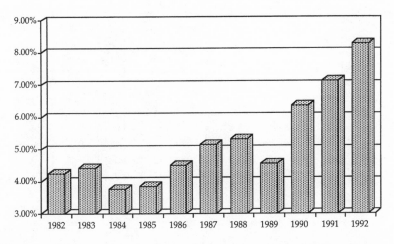

Figure 4.1. Top ten private business sales as a percentage of GDP, 1982–1992. *Source*: *Expansión*, various issues; International Monetary Fund (1994).

that the sales of just the top ten private (both foreign and domestic) firms in Mexico as a percentage of GDP nearly doubled in the ten years after the crisis hit, going from 4.2 percent in 1982 to 8.3 percent in 1992 (see Fig. 4.1). In other words, ten private firms provided more than 8 percent of GDP in 1992. *Expansión* data on 1992's top 25 (12.3%) and 50 (16.0%) private firms in Mexico show similar patterns of concentration.

Many of these top firms belong to one of Mexico's many business conglomerates, or "groups," that link together a number of different enterprises under a single system of ownership, either within a single sector or across various sectors of the economy.[11] Data published by *Expansión* on the top business groups in Mexico exhibit patterns of economic concentration similar to what has occurred at the level of the individual firm. Garrido's (1993, table 16) analysis of the top fifty-nine business groups (excluding Pemex) shows that their total sales expressed as a percentage of GDP increased from 11.9 percent in 1987 to 15.3 percent in 1990, before dropping slightly to 14.7 percent in 1991. Furthermore, the level of concentration among these groups was high and rising during this period, with the top ten groups' share of the total sales of the top fifty-nine groups increasing from 44 percent in 1987 to 56 percent in 1991 (ibid., table 18). My analysis of the private sector alone shows that the total sales of the top ten private (both foreign and domestic) groups in Mexico increased more

11 Garrido (1992) reports that nearly 70% of the top 500 firms belonged to one of the top 99 groups on the *Expansión* list in 1989.

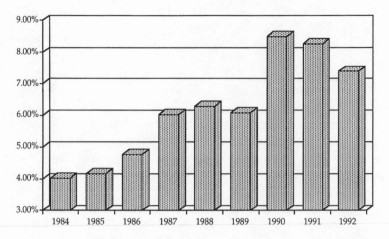

Figure 4.2. Top ten private group sales as a percentage of GDP, 1984–1992. Totals for some years were adjusted to include missing groups' data by including their principal firm's figure from the *Expansión* list of the top 500 firms in Mexico as an approximation of the group's total sales. *Source*: *Expansión*, various issues; International Monetary Fund (1994).

or less steadily from the mid-1980s onward, moving from 4.0 percent of GDP in 1984 (the first year of the data series on groups) to 8.5 percent of GDP in 1990, before declining slightly in 1991 and 1992 (see Fig. 4.2).[12]

This growing concentration within the Mexican economy prompted Garrido (1992) to conclude that the business sector has become "heterogeneous and strongly polarized" (59). On the one hand, there is an "immense majority of so-called businesspeople who support themselves with businesses of tiny scales of operation and extremely low levels of productivity, characteristically associated with the world of protectionism." This group stands in stark contrast to "a smaller group of medium businesses and another group – even smaller but powerful and competitive – corresponding to the large firms, which together make up what we can call a nucleus of modern businesspeople, with a logic of international competitiveness and profit seeking" (ibid.).

Economic Geography. The internal balance of forces within the private sector has also shifted in terms of the sectoral distribution of economic

12 My analysis of the *Expansión* data in Figures 4.1 and 4.2 takes only private foreign and domestic firms into consideration, and in that sense it differs from Garrido (1992, 1993), who also includes all state-owned companies (aside from Pemex) in his analysis.

power, which roughly parallels the economic geography of Mexico. Heredia (1992b), for example, notes that the impressive growth of new businesses had been especially strong in the northwestern area of the country (290), which tends to be more outward-oriented. Generally speaking, the northern areas of the country are more closely linked to the international and U.S. economies, and the area surrounding Mexico City tends to be more inward-oriented and state-dependent, with fewer external ties. Hernández Rodríguez (1991) presents useful data on the long-term patterns of the growth of the business sector by geographic location and type of economic activity. These figures suggest a gradual, long-term reorientation of the private sector toward the regions and sectors that are most closely linked to the international economy.

Table 4.3 breaks down Hernández Rodríguez's data on the growth of the proportion of businesspeople in the economically active population by geographic region and economic activity from 1950 to 1970.[13] Some of the fastest-growing regions were those with the most extensive external ties. In terms of the total growth rates, the fastest-growing region was the northwest, and two of the four regions that grew faster than the national average of 8.8 percent are located in the northern part of the country. The third, the Central-Pacific, includes a major metropolitan area (Guadalajara) that is also somewhat oriented toward the external market. The fourth, the Mexico City metropolitan area, is generally considered to be less tied to the international economy. Its development during this time period can probably be attributed in large part to the state's protectionist and sectoral development programs that were biased in favor of these areas. Sectorally, some of the most impressive growth in the northern regions took place in two sectors, commerce and services, that frequently have close linkages with the international economy. Overall, these were the most dynamic sectors of the Mexican economy in the growth of businesspeople as a percentage of the economically active population, particularly in the northern parts of the country (see Table 4.3).

Recent trends suggest a more rapid, abrupt transformation in the patterns of size and concentration within Mexican business in the 1980s. The strong presence of business in northern Mexico is not new, but after 1982 it became even more dynamic, at least in relative terms. Monterrey, for example, has been a major power in the Mexican economy dating back at least to the early years of this century and the time of the

---

13 These figures exclude the informal sector. The patterns displayed in Table 4.3 therefore represent growth only in the formal sector of the economy; the rapid development of the informal economy in recent decades does not distort them (telephone conversation with Rogelio Hernández Rodríguez, 12 June 1995).

Table 4.3. *Growth of Businesspeople as a Percentage of the Economically Active Population (EAP), 1950–1970*

Region[a]	Total	Agriculture	Mining, Energy, and Industry	Construction	Commerce	Services
Northwest	**16.0**	**5.4**	**26.6**	**23.0**	**34.9**	**38.1**
Northeast	**9.7**	**2.3**	**13.1**	**14.7**	**16.9**	**23.7**
North	8.1	1.5	13.9	13.1	20.3	24.8
Central-Pacific	**9.5**	**2.7**	**19.2**	**16.9**	**20.1**	**28.3**
Central-North	6.1	1.6	12.4	13.0	16.5	22.4
Central-Gulf	7.2	2.7	10.7	13.0	19.9	20.2
Central	6.7	2.0	13.0	15.3	17.2	23.6
Mexico City area	**14.7**	**4.4**	**16.5**	**13.9**	**16.5**	**16.1**
Peninsular	7.8	2.7	12.0	14.3	18.0	21.5
Pacific-South	4.1	1.5	7.1	12.3	15.3	19.6
National	8.8	2.3	14.7	15.1	18.7	21.8

Source: García (1988), cited in Hernández Rodríguez (1991, table 5).

[a] Regions are defined as follows (regions that are above the national average listed in bold): Northwest: Baja California and Baja California Sur, Sonora, Sinaloa, and Nayarit; Northeast: Coahuila, Nuevo León, and Tamaulipas; North: Chihuahua and Durango; Central-Pacific: Colima, Jalisco, and Michoacán; Central-North: Aguascalientes, San Luis Potosí, and Zacatecas; Central-Gulf: Veracruz; Central: Querétaro, Guanajuato, Hidalgo, Morelos, Puebla, Tlaxcala, and the State of Mexico minus eleven municipalities; Mexico City area: the Federal District and eleven municipalities of the State of Mexico; Peninsular: Yucatán, Quintana Roo, Tabasco, and Campeche; Pacific-South: Chiapas, Guerrero, and Oaxaca.

Table 4.4. *Regional Distribution of Industrial Employment,[a]* 1981 and
1991

Region[b]	1981	Percent of 1981 national total	1991	Percent of 1991 national total	Percent change, 1981–91
Northern industrial belt	474,170	21.3	950,177	30.9	100.4
Central industrial belt	1,321,021	59.3	1,505,142	48.9	13.9
Other regions	433,688	19.5	622,681	20.2	43.6
National totals	2,228,879	100.0	3,078,000	100.0	38.1

Note: Percentages may not add to 100 due to rounding.
Source: Velasco Arregui (1993, 169) from INEGI data.
[a] Defined as the number of industrial workers insured by the Mexican Institute of Social Security. Excludes the informal sector.
[b] Regions are defined as follows: Northern industrial belt: Baja California, Sonora, Chihuahua, Coahuila, Nuevo León, Tamaulipas, Aguascalientes; central industrial belt: Metropolitan area-Valley of Mexico, Jalisco, Veracruz, Puebla; other regions: All other areas of Mexico.

Revolution. But recent developments invigorated the northern areas while the more internally oriented regions withered. Many of the larger firms and groups also happened to be located in this region.

More precise data using measures different than the 1950–70 figures show even stronger tendencies during the 1980s. Using data on the number of industrial workers insured by the Mexican Institute of Social Security (IMSS), Velasco Arregui (1993) compares the growth of industry in the northern versus center regions.[14] Table 4.4 summarizes these findings, which demonstrate that the northern areas' industrial growth as measured by formal employment easily outpaced the rates for the center region, the other regions collectively, and for the country as a whole. In the decade covering 1981 to 1991, the number of industrial workers in the northern industrial belt grew by 100 percent, compared with a national total of about 38 percent. In contrast, industrial employment in the center region (including the Mexico City metropolitan area that had grown so much in earlier years) increased much more slowly, by about 14 percent. By 1991 the northern industrial belt held almost 31 percent of total national industrial employment, nearly one and a half

14 He also excludes the informal sector.

times its 1981 share. In fact, the seven states comprising this region accounted for a full 56 percent of the total 1981–91 increase in national industrial employment (ibid., 169). At the same time, the center industrial belt lost its dominant position, dipping from nearly 60 percent to less than 50 percent of the national total. Furthermore, much of this loss took place in the Mexico City metropolitan area, which declined from a 45 percent share of total industrial employment in 1981 to 34 percent in 1991. In those same ten years, the number of industrial workers employed in the Mexico City metropolitan area grew by a total of just 4.5 percent, far less than cumulative population growth (ibid.).

These processes highlight an emerging dualism within the private sector, in which internationally linked northern businesses gained and the domestic market-oriented groups suffered:

On the one hand, interruption of the external credit flow weakened the state enterprise sector's capacity to deliver subsidies and public contracts to business groups closely associated with the PRI-dominated system. On the other hand, although most northern sectors had also fed at the public trough, their control over liquid assets and their links to foreign markets placed them in a better position to ride out the credit austerity, to capitalize on peso devaluations, or, if necessary, to get their money out of the country entirely (Kaufman 1989, 123).

Compared with the firms that proliferated in the Mexico City area in the postwar period, northern business "tended to be less dependent on state protection . . . , more closely allied with multinational firms located in Mexico, and more extensively linked to U.S. capital and export markets." These firms found themselves "in a relatively good position . . . to profit from the liberalization of trade and capital flows" (Kaufman 1988, 100). More concretely, many of the benefits of NAFTA are also expected to flow to the northern border region (Davis 1992). Finally, northern entrepreneurs have also been more likely to challenge the government politically than their counterparts in the interior (Hoshino 1993, 512).

The private sector's trade policy preferences appear to follow the economic geography of Mexico reasonably closely. Alduncin Abitia's (1989) survey of businesspeople for the National Bank of Mexico (Banamex) indicates that the business leaders most likely to adapt to and support a deepening or at least a continuation of commercial opening were in the north and northwest, while the Mexico City metropolitan area, the center, and the east each showed significantly lower levels of business support for trade liberalization (see Table 4.5). Predictably, those areas with the highest levels of business leader opposition to trade liberalization were the southeast, west, east, and center regions (Alduncin Abitia 1989). In sum, the strongest business and industrial growth occurred in

Table 4.5. *Business Opinion on Trade Liberalization, 1988*

Region[a]	Percent of business leaders favoring trade liberalization
North	89
Northwest	75
Metropolitan	63
Center	61
East	60

Note: The survey was carried out in October and November 1988. Some 190 Business leaders were asked whether they hoped that the new trade policy (liberalization) would deepen or at least continue.
Source: Alduncin Abitia (1989).
[a] States in each region are as follows (Hernández Rodríguez 1991, 456): North: Durango, Tamaulipas, Nuevo León; Northwest: Sonora, Chihuahua, Baja California, Sinaloa; Metropolitan: Federal District, Mexico, Morelos.

the geographical areas that were most likely to favor free trade. The overall balance of forces within the Mexican private sector moved, first more slowly and then more rapidly, toward a more northern-based, outward-oriented one more independent of state control, less reliant on state protection, and more likely to support free trade.

A New Business Elite Emerges. The cumulative effect of these multiple changes within the Mexican private sector was the emergence and consolidation of a corporate, northern-oriented, outward-looking, multinationally linked, big business elite. Two additional characteristics distinguish this new elite from other historical and contemporary segments of the business community. First, it is characterized by a culture and business structure that is corporate (rather than family based), hierarchical, oriented toward external markets, and more likely to form alliances and joint ventures with multinational corporations (MNCs) doing business in Mexico. Second, this new corporate culture and the changes in size, concentration, and the sectoral and geographical distribution of business have given rise to the consolidation of power by a small number of new businesspeople who control, by means of a system of interlocking management and boards of directors, many of Mexico's most important business conglomerates. Together with the management of MNC subsidiaries, these big business elites represent a new generation of private sector leadership in Mexico.

The culture and structure of many of the larger firms in Mexico underwent an important transformation in the 1980s and early 1990s. One aspect of these changes has been the decline of the family business and the adoption of a corporate style of management. A first step in this direction was the public trading of many firms' shares on the Mexican Stock Exchange (BMV), which had previously been fairly limited in scope. Many of Mexico's largest and most important business conglomerates went public only as recently as the 1980s and early 1990s. Many businesses also began to be organized along vertical and hierarchical principles rather than the traditional family-centered business practices of years past. One manner in which this was done was through the separation of ownership and management, whereby a growing number of firms place a great deal of control over management in the hands of a director general who is not an owner or shareholder in the company (Salas-Porras 1992).

These changes in the organization of Mexican firms affected the overall view of business toward foreign trade and other areas of economic reform. The spread of this new corporate culture and structure has not been evenly distributed across the various sectors and regions of the country. In fact, these changes closely paralleled many of shifts that occurred with respect to size, concentration, sectors, and geography. Partly because of their linkages with transnational and foreign firms and markets, and because they have been relatively more economically and ideologically independent of the state, the large Monterrey business groups have adapted this new corporate culture much more readily than firms in other regions. Generally, "the most profoundly affected by this process appear to be the most internationalized groups and the groups that emerged from the process of privatization" (ibid., 152). Most of the groups that fit this categorization are in the state of Nuevo León, where Monterrey is located. In sum, these changes involve, "on the one hand, a new organizational culture (a corporate culture), and, on the other, elitism, pragmatism and an ideology of globalism, widely shared by management and shareholders" (ibid., 136).

This new corporate elite is a select group, perhaps even more so than the actual number of companies that have adopted the new corporate culture and organization would indicate. Many of the most important and largest businesses in Mexico are part of business groups, or conglomerates, that bring together different firms, from both within a single sector and across a wide variety of sectors, through overlapping management, directorship, and even ownership. Furthermore, Garrido's (1992) analysis suggests that overlapping management networks tie many of the groups themselves closely together. For example, several of the largest business groups in Mexico have as many as eight board members in common (ibid., 57). Garrido uses the term "big business" (*grandes empresarios*) to refer to those people in positions of ownership and/or control over two or more conglomerates or groups. In his study of the members of the boards of directors of both financial and nonfinancial large businesses listed on the Mexican Stock Exchange, thirty-three of the 111 studied participated in the boards of two or more groups, conglomerates or financial enterprises. Some of these people sat on the boards of as many as ten or fifteen such entities. Many of these board members linked together various nonfinancial business concerns with a number of different types of financial operations, such as private banks, stock brokerages, insurance companies, and investment funds, that control large amounts of liquid investment resources. The growing presence of these big business leaders "shows the existence of a small national nucleus of economic control" (ibid., 28). Many of these new leaders are relatively young and made the bulk of their fortunes since the 1980s, and a good number of them took an active part in the auctioning off of the many state-owned enterprises during the Salinas administration.[15]

Several of these newly powerful, younger entrepreneurs assumed leadership roles as social representatives for the private sector and Mexican society as a whole. Along with the increased importance of foreign investment and the sharply diminished role of the parastatal sector, this transformation of the Mexican business elite has transformed the identity and nature of private sector leadership. "This means that in contrast to the situation in 1983, business leadership now corresponds to transnational capital of U.S. origin and the restructured sector of national big business" (ibid., 60). This new balance of forces in Mexican business would be expected to affect trade policy coalition formation. The new private sector elite would make for more attractive and influential trade policy coalition potential members as they gained strength over the course of the 1980s and early 1990s.

Business Strategies

Using Hirschman's (1970) language, two strategies, or responses, have been especially important in recent Mexican political economy: exit and voice. Traditionally, exit had been dominant, but beginning in the

15 To cite just two examples, Carlos Slim of the Grupo Carso, which controls the privatized Teléfonos de México (Telmex), and the Banamex-Accival group's Roberto Hernández, who began his career as a stock broker, were among the more prominent and widely known members of this leadership. I treat the privatization of the parastatals at somewhat greater length in the next section.

early 1980s the voice option began to gain favor among some segments of the business community. As a result, the overall level of pressure exerted by the private sector vis-à-vis the state increased significantly in the 1980s, and this increase enhanced business participation in trade policy coalitions.

Exit. Historically, the private sector preferred not to involve itself directly in the messy details of Mexican politics as long as the "revolutionary" state protected its material interests. This system, established in the early 1940s by Manuel Avila Camacho (1940–46) to assuage the business alienation that had resulted from the populist measures undertaken by Lázaro Cárdenas (1934–40), has been called the "alliance for profits" (Mizrahi 1992, 748). "Businessmen left politics to the PRI in return for a promise that their profits would be guaranteed and their interests would not be compromised" (Maxfield 1989a, 221). The principal strategy of the private sector was traditionally exit, or withdrawal. The logic of this strategy is simple and powerful: "The acceleration of production in a mixed economy presupposes the presence of wealthy entrepreneurs able to invest in companies which provide employment, income, and purchasing power to the Mexican people, as well as increase production" (Carrillo Arronte 1987, 52).

The two related methods traditionally used by the Mexican private sector to exercise its exit option have been to withhold investment and to engage in capital flight.[16] Going back at least as far as the administration of Lázaro Cárdenas (1934–40), business would occasionally express its displeasure with certain government policies by refusing to invest in long-term industrial projects, opting instead to send its capital abroad (Carrillo Arronte 1987, Luna, Tirado, and Valdés 1987, Heredia 1992b). In Hirschman's terms, business expressed its dissatisfaction with the decline in the quality of a "product" (economic policy) provided by the government by withdrawing. The economic instability associated with the crisis of the 1980s was no exception, and the greater degree of international capital mobility in this era made the threat of exit more credible. While precise measures of capital flight are impossible to make, the conservative measures depicted in Table 4.6 show that it was a serious problem for Mexico, especially in the early 1980s, when the total for 1981 and 1982 is estimated to have exceeded $18 billion. This exodus of mobile capital resources from Mexico is reflected in the rate of private sector investment, which declined by over 11 percent in 1982 and nearly 18 percent in 1983 (see Table 4.7).

16 In a follow-up to his original theory, Hirschman (1981, 253–58) specifically discusses the use of capital flight as exit.

Table 4.6. *Estimated Capital Flight in the 1980s (U.S. $ billion)*

1980	1981	1982	1983	1984	1985	1986	1987	1988	1989
−0.3	11.6	6.5	2.7	1.6	0.7	−2.2	0.3	1.1	−2.9

Source: Lustig (1998, 23, 40–41).

Table 4.7. *Real Growth Rate of Private Sector Investment, 1981–1990 (percent)*

1981	1982	1983	1984	1985	1986	1987	1988	1989	1990
11.9	−11.1	−17.7	6.4	13.5	−0.7	1.9	15.4	1.2	7.3

Source: Pfeffermann and Madarassy (1992); International Monetary Fund (1994).

One reason for the historical lack of effective business voice was a traditional division within its ranks over its role in the political system.[17] Historically, the private sector can be divided into two broad camps. The first group, often referred to as the "radicals" (Luna, Tirado, and Valdés 1987) or the "liberals" (Carrillo Arronte 1987), is strongest in the northern region of the country, especially in and around Monterrey. With roots dating back to the prerevolutionary nineteenth century, this group has consistently been the more economically liberal and publicly outspoken of the two. Economically, it has traditionally been closely linked to the international economy, especially to the U.S. market. Politically, it has been the less state-dependent and more confrontational of the two groups, operating primarily through the business organizations COPARMEX and CONCANACO, the CCE, the Mexican Businessmen's Council (CMHN), and (to a lesser extent) CONCAMIN.

The second group, the "moderates" (Luna, Tirado, and Valdés 1987) or "nationalists" (Carrillo Arronte 1987), is concentrated mostly in the center of the country, especially around the Mexico City area. It emerged and gained strength largely as a result of government policy, especially the mandatory business chambers law and the ISI policies adopted beginning in the 1940s. Consequently, this group has depended heavily on

---

17 Among the numerous works on the subject of business-state relations in Mexico, see Shafer (1973), Hamilton (1982), Story (1986), Arriola (1988), Camp (1989), Luna (1992), Puga (1993a), Valdés Ugalde (1997), and Roett (1998).

state protection and the domestic market. It channeled most of its political action through the industrial and small business organizations, especially CANACINTRA. Legally a chamber within CONCAMIN's umbrella industrial confederation,[18] CANACINTRA represented thousands of protectionist small industrial firms closely linked to the ruling party, PRI. Although strong economically, the radical faction historically had a more politically distant relationship with the PRI government than the moderates, who enjoyed greater involvement in policy coalitions via the postrevolutionary alliance between labor, the state, and local capital (Davis 1992).

Until the early 1980s, most businesspeople preferred to act as more or less silent partners, pressuring the state (primarily via exit) only when they felt that their individual interests were not being respected. This system remained remarkably stable for several decades. A small group of business leaders within the radical faction had called for increased business participation in the political system off and on for years, but for most of the postrevolutionary period their pleas fell on deaf ears apart from the occasional, temporary outburst (Luna, Tirado, and Valdés 1987). As long as business rights were respected and profits protected, this strategy made sense; business leaders perceived no need to use voice to push for a direct role in the policy-making process.

The first signs of an institutional shift in business-government relations date back to the creation of the CMHN in 1962. The CMHN is a secretive, exclusive grouping of a small number of Mexico's "captains of business" (Valdés Ugalde 1997, 159). Its original founders numbered a dozen, and by the 1990s membership was restricted to thirty-seven members. Though less politically confrontational than COPARMEX and CONCANACO, the CMHN joined the ranks of the radical faction of business organizations (Luna, Tirado, and Valdés 1987). The ultimate goal of the council, according to founding member and former CMHN president Juan Sánchez Navarro, was to create a mechanism for informal business consultation with the President and high-level government officials on matters of economic policy (cited in ibid., 161–62). Over time, the CMHN would become perhaps the most powerful business organization in Mexico. It laid important institutional groundwork for business-government negotiations in the 1980s and 1990s by participating informally in policy debates and by influencing other business organizations (Schneider 1999).

18 Luna, Tirado, and Valdés (1987) place CONCAMIN within the radical faction, as a moderate (as opposed to strong) critic of government policy. Historically, it has also reflected the interests of the moderate/nationalist business faction. CONCAMIN's policy positions shifted toward those of the liberal, radical camp and away from those of its subsidiary CANACINTRA during the 1980s.

In response to what it viewed as leftist redistributive policies adopted by Luis Echeverría (1970–76), including 1975 land expropriations in the state of Sonora, private sector leaders founded the CCE in 1975. This peak organization (*cúpula de cúpulas*) represents some 900,000 businesspeople from virtually every sector within an organizational structure that brings the leading business organizations in Mexico together under the same institutional roof (Luna and Tirado 1992). The initial push behind the CCE appears to have come from the radical pole of the business community, especially the Monterrey groups (Valdés Ugalde 1997, 189–90). The CMHN has also played a central role in the life of the CCE, providing most of its funds and many of its presidents, including Sánchez Navarro as its founding president (Valdés Ugalde 1997, 189; Schneider 1999, 17). The institutional groundwork for active business participation in policy coalitions dates back to the founding of the CMHN and CCE in the 1960s and 1970s, though open business political participation remained both limited in scale and temporary in duration until the 1980s.

On September 1, 1982, President José López Portillo issued an executive decree nationalizing Mexico's private banking system. At the same time, he also imposed strict exchange controls. His rationale for making these moves was to stem the flow of capital leaving the country and to give the government greater control over the country's financial system (Maxfield 1990). As in the past, this move caused the private sector to engage in rapid exit. The data in Tables 4.6 and 4.7 show that although capital flight began to ease a bit after the nationalization and the imposition of exchange controls, the rate of private sector investment plummeted even faster.[19] Data collected in a survey of 200 Mexican businesspeople in mid-1985 by Sylvia Maxfield link the lack of investment directly to the bank nationalization. Some 74 percent of those surveyed indicated that confidence in the government was an "extremely important" variable affecting their investment decisions, and 92 percent said that confidence in the government was at least "important" to their investment decisions. Only 9 percent said it was "not very important." Of the various policies of the López Portillo administration that could have decreased investor confidence, 96 percent of those surveyed felt that the bank nationalization was an "extremely important" one. The remaining 4 percent said it was "very important" (Maxfield 1989a, 227, 229). In light of the developments in international financial integration and in Mexico's capital markets during this period, exit became an even

19 The gap between capital flight and investment after September 1982 is accounted for mostly by the exchange controls that limited capital flight and the ensuing diversion of assets into short-term, highly speculative financial markets (Maxfield 1989a, 230).

more viable business response to what it viewed as an encroachment upon its rights by an all too capricious state.

Voice. In addition to disinvestment, the bank nationalization induced a vigorous political reaction by the private sector. For many businesspeople, the government had not simply moved against the interests of a very important sector of the business community; it had violated an unwritten rule of the game by seizing the bankers' private property. Furthermore, "the bank nationalization occurred without the traditional step of negotiation between the government and the affected sector – in this case, the bankers" (Luna, Tirado, and Valdés 1987, 18). Finally, given the powers of the state as specified in the Mexican constitution, the state could potentially undertake similar measures in the future: "That the private banks lost control of finance was less important than the possible repetition of the phenomenon" (Hernández Rodríguez 1986, 247). José María Basagoiti, a director of COPARMEX, summarized business's fears succinctly when he stated that, after the bank nationalization, "anything could happen in Mexico" (quoted in ibid., 260).

Despite the de la Madrid administration's early efforts to repair the damage of the nationalization and restore private sector confidence in the Mexican government, the mid-1980s witnessed a greater degree of agreement within business that a more politically confrontational strategy was necessary to protect their interests. Still employing widespread disinvestment and exit, various individuals and organizations within the private sector began to push for greater political space. In 1983, Basagoiti blamed the growth of government on the lack of effective political participation by the Mexican citizenry. In 1984, Jorge Chapa, a former president of CONCANACO, declared that private sector groups must come forward to counteract the interventionist nature of the state (Hernández Rodríguez 1986, 258). Some divisions persisted within the wider ranks of the private sector over the precise manner in which to respond to government activism, but momentum for consensus was building. Almost 100 percent of businesspeople surveyed in 1985 believed that more than half of the business community sympathized with businesspeople engaged in open political activities on behalf of the PAN (Maxfield 1989a, 232).

The private sector channeled most of its political activities through business organizations and political parties, especially the PAN. The ruling PRI is organized into three separate corporatist structures representing labor, peasants, and the popular classes. Formally excluded from this schema, business has historically used business organizations as its principal outlet for voice, even though most of these organizations were legally prohibited from engaging in "political" behavior. In the 1980s,

COPARMEX and CONCANACO, along with the peak organization CCE, were the most strident defenders of the political rights of business. These groups initiated the "Mexico in Freedom" movement, organizing demonstrations in the fall of 1982 in several cities to demand political democracy and the reversal of the "socializing actions" taken by the state since 1970 (Bravo Mena 1987, 99). When the government tried to restrict the activities of this movement, COPARMEX responded with a strongly worded statement: "The position of the PRI . . . is a veritable attempt to limit freedom of expression among citizens belonging to any of this country's social assemblies. . . . If we want to know, once and for all, whether the party in power wants to lead our country to totalitarianism, this attempt to silence consciences, minds, and demonstrations should eliminate any doubts among the citizenry" (quoted in ibid., 100–101). Though the Mexico in Freedom movement eventually petered out, other types of business political activity continued to flourish into the 1990s.

This new political outlook of the private sector broke sharply from the past, when the private sector never questioned the legitimacy of the political system, "even in the most icy moments" of business-state relations (Hernández Rodríguez 1986, 259). For example, when Echeverría's populist measures began to sour relations in the 1970s, the politicized minority of the business community still lacked a common political agenda (Escobar Toledo 1987). Once López Portillo granted policy concessions in the early years of his *sexenio*, even the most hardline business opposition quieted down. In contrast, in the 1980s, "for the first time since the Revolution, reconciliation between big business and government was not followed by business' political retreat" (Heredia 1992b, 277). Business now had a longer time horizon and its goals were more political and less narrowly instrumental.

Certain businesspeople also became much more active in electoral and party politics, most prominently within the PAN. The PAN experienced unprecedented success in the 1980s, much of it occurring at the regional level, where its support was more highly concentrated (Loaeza 1992). The PAN's first measure of success occurred when it fared well in the 1983 municipal elections in Chihuahua (Heredia 1992a). The 1986 governor's races in Chihuahua and Sinaloa represent the first truly troublesome electoral challenge to the PRI. The PAN ran business leaders Francisco Barrio Terrazas in Chihuahua and Manuel J. Clouthier del Rincón in Sinaloa. Each lost, but there were widespread suspicions of fraud perpetrated by the PRI (Maxfield 1987). Determined to fight on, the PAN eventually took two governorships, winning in Baja California in 1989 and in 1992 in Chihuahua, where Barrio Terrazas was the victor.

The goals of private sector actors in exercising voice were not merely to extract specific short-term policy concessions, but rather to challenge the legitimacy of the system itself and secure a permanent role in the political system to protect and promote their interests in the future. Despite the shift in structural power relations in favor of business (see Chapter 3), exclusive reliance on exit now seemed inadequate to important segments of the business community. Business now wanted not just veto power, but a direct say in policy formulation, to share power. Entrepreneurs asked "that citizens and certain businessmen begin participating in political life so as to restrain, moderate, and perhaps even win political power" (Luna, Tirado, and Valdés 1987, 30). As the then-president of COPARMEX, Alfredo Sandoval, declared in 1985, "instead of reacting, we want to participate in the process of making decisions over the long-term" (quoted in Hernández Rodríguez 1986, 262). Rather than trusting the PRI-controlled government to look out for their best interests, important groups of Mexican businesspeople now sought to play an active, direct role in their country's political system and policy-making processes.

In the 1980s, the Mexican private sector employed a forceful combination of exit and voice strategies to pressure the state. It should be noted that it was not necessarily always the same exact members of the business community engaging in each of these two strategies. For example, one study shows that much private sector electoral activity has been carried out by small and, more common, medium-sized northern businesspeople (Mizrahi 1992). Meanwhile, big business, including the expropriated bankers, continued to rely on exit while also seeking out a more direct role in policy formulation. In tandem, these two strategies of political pressure and the exertion of structural leverage threatened the political position of state leaders and encouraged them to shore up their societal bases of support.

STATE PARTICIPATION IN TRADE POLICY COALITIONS

Parallel to developments within business, the state's participation in trade policy coalitions changed a great deal in the 1980s and early 1990s. From the 1940s through the 1970s, the state's internal perspective on trade leaned heavily in favor of closure. For years state policy makers sought to establish and fortify coalitions with those societal groups that supported protectionist policies. Factions within the state that supported a policy of opening were generally isolated from positions of real political authority. Additionally, state policy sought to strengthen protectionism's winners and weaken its losers within the private sector. Key state policy makers courted winners' support and kept losers at bay.

Trade Policy Coalitions in the 1980s

Beginning in the 1980s, these patterns began to reverse course, as a new generation of young, foreign-educated technocratic elites rose to power in the de la Madrid and Salinas administrations. These new state leaders also managed to establish new ties with the business sector, in particular with the new big business elite that emerged at the same time. State policy strengthened this new big business sector at the expense of the more traditional, inward-oriented private sector bases of political support. This section discusses the ideological and institutional shifts within the state bureaucracy that modified the state's overall perspective on free trade in the 1980s and early 1990s. It also examines the measures undertaken by the state that favored business's potential free trade coalition members and undermined the protectionist coalition's private sector base of support.

State Interests and Institutions

The structure of power and authority within the state exerts direct effects on the policy process. Similar to what occurred within business, changes within the state, especially the expanded influence of market-oriented reformers within the policy-making bureaucracy, helped strengthen the state's potential membership in the free trade coalition in the 1980s. These processes can be divided into two separate but related realms: (1) the increasing influence of neoliberal-style technocrats within the state bureaucracy, and (2) the greater presence of the business sector in the state bureaucracy.

The Tecnoburócratas. The most important change within the state was the rise of politically savvy, free-market technocrats. Paralleling the historical divisions in the private sector, within the state bureaucracy we can speak of two divergent tendencies: the "neoliberal" and the "nationalist" (Cordera and Tello 1981). Over time, the relative capacities of state bureaucrats supporting each of these two macroeconomic policy models has fluctuated. Beginning in the 1930s under Cárdenas, the nationalist faction enjoyed greater policy influence. During the 1950s and 1960s Stabilizing Development period, the general balance of forces favored orthodox macroeconomic policies. During the borrowing and oil boom of the 1970s, the pendulum swayed back toward the nationalists (ibid., Heredia 1992a). Finally, in the 1980s, power shifted decisively toward a heavily neoliberal orientation that now encompassed trade and that helped reorient the state's participation in trade policy coalitions.

This last power shift was closely related to changes in the composition of the Mexican state bureaucracy's personnel from 1982 to 1992. Centeno and Maxfield (1992) discuss the rise of a new class of state

Table 4.8. *Education of Cabinet Members, 1964–1988 (percent)*

Administration	Master's or Ph.D.	Mexican private or U.S. university	Economics or administration
Díaz Ordaz (1964–70)	6.7	23.3	10.0
Echeverría (1970–76)	22.2	25.0	22.2
López Portillo (1976–82)	19.4	16.1	25.8
de la Madrid (1982–88)	35.3	44.1	50.0
Banking sector, 1983[a]	31.7	48.7	70.9
Planning sector, 1983[b]	44.8	51.7	59.9

Source: Centeno (1990, 176, 212).
[a] Figures are for the whole sector (above Director General, $N = 189$), rather than just the cabinet level.
[b] Figures are for the whole sector (above Director General, $N = 172$), rather than just the cabinet level.

bureaucrat in Mexico, the "*tecnoburócrata*" (technobureaucrat). The *tecnoburócrata* is a relatively new actor in the Mexican political economy, combining the technical and bureaucratic elements of governing together to specialize in both policy formulation and implementation. *Tecnoburócratas* tend to be young, urban, highly educated, and neoliberal. As opposed to their nationalist counterparts (similar to Centeno and Maxfield's old-style *políticos*), most of whom studied law at the public National Autonomous University of Mexico (UNAM), many of the *tecnoburócratas* obtained graduate degrees in economics or administration in private Mexican universities and/or abroad (mostly in the U.S.). Table 4.8 charts the educational backgrounds of the cabinet members of each administration from 1964 to 1988. A fairly consistent rising pattern is observed in each category over time, with the exception of temporary drops in two categories under López Portillo. By the mid-1980s, 35 percent of de la Madrid's cabinet members held a master's or Ph.D. degree, 44 percent had attended either a private Mexican university or a U.S. university, and 50 percent had studied either economics or administration. These trends continued under Salinas, who formed a cabinet that was 30 percent U.S.-educated, with half of its members (and 48% of the elite as a whole) claiming graduate degrees and 46 percent having studied economics (Centeno 1990). "The 'up-and-comers' are more likely to be familiar with macroeconomics than with the more 'humanistic' concerns of a traditional legal education, and to have spent part of their youth not in the regional and (at least limitedly) class melting pot of UNAM, but in private institutions frequently associated with politically conservative and economically orthodox thought" (Centeno and Maxfield 1992, 68).

These changes also signaled shifts in the institutional balance within the Mexican state. The presence of these new *tecnoburócratas* was more highly concentrated in the financial/banking and planning agencies,[20] and the influence of these agencies and their administrators within government rose sharply in the 1980s. Many of the patterns in educational backgrounds for de la Madrid's cabinet discussed above are magnified within the banking and planning agencies of the state. Table 4.8 shows that the percentages of high-level banking sector personnel who attended a private Mexican or a U.S. university and who previously studied economics or administration are higher than the overall cabinet's figure. Those in the planning agency were also more likely to hold graduate degrees, scoring higher than the general cabinet on all three indicators. Additionally, the banking and planning *tecnoburócratas* tended to be very young, with 53 percent of the Ministry of Finance's (SHCP) and 85 percent of the Ministry of Programming and Budget's (SPP) highest levels staffed by people who were born after 1939 (Centeno 1990, 216).[21] A concomitant shift in the balance of power among the various state institutions in favor of the banking and planning agencies accompanied these changes. "Personnel in the category we call *tecnoburócratas* were able to translate control over technical functions to more general command of government as the relative weight of institutions they dominated grew within the hierarchy of state agencies" (Centeno and Maxfield 1992, 64). As a result, those with a "statist/nationalist bent" were excluded from high government posts in the most influential agencies (Teichman 1992).

In the Mexican political system, these types of changes typically initiate from the very top of the state's hierarchy, at the level of the President. Both de la Madrid and Salinas arrived to the presidency via SPP, while López Portillo had come from SHCP. The naming of de la Madrid – a relative political unknown at the time – as the PRI's presidential candidate in 1981 "assured that the new generation of bureaucrats would now dominate Mexican politics" (Centeno 1990, 243). And Salinas, another dark horse pre-candidate, "was considered the technocratic candidate *par excellence*" in 1987 when de la Madrid chose the SPP chief to succeed him (ibid., 438). Consequently, the number of cabinet members with experience in the planning and financial areas increased noticeably over just a few *sexenios*. Almost half of de la Madrid's

20 Especially important here are the Ministries of Programming and Budget (SPP) and Finance (SHCP), as well as the Office of the Presidency.
21 Centeno (1997) provides many similar measures in book form.

appointments came from SPP, while 83 percent of Salinas's came from just two agencies combined, with 33 percent from SHCP and 50 percent from SPP (Hernández Rodríguez 1987, Centeno 1990, Centeno and Maxfield 1992, Heredia 1992a). The Salinas administration was particularly successful in consolidating power among a few banking and programming sector *tecnoburócratas*: "the Salinas clique was the smallest in the history of the regime. . . . An exclusive *camarilla*,[22] composed of Ivy League graduates fluent in English and Econometrics, now controlled Mexico" (Centeno 1990, 466–67).[23]

One of the most important effects of these developments was to bring into power a new cadre of neoliberal free traders in the most influential positions in the Mexican government in the 1980s and 1990s, and to undercut simultaneously the position of much of the protectionist coalition's state membership base of nationalists. At the outset of the decade, the state had been divided over the question of trade liberalization. By about 1985, the new band of free traders overseen by de la Madrid and headquartered in the Bank of Mexico, SPP, and eventually SHCP constituted a relatively united front that would sponsor and push the first round of trade liberalization through the policy bureaucracy, spearheading the new free trade coalition. The direction of the negotiations for the Economic Solidarity Pact by the members of this group extended its influence further and helped secure its hold over trade policy. By the time NAFTA came about, one of the de la Madrid free trade team's key leaders (Salinas) had become President, and the "champions of all-out laissez-faire and export promotion now occupied the apex of the policy making pyramid" (Vega Cánovas 1991a, 67–68).

The Presence of Business in the State. New connections also began to develop between the business sector and the state during the 1980s. Traditionally, there had been very little overlap between the state and business. Though government officials would sometimes enter the private sector after leaving office, the reverse exchange of businesspeople moving into high-level government posts was less common. Business and political leaders generally had different social, professional, geographic, economic, and educational backgrounds (Camp 1989). These tendencies led Smith (1979) to conclude that a "power elite," or a group of people possessing both economic and political power, did not exist in Mexico.

22 A *camarilla* refers to a small coterie of political allies or advisors who follow a candidate up Mexico's political ladder.
23 Both of Salinas's hand-picked presidential candidates, first Luis Donaldo Colosio and later – after Colosio's March 1994 assassination – Ernesto Zedillo, had been central figures in the Salinas *camarilla*.

Though these groups still differ in critical ways, they have become more similar in recent years.[24]

Centeno and Maxfield (1992) argue that a sizable business presence emerged within the government agencies in the 1980s. They base this conclusion on data collected mostly from biographical dictionaries on the background of bureaucratic elites in 1983. Although they do not have data for any of the other *sexenios*, they do break down the bureaucrats into two separate generations: (1) those whose first government job was before 1970, and (2) those whose first government job was after 1970.[25] Differences between the generations should be a good proxy for changes over time in the makeup of the government bureaucracy and serve as a good indicator of what is to come in the future as the younger generations move up through the ranks. In terms of social background, the authors found that 77 percent of elites who entered the government after 1970 had fathers whose occupation was either "professional" or "businessman," compared with approximately 70 percent of the pre-1970 elites (ibid., 66).[26]

A 7 percent difference between the social backgrounds of these two generations does not necessarily imply a fundamental redefinition of the Mexican bureaucrat. A more direct measure of the growing presence of businesspeople in the bureaucracy, the number of government elites who came out of private sector, suggests a more noteworthy transformation. Traditionally, this overlap has been relatively small. But the percentage of bureaucratic elites who had previous experience in private business was much larger (32%) for those who entered the government after 1970 than those who came in before 1970 (21%) (Centeno and Maxfield 1992, 73).

Impressionistic evidence suggests that these ties appear to have gotten more extensive after 1983 (see Luna, Tirado, and Valdés 1987, Maxfield 1987, Teichman 1992). For example, Centeno and Maxfield (1992) cite a paper by Smith (1991) in which "he sees 'a new private sector government alliance' and 'a remarkable business presence in government'" (72). Puga (1993a) refers to the incorporation of business into positions of public sector authority as "the consolidation of a broad sector that concentrates power and income and that could constitute, in the medium-term, a modern national oligarchy" (67). More concretely, Centeno (1990) describes "the complete absence of those from humble

24 Camp (1989) argues that these trends continued until the early 1980s (where most of his data end), but he also says that developments that might facilitate a greater exchange between the private sector and the state had already begun to take hold.
25 They also break them down by age, with a birth year of 1940 as the dividing point, and those data support more or less the same conclusions.
26 In each case, the remainder were distributed among the following categories: government official; peasant, laborer, or artisan; and other or don't know.

backgrounds" within the Mexican bureaucracy under the Salinas regime. Using slightly different measures (from cabinet-level bureaucrats only), his analysis of those from the twenty-four original Salinas cabinet members for whom data were published in the 1989 Biographical Dictionary of the Mexican government shows that half of this group had fathers who had worked in business (ibid., 460).

These kinds of data lead Centeno and Maxfield (1992) to conclude that the Mexican state's bureaucracy is not representative of the classes for whom the Revolution was fought: "If the bureaucracy 'belongs' to any social class, it is to professional and private industrialist fractions of the middle sector" (67). Beginning in the 1980s, business found better representation within the government bureaucracy. The new Mexican *tecnoburócrata* supported more market-oriented economic policies and also appeared to have closer ties to the private sector than his or her predecessors did. The emergence and fortification of the market-oriented, business-friendly *tecnoburócratas* and their ties to business helped strengthen the free traders' position within the state (Luna, Tirado, and Valdés 1987, Maxfield 1987, 1989a).

State Initiative

A more subtle and perhaps more intriguing aspect of policy coalition formation is the manner in which state policy can promote certain transformations within society, and how the state might subsequently respond politically and economically to those changes. This aspect of the problem can also be tied back indirectly to some of the changes that took place within the state bureaucracy. Government initiatives that effect changes within society may serve to alter the potential bases of societal support for certain policies and certain factions within the state. State and society are intertwined: Changes in society affect the state, and vice versa, in a continuing and unending pattern of reciprocal interaction. The state can induce changes in society that may later detract from, limit, add to, or enhance the state's capacity to govern. In this view, "economic institutions are created not to enhance the political life chances of all members of an incumbent regime but rather to privilege the economic and political fortunes of particular segments of the polity: interests that are better served by new kinds of economic policies" (Bates and Krueger 1993, 465). For example, the power shifts within the state favoring the financial and planning ministries may represent "an attempt to stabilize the fortunes and protect the political triumph of particular interests" served by these changes (ibid.). Coming full circle, the end result of this type of dynamic "is not economic decisions that are apolitical; rather, it is economic decisions that enhance the political prospects of politicians" (ibid.,

467). Two related aspects of the Mexican case in the 1980s and early 1990s illustrate this logic: (1) how state policy affected the relative fortunes of different private sector actors, and (2) how the state managed the political challenge of realigning itself with the favored segments of the business community. The Mexican state moved away from its traditional base of support and consolidated its ties to a new, stronger one to form, strengthen, and consolidate a free trade coalition.

State Actions Affecting the Internal Makeup of Business. State policies can alter the relative strength of existing politico-economic constituencies or even create new constituencies (or eliminate old ones) capable of participating in policy coalitions (see Frieden 1991a, 28). Several types of state policies in the 1980s helped alter the balance of forces in the private sector in ways that favored the free trade coalition's constituency. Chapter 3 discusses the de la Madrid and Salinas administrations' policies regarding the bank nationalization, capital markets, and foreign investment laws that hastened the development of a new, financially linked private sector elite.

The government's broader package of stabilization and structural adjustment reforms also helped transform the state's potential and existing private sector constituencies. One important component of this program was the privatization of much of the state enterprise sector of the economy. In addition to the banks, the government privatized several other state-owned companies in the 1980s and early 1990s. Between 1983 and 1992, 215 state-owned enterprises were sold off, and another 594 were either closed, merged, or transferred by the state (Bazdresch and Elizondo 1993, 51). Altogether, from 1982 to 1993, the Mexican state divested itself of some 942 parastatal entities, and by 1993 only 213 remained in state hands (Garrido 1993, 36). From 1989 to 1992 alone, the government sold state-owned assets valued at 6.5 percent of Mexico's 1991 GDP to private investors (Valdés Ugalde 1994, 234). Some of the more prominent examples of the privatized firms include companies from the sugar, automobile, food processing, tobacco, fertilizer, copper, airline, and telecommunications industries (Bazdresch and Elizondo 1993, 52).

Essentially starting from scratch and operating in a new policy environment, these privatized companies have a different economic and political perspective than most of the small, medium, and even large national industries that began to develop in the 1940s and 1950s and that have traditionally been more dependent on state patronage and protection. Furthermore, as one might expect, the purchases of the most expensive and most prominent parastatal firms have been made by the larger domestic and foreign business conglomerates that have access to the resources necessary to acquire them. The Cananea mining company, for example, was auctioned to Jorge Larrea's Grupo Industrial Minera México, which now controlled nearly 95 percent of national copper production and 6 percent of world production (Puga 1993a, 194). And Teléfonos de México (Telmex), Mexico's telecommunications monopoly, went to Carlos Slim, who had made his fortune as the head of the Inbursa brokerage group in the 1980s, and his Grupo Carso, which bought 20 percent of Telmex's stock and 51 percent of its voting options (ibid., Bazdresch and Elizondo 1993, 59). Many of the new owners of these privatized firms came from "the ranks of new private financiers that rose to power during the financially volatile 1980s" (Heredia 1992a, 25), and their acquisition of these companies fortified the development of the new, independent, financially connected entrepreneurial class. Additionally, these new entrepreneurs faced a relatively more hospitable international context and fewer market opportunities domestically, further encouraging their generally outward orientation. Because of their internal perspective and the opportunities offered by the external environment, these new businesspeople were generally more inclined and able to compete successfully with foreign competition and to participate in the free trade policy coalition.

Decreases in fiscal expenditures also facilitated the decline of the state-dependent business sector in the 1980s. Many of these companies had previously received high levels of direct and indirect subsidies from the government, and in conjunction with rapid inflation and sluggish domestic demand, the efforts to cut government spending hit them hard, sending many into bankruptcy. In addition, many of these firms had in the past sold a high proportion of their products to the parastatal sector (often at artificially inflated prices) and/or received subsidized inputs from state-owned firms. When the bulk of the state enterprise sector was sold off, it left many state-dependent firms in the lurch. "While in 1980 public sector revenues to small and medium industries were valued at 473.6 million pesos, in 1991 this figure was only 282.6 million" (Davis 1992, 25).[27]

Government policy toward privately held debt gave another boost to the largest firms and groups during the 1980s. In 1983, the government established the Fund for Exchange Risk (FICORCA) to provide financial assistance to indebted private firms. With FICORCA, the government set up a mechanism through which it would protect private borrowers from the risk of currency devaluation by covering the difference between the exchange rates at which the private sector took out and repaid dollar-

---

27 Davis does not indicate whether these are real or nominal figures, but we can probably assume that they are expressed in real terms. If they are expressed in current prices, the real decline would be much sharper.

denominated loans. This fund subsidized approximately half of the private sector's debts, for a total of $12 billion, but most of these benefits accrued only to the very largest firms in Mexico (Maxfield 1990, Pozas 1993). For example, just twenty large groups and businesses accounted for 80 percent of FICORCA's resources (Garrido and Quintana López 1988, 50). Moreover, these large firms "were those that assumed the leadership of the non-traditional export expansion" associated with Mexico's new export-oriented development model (Garrido 1991, 23).

Finally, positive feedback loops created by trade reform itself also fostered shifts within the business sector. Trade policy shifts are not entirely exogenous. Earlier reforms can gain momentum and help strengthen the free trade coalition's potential business sector membership base for later policy episodes. Once Mexico's reform process had gained a certain degree of momentum after mid-1985, it began to feed off of itself to begin creating a new group of proexport interests and weakening or even eliminating many import-competing interests in the private sector. This positive feedback loop helped clear the path for the liberalization measures that followed and provided greater potential support for each subsequent round of reform. Many of the firms that had opposed trade reform in the late 1970s and early 1980s had either adjusted or gone out of business by the latter part of the decade. "Before the introduction of the Mexican reform program in 1985, business held a strong stake in Mexico's protectionist regime. The majority now see their future tied to Mexico's more outward-looking policy mix" (Vega Cánovas 1991a, 4). As each policy episode passed, free trade gradually gained more support within the private sector. Reforms that were pushed through in 1985 by the narrow Bank of Mexico and World Bank-led sponsorship generated a broader base of private support that was recruited into the free trade coalition for the 1987–88 Solidarity Pact talks and the 1991–92 NAFTA negotiations (cf. Gil Díaz and Zepeda Payeras 1991).

On the whole, government policy strengthened the free trade coalition's private sector constituency of big business free traders during the 1980s and early 1990s.[28] Collectively, these changes "pointed toward the

---

28 The most important exception to this was the government's crawling peg exchange rate policy, which gradually led to a highly overvalued currency that eventually crashed in the 1994 peso devaluation. The steady increase in the real value of the peso undermined the competitive advantage gained by the tradables sector from sharp devaluations preceding the Economic Solidarity Pact in 1987 (Lustig 1998). These initial devaluations helped ease opposition from import competers and court supporters from exporters for free trade by making Mexico's imports more expensive and its exports cheaper. By the time the peso became overvalued and generated large trade deficits in the early 1990s, political support for free trade was strong enough to sustain the power of the free trade coalition through and beyond NAFTA's inauguration.

strengthening of the large business groups and the formation of new ones; toward the formation of monopolies and toward a pronounced stratification of business that tended increasingly to separate the largest exporting businesses from the smaller industrial concerns destined to cope with an increasingly competitive domestic market" (Puga 1993a, 192). At the same time, the state shifted its business alliances away from the inward-oriented industrialists and toward "the newly rising export-oriented firms and groups" (Heredia 1992a, 28).

Coalition Building. Beyond fomenting change within the business sector, key actors within the Mexican state also attempted to establish political alliances with private actors, especially those favored by recent developments in the business community: outward-oriented, big business. Politicians faced growing, double-barreled pressure from business exit and voice and recognized – even encouraged – the power shifts that had been taking place within business. The outward-oriented financial and planning sector state elite responded to this new reality by consciously establishing and reinforcing ties to a new coalition of support led by big business elites.

Partly as a result of the political activation of business discussed above, the Mexican state's official party, the PRI, faced increasing levels of electoral challenge, first from the right and later from both the right and the left. These pressures heightened the state's electoral vulnerability and threatened the political position of incumbent leaders. After dominating the electoral arena since 1929, the PRI maintained ever-decreasing margins of victory in many national, state, and municipal elections after the 1970s. Many believe that it had to resort to varying degrees of electoral fraud to maintain its hold on power (see Baer 1990). Figure 4.3 shows that the PRI experienced a fairly consistent decline (1976 and 1991 being the only exceptions) in the total share of votes for single-member district seats in the Chamber of Deputies. The vote for the PRI fell from over 90 percent in 1961 to 52 percent in 1988, before recovering somewhat to approximately 63 percent in 1991. The presidential votes have varied more, but the overall pattern is even more striking: The PRI received an average of nearly 90 percent of the votes from 1958 to 1976, but only 50.36 percent in 1988 (see Fig. 4.4).

Apart from the simple numerical challenges, tremendous public opposition to reported PRI-sponsored electoral fraud also began to emerge. After the 1986 gubernatorial and municipal elections, for example, "PRI cheating in the vote count was exposed in the press, leading to anti-PRI demonstrations and denunciations from both the political right and left" (Weintraub 1990, 42). Despite electoral reform laws passed in 1986 and 1989, opposition leaders continued to accuse the PRI of stealing

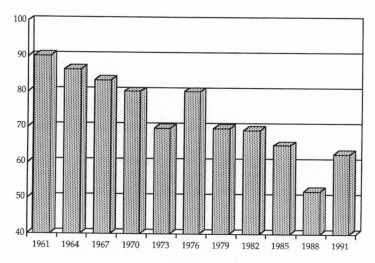

Figure 4.3. PRI votes for the Chamber of Deputies (percent), 1961–1991. *Source*: Baer (1990, 42) for 1961–85; *New York Times* (15 July 1988, 22 August 1991) for 1988 and 1991.

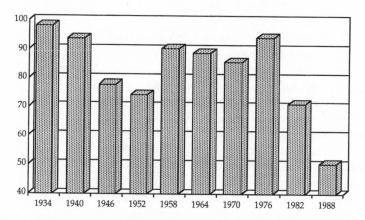

Figure 4.4. PRI votes for President, 1934–1988 (percent). *Source*: Grayson (1990).

elections that it had rightfully lost, such as the 1988 presidential race and the 1989 gubernatorial race in Michoacán (Cárdenas 1990). The PRI did start to loosen its grip slightly, allowing the PAN's 1989 victory in the Baja California gubernatorial race and small opposition gains in the Senate (four seats to the PRD in 1988) and Chamber of Deputies, where in 1988 the PRI captured 249 of the 300 single-member seats (after having held more than 290 since 1979). This left the PRI with 260 out of 500 total seats (Weintraub 1990, 47).[29]

But despite these opposition gains in the 1980s, the PRI was unwilling to relinquish its tight grip on power. For example, many analysts believe that the left-leaning son of former President Lázaro Cárdenas, Cuauhtémoc Cárdenas, actually received a plurality of votes in the 1988 presidential election. After an alleged late night computer breakdown was repaired, the official results gave the PRI 50.36 percent to Cárdenas's National Democratic Front's (FDN) – now the Democratic Revolutionary Party (PRD) – 31.12 percent (Grayson 1990). In addition, one knowledgeable observer claims that while conceding the PAN's 1989 victory in Baja California, "at the same time, the PRI stole elections from the PRD in Cárdenas' home state of Michoacán" (Pastor 1990, 11). Furthermore, many characteristics of the electoral system served to sustain PRI dominance by allowing only minimal opposition participation. For example, the Federal Electoral Commission, the agency responsible for monitoring elections in the 1980s, was still dominated by PRI officials (Pastor 1990, 11). Also, certain reforms in the late 1980s, while granting some concessions to the larger opposition parties, made it possible for the PRI to maintain a majority in the Congress with only a plurality (as low as 35%) of the votes (see Gilly 1990, 282). During the 1988 presidential campaign, PRI candidate Salinas admitted that the party was loath to relinquish power: "Our goal is to modernize to remain the majority, and not to weaken ourselves and fall into the burdens and shackles of parliamentary coalitions where the minorities end up governing" (quoted in Bailey and Gómez 1990, 303).

Much opposition to the PRI has been concentrated in the most urban, industrialized, and "modern" areas of the country. For example, Chamber of Deputies voting data from the 1985 midterm elections show that the PRI did most poorly in the Federal District, Baja California, Chihuahua, Jalisco, and Mexico state. "In these critical areas, the PRI ran from 10 to 15 percentage points below its national average of 65 percent of the vote" (Baer 1990, 43). At a broader level of aggregation, the PRI "consistently wins almost 20 percent more votes in rural districts than in urban congressional districts" (ibid.). This meant that the party increasingly relied on poor, rural constituencies for support while at the same time confronting the stepped-up pressure from the business sector in the dual form of disinvestment (exit) and political mobilization (voice).

29 Two hundred seats were decided via proportional representation and were more or less equally split between the PAN and PRD, leaving the opposition with a total of 240 Chamber of Deputies seats. The opposition pushed the PRI out of its majority position for the first time in 1997.

Trade Policy Coalitions in the 1980s

By the mid- to late 1980s, the Mexican state and its official party faced a dilemma. State and party leaders wanted to maintain power, but they were becoming increasingly vulnerable to the political and economic pressures exerted by business and other actors. Private sector disinvestment was exacerbating the economic stagnation that associated with the debt crisis, and business political participation through the PAN was beginning to make some inroads on the PRI's electoral hegemony. At the same time, the leftist opposition was also beginning to mount a serious challenge to the PRI (see Klesner 1994, 1997). Politically, party leaders needed to bolster support for the PRI in the urban and northern areas of the country where its opposition was strongest. Economically, state elites felt pressured to do something to boost investor confidence and attract scarce investment capital into the economy. In short, state and party leaders needed to renovate their alliances with their politico-economic coalitions of support to survive in power.

One response of the incumbent political elite to this dilemma was the gradual incorporation of business into the PRI. As the private sector began to increase its use of voice in the electoral arena in the 1980s, the PRI responded aggressively. Although this response likely included some degree of electoral fraud, it also involved an attempt to incorporate part of the business community into the party by forming alliances with individual business leaders and choosing business candidates to run against the PAN where private sector interests were strongest. Examples of the PRI running its own business candidates against the PAN include, among others, the 1983 elections in Sinaloa, the 1985 state elections in Sonora and Nuevo León, and the 1986 gubernatorial race in Chihuahua (Maxfield 1989a, 231). The party also opened channels for businesspeople to participate in political campaigns through finance committees and named several businesspeople to the cabinets of PRI state governments, including those in Nuevo León and Chihuahua (Mizrahi 1992, 769–770).

While this strategy appeared to have succeeded (at least temporarily) in dampening some of the private sector's enthusiasm for the PAN (Heredia 1992a, Loaeza 1992),[30] it also increased the influence of busi-

---

30 The PAN's fortunes were mixed in the 1990s. It still received a fairly high level of regional support in the northern areas of the country, exemplified by its victory in the 1992 gubernatorial race in Chihuahua. The strong showing by Diego Fernández de Cevallos in the 1994 presidential race suggested that the PAN had reemerged as the leading opposition party, but in 1997 the PRD's strong showing in midterm congressional elections and Cárdenas's victory in the race for mayor of Mexico City presented new challenges to the PAN. As the first opposition party to govern at the state level, the PAN's loss of the governorship of Chihuahua in 1998 shows that it has also suffered the drawbacks of incumbency during a crisis. See Rodríguez and Ward (1995) for an original analysis of opposition government in Mexico.

ness within the PRI, where business had never before been a major player. Luna, Tirado, and Valdés (1987) recognized this process just as it was beginning: "if pressure by the business sector and the PAN continues in the future, the PRI and the government will recruit more and more businessmen into their ranks. This, and not the noisy politicking of the PAN, in fact seems to be the most expeditious route to political power for businessmen" (42). The creation of the PRI's "business cells," a mechanism designed to incorporate businesspeople into the party's 1994 campaigns, confirmed much of this prophecy. By the latter part of the 1980s, state and party leaders were actively recruiting businesspeople into their own ranks, departing abruptly from the historical arrangement under which state leaders had kept their big business silent partners at arm's length from the political process. For the first time, these leaders began in the 1980s to solicit explicitly the active, outward participation of business in PRI politics and government. "President Miguel de la Madrid and, above all, President Carlos Salinas de Gortari have sought a new alliance between business and the government. This alliance presupposes more open political participation on the part of business and is therefore qualitatively different from the 'alliance for profits'" (Mizrahi 1992, 769).

The corollary to the increase in the private sector's participation in party life was a loss of labor influence within the PRI. "Basically, the period from 1980 to 1990 witnessed a fundamental transformation in the structure of power within the PRI which, among other things, reduced labor's say in national policy making" (Davis 1992, 16). Besides the push for inclusion in the political system by business, this reduction in the role of labor was related to divisions within the labor movement itself. These divisions were primarily the result of: (1) a push by rank-and-file union members for democratization of the unions that undermined working-class cohesion, and (2) the increase in the size of the nonorganized, informal labor sector that drew support away from organized labor, one of the three poles of the PRI. "With reduced solidarity the result, the labor movement itself had less bargaining power with government policy makers" (ibid., 18).

In addition, the power of the PRI itself, still considered to be one of the last bastions of labor support despite business's recent gains in the party, declined in the 1980s and early 1990s in relation to other components of the state, especially the Presidency and the Programming and Finance Ministries (Centeno and Maxfield 1992, Davis 1992). Centeno (1990), for example, describes the difficulty in the late 1980s of finding press references to PRI labor linchpin Fidel Velázquez, whose every political move and weekly briefings had previously been front-page news. Many old popular party ties were severed, and new lines of contact with society often ran through the executive rather than through the party. A good example of this institutional power shift was the prominent role of Salinas's National Solidarity Program (Pronasol) poverty alleviation program, overseen for a time by *salinista* Luis Donaldo Colosio while he headed the Ministry of Social Development. Pronasol bypassed the traditional corporatist structures of the PRI in favor of direct executive-popular class linkages. Pronasol was credited with restoring some of the regime's popular sector support by distributing resources in some of the most politically contested regions, though critics have questioned its overall effectiveness as a poverty reduction program (see Dresser 1991, Davis 1992, Pastor and Wise 1997, Trejo and Kaufman 1997).

These shifting and expanding ties between business and the state interacted closely with government policy. In general, the incorporation of business as a political ally helped make the party platform and government policy much more probusiness. As business's political influence grew, the PRI government increasingly pursued policies, such as fiscal restraint, reduction in the size and scope of the public sector, and trade liberalization, that could have been lifted straight from the PAN's platform. In 1987, one author predicted that the

> PRI strategy of response to business participation in opposition party politics will guarantee changes in the content of public policy, making it more probusiness. PRI candidates and elected officials will increasingly echo the preferences of big business for less state intervention in areas of production and commercialization which compete with the private sector and in redistributive activities. They will also support opening Mexico to the international economy and policies of strict wage control (Maxfield 1987, 11).

Five years later, Mizrahi (1992) confirmed that "the government has adopted radical economic policies, many of which had been banners of the opposition" (770). Similarly, "in the final analysis the policies of Carlos Salinas de Gortari are satisfying the demands presented by the PAN in its historical program" (Gilly 1990, 282).

The state's realignment of political and economic coalitions came to the forefront in trade policy. A new generation of state policy makers more responsive to the interests of big business came to power in the 1980s and began to implement trade policies likely to be favored by large, outward-oriented firms. Entrenched interests within both the state and the private sector resisted these changes, but with the support of the President (as well as the World Bank), free trade's political sponsors initiated a trade reform program beginning in mid-1985 and fomented the growth of the nascent free trade coalition. At the time, the credibility and permanence of this trade reform program were not at all clear.[31] The subsequent rounds of liberalization in the late 1980s and early 1990s then became both a cause and consequence of the restructuring of the state's alliances with the private sector. State policy makers designed a trade policy regime that would benefit precisely those groups in the business community whose power had already begun to increase in the 1980s. Each subsequent round of liberalization thus served to accelerate developments that had their own momentum. By the time of the 1987–88 Economic Solidarity Pact negotiations, the big business free trade constituency was sufficiently well developed to be explicitly incorporated into the free trade coalition by the now more united state free trade contingency through the pact's peak-level concertation mechanisms. It was during this time that the free trade coalition took over the trade policy-making process in Mexico. By the beginning of the 1990s, the government was poised to consolidate its own political and economic position by fortifying its new free trade coalition with the private sector.

31 Following a long tradition, many businesspeople expected the reforms to be reversed by the time the next government devised its own trade policies (interviews with various business leaders).

5

Assembling Teams and Building Bridges

INTRODUCTION

Mexico's participation in the NAFTA negotiations with the United States and Canada represents the final stage in the development of the free trade coalition and the incorporation of big business as an active partner in trade policy. The establishment of this free trade coalition between the state and the private sector was one of the keys behind the government's pursuit of a free trade agreement with the United States (and eventually Canada). "Its new alliance with the business sector has given the government important support to push forward this [NAFTA] proposal, with big business spearheading the process" (Pozas 1993, 84). This alliance joined together big business elites with a new generation of like-minded, financial- and planning-oriented free trade state elites that by now controlled almost all of the Mexican state's economic policy bureaucracy. This chapter examines the breadth, depth, and nature of private sector participation in trade policy and the related evolution and relative strength of competing cross-cutting business-state coalitions leading up to and during the NAFTA negotiations of 1991–92. The next section describes some of the initial efforts put forth by the Salinas administration to reassure wary investors. The following section traces the origins and makeup of the state's NAFTA negotiating team. The fourth section discusses the private sector's incorporation into the official negotiating framework and the institutional mechanisms created to channel business participation. The final section considers two possible explanations for this new consultative style of policy making.

CONSOLIDATING THE FREE TRADE COALITION

Following de la Madrid's efforts to restore business confidence and repair public-private sector alliances, new President Carlos Salinas de Gortari came into office in December 1988 convinced that he needed to step up his efforts to recruit private sector support if Mexico's new economic model was to lead the country successfully out of the economic crisis in which it had been mired for six years. Salinas moved quickly to adopt a series of measures designed to bring the private sector back into the fold and to boost society's confidence in the government after the complications of the 1988 elections had weakened the incoming President, a career technocrat who initially appeared to lack the personal charisma to attract the political support necessary to overcome the country's political and economic crises. These measures ranged across several different areas of the state's domain, and they came to symbolize much of what the Salinas administration would stand for over the course of the *sexenio*.

Salinas acted quickly and boldly to curry private sector favor by naming Claudio X. González, president of the multinational firm Kimberley-Clark de México, to serve as a presidential advisor for economic affairs, with a special emphasis on foreign investment. González, who served as president of the Business Coordinating Council (CCE) from 1985 to 1987, is known for his orthodox economic views (Puga 1993a, 182). His appointment in the second week of the Salinas presidency was clearly an effort to court business sector support by bringing one of its own into the uppermost reaches of the economic policy bureaucracy, where González would have enviably close contact with the President. González was the most prominent businessperson to have been appointed to such a position in the Mexican government. His incorporation into the Office of the Presidency is a much bolder example of the entrance of businesspeople into the state bureaucracy discussed in Chapter 4.

Salinas also struck simultaneous blows against labor and corruption within the public enterprise sector when he arrested the oil workers' militant union boss, Joaquín Hernández Galicia ("La Quina"), on various criminal charges, including illegal importation of arms and murder (Samstad and Collier 1995, 26). La Quina had ruled the PEMEX union with a mixture of corruption and authoritarian control, and attempted to undermine the Salinas candidacy in 1988 by tacitly supporting Cárdenas (ibid.). His arrest presaged the subsequent restructuring both within the PRI and between the PRI and other arms of the state that undercut the political power of labor. These moves against the official labor movement also helped raise the private sector's confidence in the Salinas government.

The deregulation of the economy also bolstered private sector support for the new administration. One of the most common business complaints about their day-to-day interactions with the government was the extent to which government regulations obstructed business operations. A new office for deregulation was created in the Trade and Industrial

Development Ministry (SECOFI) to oversee the dismantling of many of the regulations seen as impeding the development of the business sector and economic growth. The many regulatory items under the jurisdiction of this office included numerous levels of extensive bureaucratic red tape to obtain business permits and licenses, and an intricate program of domestic price controls that necessitated a continuous process of direct oversight of business practices by low-level SECOFI officials (interviews with business and government officials). The new office was headed up by Arturo Fernández, a young, University of Chicago-trained economist who would later become Rector of the Autonomous Technological Institute of Mexico (ITAM), a private university with close connections to the business community. ITAM is also well known for neoclassical economics and as the intellectual home of many of Mexico's new generation of state elites. Under Fernández's direction, the deregulation of the Mexican economy helped to improve the image of the government (and SECOFI in particular) in the eyes of many Mexican businesspeople (interviews with business leaders).

Several probusiness policies initiated by the de la Madrid administration and sustained by Salinas also continued to attract private sector support. For example, the process of privatization of state-owned enterprises initiated in the 1980s gained more momentum under Salinas, who auctioned off several of the largest and most important parastatals, including Telmex and the banks (see Rogozinski 1993). Salinas also renewed the Economic Solidarity Pact (PSE) under a new name, the Pact for Economic Stabilization and Growth (PECE), transplanting the name "solidarity" to his pet poverty alleviation program, Pronasol. The new pact continued to operate and conduct weekly peak-level meetings between government, business, and labor leaders. The pact received much of the credit for controlling and lowering inflation during the Salinas administration, which saw the annual rate of growth of consumer prices fall from almost 160 percent in 1987 to under 20 percent in 1989, before rising briefly to about 30 percent in 1990. The rate of inflation soon dipped below 20 percent in 1991 and 1992, and it eventually fell into single digits, topping out at 8 percent in 1993 and 7.1 percent in 1994 (data calculated from Banco de México n.d.). Business rhetoric had emphasized precisely these kinds of measures for the past several years, and they were especially popular among the larger segments of business that tend to reap relatively greater benefits and incur relatively fewer losses from these programs. Their burgeoning success helped to shore up private sector support for the new administration.

Much of the business community reacted positively to the new policies pursued by de la Madrid and deepened under Salinas. This was especially true at the upper echelons of the private sector, among the big business elite. CCE president and financier Agustín Legorreta expressed in mid-1988 his support for the new mode of governing the Mexican economy:

During its 12 years of existence, the CCE has lived through the breakout of inflation, crisis and recurring recoveries, the illusion of the petroleum bonanza, the disproportionate growth of the foreign debt, the nationalization of the banks, the growing obesity of the public sector and, *now, the policies of the present administration* to make the government stronger by reducing its size, to substitute closed protectionism with the opening of foreign trade, to restructure the productive apparatus, modernizing it and making it more competitive and to eradicate definitively inflation (quoted in Puga 1993a, 182–83, emphasis in original).

These measures further eased many private sector concerns about the economic role of the state, and they helped pave the way for the state's incorporation of big business as an active partner who would be central to the consolidation of free trade coalition's position in the trade policy-making apparatus. The Salinas administration's principal focus in trade policy was NAFTA. The Salinas government had not originally anticipated pursuing a free trade agreement with the United States or Canada, at least not openly. On several occasions, candidate and President Salinas had publicly declared that his administration would not request a free trade agreement with the United States. The administration's original national development and foreign trade plans did not mention the possibility of a trade agreement with Mexico's northern neighbors, emphasizing instead a multilateral and sectoral strategy for gaining the market access necessary for the success of the country's new export-oriented development model. The 1989–94 National Development Plan, for example, called for Mexico "to make use of the advantages of the GATT to conduct multilateral negotiations" and "to utilize bilateral negotiations to gain permanent access to foreign markets for Mexican exports, to counteract the diversion of trade that could result from the trade integration of regional blocs" (reprinted in Arriola 1994a). The 1990–94 National Industrial Modernization and Foreign Trade Program also emphasized the GATT, as well as negotiations to open markets to the south of Mexico through the Latin American Integration Association (ALADI). With respect to trade with the United States, this plan called not for the comprehensive regional trade treaty that would eventually come to pass, but rather for continued reliance on sectoral accords between the two countries in such sectors as steel and textiles (SECOFI 1991). As Salinas himself summarized the situation in early 1990, "we are promoting sector by sector agreements to guarantee our exports greater and more secure access to the North American market" (quoted in Arriola 1994a).

Salinas appears to have made the decision to pursue a free trade agreement with the United States (the decision to include Canada came later) shortly after his visit to the February 1990 annual meetings of the World Economic Forum in Davos, Switzerland. The President had hoped that his appearance at the meetings would help diversify Mexico's foreign trade relations, three fourths of which were concentrated with the United States. In his keynote address at Davos, Salinas touted the many remarkable achievements of his country's recent economic reforms and spoke of the propitious environment for foreign participation in the Mexican economy. Salinas's reliance on the sectoral approach and third party markets and his lack of public support for negotiating a free trade agreement with the United States were apparent in an interview he gave at Davos:

The differences between the economies of Mexico and the United States are so large that we are not contemplating entering a common market in the foreseeable future; nevertheless, we do want closer trade relations with the United States and Canada. That is the reason for the stimulating [sectoral] agreements we have already reached with those two great nations. But at the same time, we want to have a more active presence in the European Community and the Pacific Rim, and to strengthen our historical ties to Latin America (ibid.).

The response the Davos speech received from the Europeans and others present at the meetings, though polite, disappointed Salinas and reportedly inspired him to rethink his diversification strategy. In early 1990, Eastern Europe had just begun to open up after the fall of the Berlin Wall in November 1989, and the eyes of Western Europe fixated on events unfolding in the east. Plans for future investment also aimed at this untapped market. Mexico surely must have seemed very distant to the Europeans in early 1990, as evidenced by the overflow crowds attending the Eastern European meetings and the number of empty chairs at the Mexico panels (see Golob 1992). According to several people familiar with the situation, Salinas reversed strategy on the plane ride home from Davos, deciding instead to explore the possibility of a free trade agreement with the United States partly because he now believed that the European and Asian support and participation he had sought would not be forthcoming (interviews with government officials). Salinas did not want Mexico to end up on the outside looking in on what he viewed as the increasing regionalization of international trade: "Look at the blocs that are being created: Europe in 1992, the Pacific Basin countries, the United States and Canada. I don't want to be left out" (quoted in Gilly 1990, 285).

A little more than a month after the Davos meetings, the *Wall Street Journal* broke a story reporting that Mexico had approached the Bush administration about the possibility of negotiating of a free trade agreement between the United States and Mexico. In April 1990, the Mexican Senate called a National Forum of Consultation on Mexico's foreign trade relations, which concluded in May by recommending the negotiation of a free trade agreement with the United States. Bush and Salinas met on June 10 and 11, and on June 11 the two countries issued a joint communiqué in which they announced their intentions to negotiate a free trade agreement between them. By February 1991, Canada officially joined the NAFTA negotiations. The trilateral trade negotiations began on June 12, 1991, in Toronto and concluded on August 12, 1992, in Washington, D.C. (Arriola 1994a, various SECOFI documents).

The remainder of this chapter shows how the actual process of negotiating NAFTA with the United States and Canada both served and benefited from the consolidation of the power of the free trade coalition. This consolidation, crucial to the successful negotiation and implementation of NAFTA, was achieved largely via the incorporation of big business into the negotiations by a unified team of state bureaucrats. To achieve this, the new generation of state policy elites sought to establish direct ties to certain powerful groups within the private sector by officially including them in the negotiating framework set up by the government.

THE STATE'S NEGOTIATING TEAM

The new, free trading state elite that had emerged in the 1980s came to control virtually all of the economic policy bureaucracy in Mexico in the Salinas administration. This group still held control over the financial and planning sectors of the state, including the Bank of Mexico (Banxico) and the Ministries of Finance and Public Credit (SHCP) and Programming and Budget (SPP). Under Salinas, a planning person who had spent his entire bureaucratic and political career in SHCP and SPP, this group extended its influence to agencies that had traditionally been the territory of some of the more nationalist factions, most notably SECOFI. In a style characteristic of the hierarchical and patronage-based Mexican political system, these changes began at the very top of the pyramid, at the level of the President and his cabinet, and made their way down to the lower levels of the economic policy bureaucracy.

The Salinas Team

Within the bureaucracy as a whole, data from the Mexican *Diccionario Biográfico* (Biographical Dictionary) suggest that the development of the new, foreign-educated financial-planning state elite of earlier years continued at an even faster pace under the new Salinas administration. For all those included in the 1989 edition's statistical analysis, Centeno (1990) finds that the new generation tended to come from urban origins, and that the number of bureaucrats with peasant and worker backgrounds declined. Some 48 percent of the mid- to upper-level bureaucrats included in the analysis held graduate degrees in 1989.

Similar measures show even clearer patterns of change in the same direction at the cabinet level, where a full 50 percent of the twenty-four original Salinas cabinet members held graduate degrees, compared with 35 percent under de la Madrid and less than 20 percent under López Portillo (Centeno 1990; see also my Chapter 4, Table 4.7). This group continued the move away from a concentration in law (21%) and toward undergraduate study in economics (46%). About 30 percent of the original cabinet studied in the United States. In terms of bureaucratic-institutional backgrounds, one third of the cabinet had previous experience in the Ministry of Finance, and half of the entire cabinet had previously served in Programming and Budget, where SPP Minister Salinas had successfully built up a strong contingent of political allies who would follow him into the next *sexenio*. The new cabinet averaged fifty-two years of age, but this figure obscures a subtle division of the cabinet into two distinct age cohorts. The first of these groups fell in the mid- to late fifties age bracket, while the members of the second were much younger, in their late thirties and early forties (Centeno 1990, 460–62). Much of the younger cohort worked in the economic sphere of the cabinet.

At the level of the economic cabinet, the precocious Salinas financial-planning team filled the most important positions. These people epitomized Centeno and Maxfield's (1992) new hybrid *tecnoburócrata* category of state elites. Most of this new generation came from privileged private sector backgrounds, studied at private Mexican universities and/or in the United States, received undergraduate degrees in economics or administration, and held graduate degrees (many with Ph.D.s) in economics. Most of them also began their careers and rose to power within the financial and planning sectors of the state bureaucracy, most commonly in SPP, where they had hitched their wagons to Salinas's rising political star beginning in the late 1970s and continuing through the 1980s.

Moving to the very top of the economic policy bureaucracy, the data suggest that the formula for success included youth, private Mexican and/or U.S. education, graduate degrees in economics from top U.S. universities, and a career path that passed through the financial and planning arms of the state bureaucracy.[1] The President himself, forty years

---

1 Unless cited otherwise, the following biographical data come from my own analysis of the 1992 *Diccionario Biográfico* (Presidencia de la República 1992).

old at the time of his inauguration in December 1988, studied economics at the public UNAM before he left for Cambridge, Massachusetts, to enter graduate school. Salinas obtained a master's in Public Administration from Harvard and a master's and doctorate in Political Economy and Government from Harvard's John F. Kennedy School of Government. He began his career in the Ministry of Finance, where he worked from 1974 to 1979, and made his rise to power within Programming and Budget between 1979 and 1987. While at SPP, Salinas managed to compile a strong team of like-minded *tecnoburócratas* with personal, educational, and professional backgrounds similar to his own.

A collection of the most important economic advisors to President Salinas included, in alphabetical order, Pedro Aspe (SHCP), Luis Donaldo Colosio (PRI, Ministry of Urban Development and Ecology (SEDUE), Ministry of Social Development (SEDESOL)), José Córdoba (Presidential Chief of Staff), Jaime Serra (SECOFI), and Ernesto Zedillo (SPP, Education). Aspe took the reigns at Finance after his rapid rise through the ranks of SPP beginning in 1985 and culminating in October 1987 when he took over as Minister of SPP after Salinas's nomination as the PRI's presidential candidate. Colosio, a previous SPP bureaucrat and representative from Sonora in the Chamber of Deputies, was strategically placed at the head of the PRI, where he utilized his experience from managing the 1988 Salinas presidential campaign to oversee the restructuring of the party along the lines of the new Salinas project. He was later tapped to head SEDUE and its successor, SEDESOL, which administered the popular Pronasol poverty alleviation program. Colosio remained at SEDESOL from May 1992 until November 1993, when Salinas chose him as the PRI's 1994 presidential candidate. Córdoba, arguably Salinas's most influential advisor despite being ineligible for the presidency,[2] emerged from SPP to take on a new position as Salinas's Chief of Staff, which gave him responsibility for a wide range of policy areas. Jaime Serra applied his previous experience in Finance to SECOFI, which would lead the NAFTA negotiations for Mexico. Ernesto Zedillo succeeded Aspe at Programming and Budget until Aspe's Finance Ministry subsumed SPP in 1992. He then moved to Education, where he continued to advise the President on economic matters as a member of the cabinet until he was named in November 1993 to manage the Colosio presidential campaign. Zedillo eventually stepped in as the PRI's presidential candidate after Colosio's March 1994 assassination in Tijuana.

Table 5.1 highlights some of the most relevant characteristics of the

---

2 Córdoba was constitutionally barred from running for the presidency because he was born in France to exiled Spanish Republican parents. The Mexican Constitution required that the President be born in Mexico to native Mexican parents.

Table 5.1. *The Salinas Economic Team*

Name	Position	Age in Dec. 1988	B.A.	Course of study	U.S. study?	Graduate school	Graduate degrees[a]	Subject	Financial/ planning experience
Carlos Salinas de Gortari	President	40	National Autonomus Univ. of Mexico	Economics	Yes	Harvard	MA/Ph.D.	Administration; Political Economy and Government	SHCP, SPP
Pedro Aspe Armella	Finance	38	Autonomous Technological Institute of Mexico	Economics	Yes	MIT	Ph.D.	Economics	SHCP, SPP
Luis Donaldo Colosio Murrieta	PRI, SEDESOL	38	Monterrey Technological Institute	Economics	Yes	UPenn	MA/Ph.D.	Planning	SPP
José Córdoba Montoya	Chief of Staff	38	École Polytechnique, Paris, France	Engineering	Yes	Sorbonne; Stanford	MA/Ph.D.	Economics	SPP
Jaime Serra Puche	Trade	37	National Autonomous Univ. of Mexico	Admin.	Yes	Yale	MA/Ph.D.	Economics	SHCP
Ernesto Zedillo	SPP, Education	36	National Polytechnic University	Economics	Yes	Yale	MA/Ph.D.	Economics	Banxico, SPP

Source: Presidencia de la República (1992).
[a] An "MA/Ph.D." or "Ph.D." entry means that the person attended a doctoral program; the *Diccionario Biográfico* does not always specify whether or not the Ph.D. was actually completed.

personal, educational, and career backgrounds of the Salinas economic team. The similarities within it and between the President and his advisors are striking. This group was uniformly young, ranging in age from 36 to 38 for an average of 37.4 years of age. All but one of them did their undergraduate work at a private Mexican university, the only exception being Serra, who like Salinas went to UNAM. Three out of the five majored in economics as undergraduates, and every one of them received a graduate degree from a top U.S. university, four of them in economics and the fifth (Colosio) in planning. They also followed very similar financial-planning career paths, with four of the five emerging from Programming and Budget and the fifth (Serra) from Finance.[3] In sum, the key members of the Salinas economic team consisted of a group of young, talented U.S.-trained economists with government experience in finance and planning.

The sharp divisions between and within different government economic agencies that had existed early in the de la Madrid administration were largely absent under Salinas. Although differences of opinion on specific issues would arise on occasion,[4] the overall politico-economic perspective of this group was remarkably consistent. As a group, these technocratic politicians operated under the same basic assumptions, the same economic and political views of how the world worked. This extraordinary degree of unity gave momentum to the NAFTA process. In fact, Mexico's pursuit of NAFTA itself partly reflects the influence and character of the small Salinas coterie. According to several observers close to the situation, Salinas made the original decision to request a free trade agreement with the United States with the assistance of three of his top economic advisors: Aspe, Córdoba, and Serra (interviews with government officials). This same central team of advisors also helped consolidate the state's new coalition with big business, a natural ally of this group, which viewed the private sector as the engine of future investment, employment, and economic growth. The actual consolidation of this trade policy coalition took place primarily through Serra's SECOFI offices, which directed Mexico's overall NAFTA efforts.

---

3 Zedillo also had significant prior experience in the orthodox Bank of Mexico, where from 1983 to 1987 he directed the Bank's FICORCA program, which gave debt relief to the private sector in the form of exchange rate protection (see Chapter 4).

4 A prime example here is the reported dispute over the need to devalue the peso between the August 1994 elections and the 1 December 1994 inauguration of the new administration. President-elect Ernesto Zedillo was reported to have pushed for a devaluation against Finance Minister Aspe and Chief of Staff Córdoba, who apparently argued that a sharp exchange rate adjustment was not immediately necessary. Aspe and Córdoba's position prevailed, and the December 1994 devaluation triggered the first major crisis of the Zedillo administration.

Assembling Teams and Building Bridges

Changes within SECOFI

The nomination of Jaime Serra to head up the Ministry of Trade and Industrial Development is especially important for the NAFTA question. Previous liberalization initiatives went forward over the protests of SECOFI, or at least without its overt cooperation. This ministry's traditional ties to protected industry, its explicit institutional linkage between trade and industrial programs, and the presence within it of entrenched bureaucratic interests who had come of age politically in the high-growth, closed economy era kept most of its leaders out of the free trade coalition. In fact, SECOFI frequently spearheaded the protectionist coalition to oppose policies of trade opening in the 1970s and 1980s. The few free traders within SECOFI represented a small minority, and those within the agency who did favor some degree of liberalization were generally less enthusiastic about rapid trade opening than their counterparts in other agencies, such as the Bank of Mexico, Programming and Budget, and Finance. This bureaucratic obstacle could present problems for an administration that put free trade at the center of its national development strategy (see the 1989–94 National Development Plan, reprinted in Arriola 1994a), given SECOFI's central role in trade policy making and implementation. Furthermore, the agency had strong ties to traditionally protected industry, which SECOFI-administered tariffs, import licenses, and official pricing mechanisms protected. This made SECOFI's support and active participation necessary to help quell opposition to trade reform and to establish new ties with pro-free trade private sector factions during the Salinas presidency. The consolidation of the free trade coalition required that SECOFI come fully on board with the reforms to ensure their deepening, stability, and permanence.

Serra's background, political experience, and direct personal involvement in Salinas administration trade policy helped promote the preparation and negotiation of the free trade agreement with the United States and Canada. Serra also changed the way that SECOFI as an institution approached its role in trade policy by altering the internal structure and balance of forces within the agency. Age thirty-seven when named to the SECOFI post, Serra had studied public administration at UNAM before getting his master's in economics in 1975 from the Colegio de México, one of Mexico's most prominent research and teaching institutions. From there, he moved on to Yale, where he earned a Ph.D. in economics in 1979 with a dissertation on Mexican fiscal policy. Prior to SECOFI, all of his postdoctorate professional career had been spent as an economics professor at the Colegio de México (1979–86) and Stanford (1982) and in SHCP. Serra occupied various positions in Finance from 1979 to 1988, including Head of Advisors to the Minister in 1986 and Undersecretary of Incomes Policy from 1986 to 1988. This strong background in finance led Salinas to appoint Serra as Minister of Trade and Industrial Development, despite the fact that he had not belonged to Salinas's tight Programming and Budget clique. Salinas clearly wanted an outsider in the SECOFI post, someone, like Serra, who did not cut his bureaucratic teeth on ISI, who did not owe too many political debts to people wedded to the protectionist model of development, and who had the capacity to undertake radical reforms of the ministry.

Shortly after taking over, Serra initiated an institutional and personnel overhaul of the Ministry of Trade and Industrial Development, cleaning house of the old protectionist order and leaving in its place a new generation of young, foreign-educated free traders and an institutional structure that reflected the new realities of an open economy. SECOFI is divided into a series of subministries, or undersecretariats. Prior to 1990, SECOFI had been divided into three separate undersecretariats: foreign trade, industry, and internal commerce (*comercio interior*).[5] Until Serra's arrival, the overall balance among these three basic divisions had been relatively even. But after the late 1980s, the strength of the industry and internal commerce undersecretariats withered. Industry's bureaucratic territory shrank as most sectoral programs were discarded in favor of a more "horizontal" program designed to level the playing field for all sectors of business. Similarly, a large portion of the internal commerce area was dismantled as the elimination of the official pricing system and the deregulation of the economy proceeded. The Serra regime cut many resources and personnel in these undersecretariats, especially at the lower levels of the bureaucracy charged with implementation and enforcement (interviews with SECOFI officials, SECOFI documents).

Along with these cutbacks came changes in the basic characteristics of SECOFI personnel, especially at the higher levels of the agency, which grew during these years (interviews with SECOFI officials). Much as Salinas did with his group of high-level economic advisors, Serra brought with him from Finance a team of young free-market economists when he took over at SECOFI. The new Undersecretary for Foreign Trade, Herminio Blanco, was a thirty-eight-year-old University of Chicago-trained economist with experience in SHCP and the Office of the Presidency. Pedro Noyola had a Stanford Ph.D. and was just thirty-two when he stepped in as Undersecretary for Foreign Trade in place of Blanco, who moved over to SECOFI's NAFTA office in 1990 (see below). The new team even extended its influence to the Undersecretariat for Industry and

---

5 In very broad terms, foreign trade dealt with tariff policy and general foreign trade policies, industry with the individual sectoral industrial development programs, and internal commerce with domestic business regulations and official pricing policies.

Foreign Investment, where Fernando Sánchez Ugarte took his graduate training in economics from the University of Chicago and his valuable SHCP experience to his new job as Undersecretary at age thirty-eight. This area had traditionally been closely linked to the ISI model of development and the sectoral programs that had subsidized and protected certain sectors. Under Salinas and Serra's guidance, Sánchez Ugarte eliminated most of these instruments of Mexican industrial policy. True to his Chicago roots, Sánchez Ugarte described his office's "New Focus":

to create competitive markets that motivate efficient investment by private entrepreneurs and to create productive employment. This contrasts with the past, which was characterized by excessive and at times redundant protection, excessive participation of the government in industry, and excessive regulations that contradicted [existing] protection (Sánchez Ugarte, n.d.).

In the same document, Sánchez Ugarte goes on to cite the related steps of stabilization, trade opening (and its consolidation), and deregulation that preceded his efforts to reform the industrial domain of SECOFI.

These changes helped redefine SECOFI as an institution. It had worked to oppose or least slow down earlier efforts at trade reform, but under Serra it closely reflected the overall profile of the Salinas team of free traders. Differences between the different undersecretariats, though still present, were now far narrower. One SECOFI official put it this way: "We are all from the same universities, and we all subscribe to the same economic theories" (interview). The different branches of SECOFI were now pursuing the same basic free-market goals. The most important of these goals was the negotiation of NAFTA.

The NAFTA negotiations provoked another important institutional change within SECOFI. In February and March of 1990, Jaime Serra and Herminio Blanco began preparations for the impending (but still confidential) North American free trade negotiations. At the time, Blanco still served as Undersecretary for Foreign Trade, but NAFTA issues had begun to take up an increasing proportion of his time and that of his staff, much of which became devoted full-time to NAFTA issues (interviews with SECOFI officials). After the June 1990 Bush-Salinas joint communiqué, it became apparent that a new institutional mechanism would be necessary to coordinate Mexico's participation in the NAFTA negotiations. On September 5, 1990, under the instructions of President Salinas, Serra created the new Office for the Negotiation of the Free Trade Agreement and named Blanco to direct it (SECOFI documents).[6]

---

6 At the same time, an Intersecretarial Commission presided over by SECOFI was created to hold monthly meetings on the status of the negotiations among the following agencies: Foreign Relations, Finance and Public Credit, Programming and Budget, Labor, the Bank of Mexico, and the Office of the Presidency.

This office attained de facto undersecretariat status in short order, attracting many of the government's best, brightest, and youngest people. Soon it would surpass the other three undersecretariats in importance, and in February 1993 it officially became the Undersecretariat for Foreign Trade Negotiations, with Blanco serving as its Undersecretary (Blanco 1994).[7]

Blanco moved quickly to assemble a team of negotiators to staff SECOFI's new NAFTA office. Blanco himself was at the time a forty-year-old graduate in economics of the Monterrey Technological Institute (ITESM), which along with ITAM has one of the country's top economics programs. He spent much of the expansionary 1970s (1972–78) away from Mexico getting his master's and Ph.D. in economics from the University of Chicago, where he wrote a doctoral thesis on investment and uncertainty. He began his political-bureaucratic career as an advisor to the Minister of Finance before moving on to teach at Rice University from 1980 to 1985. He served as an economic advisor to de la Madrid from 1985 until his SECOFI appointment in December 1988. Blanco brought along his top advisor from the Undersecretariat for Foreign Trade, Jaime Zabludovsky, to serve as the new Office for the Negotiation of the Free Trade Agreement's Coordinator General, a position equivalent to Deputy Undersecretary. Zabludovsky held an undergraduate degree in economics from ITAM and a master's and Ph.D. in economics from Yale when he took on his new job in 1990 at thirty-four years of age. He had been an economic researcher for the Bank of Mexico before moving to the Office of the Presidency, where he was an economist for the Committee of Economic Advisors from 1985 to 1988. In 1988 he moved with Blanco to SECOFI's Undersecretariat for Foreign Trade, where he spent a year as the Director General of Trade Policy before becoming an advisor to the Undersecretary in 1989. In the new NAFTA office, Zabludovsky's main responsibilities were to serve as Blanco's deputy during the preparation and negotiation of NAFTA and to oversee the daily operations of the office and the Mexican negotiating team. He was the "man on the ground," with as much daily, detailed contact with the negotiations as anyone in the Mexican government.

Blanco and Zabludovsky organized the SECOFI free trade agreement office to reflect the structure of the actual NAFTA negotiations, which were divided first into seventeen, then nineteen, and finally eighteen different groups (or tables) based mostly on general themes, such as

7 One post hoc measure of the importance of this office (and of NAFTA) is the fact that new President Zedillo named Blanco to replace Serra as Minister of SECOFI in December 1994.

Table 5.2. *Profile of the SECOFI Negotiating Team*

Characteristics of the lead negotiators	Number	Percentage
Average age in June 1991	40.9	—
Father had professional occupation	5	71.4
Studied at Mexican private or U.S.		
university	6	85.7
Private Mexican university	(5)	(71.4)
U.S. university	(4)	(57.1)
Studied economics as an undergraduate	6	85.7
Graduate degree	6	85.7
Master's	(6)	(85.7)
Ph.D.	(3)	(42.9)
Financial-planning sector experience	5	71.4
Programming and Budget	(2)	(28.6)
Finance and Public Credit	(2)	(28.6)
Bank of Mexico	(1)	(14.3)

Note: N = 7, out of a total of 12 lead negotiators. See Table 5.1, note a, regarding graduate degrees.
Source: SECOFI documents; Presidencia de la República (1992).

market access, rules of origin, and dispute settlement, as well as on a few key sectors, including automotive, textiles, and agriculture (interviews with government and business officials, SECOFI documents). Blanco and Zabludovsky assembled a team of twelve lead negotiators to direct the Mexican contingents of the eighteen final negotiating tables.[8] Below the lead negotiators were other SECOFI representatives, both from the NAFTA office and from other areas of the ministry, as well as representatives from the other affected state agencies (e.g., SHCP for financial services, the Ministry of Agriculture for agriculture, etc.). The politico-economic profile of the new SECOFI office closely resembled that of the Serra and Salinas economic advisory teams. Along with Blanco and Zabludovsky, these people (and their individual staffs) collectively made up a group of young, U.S.- and/or private Mexican-educated, financial-planning economists. Table 5.2 provides a broad profile of the personal, educational, and career backgrounds of the seven (out of twelve total) lead negotiators whose entries appear in the 1992 *Diccionario Biográfico*.[9] Again, this was a young group, ranging in age from thirty-five to

8 The number of lead negotiators is less than the number of tables because some negotiators directed more than one table.
9 My interviews with six of the twelve lead negotiators (including three of the five for whom data were not published) and others suggest that the profiles of the remaining five were similar to those presented in Table 5.2.

forty-seven, with an average age of about forty-one. They generally did not come from particularly humble backgrounds, as five of the seven had fathers whose occupation could be classified as "professional" (doctors, lawyers, engineers, etc.).[10] Five of the seven went to college at a private Mexican university, including two at ITAM and two at ITESM, and four had studied in the United States at one time or another. All but one of the seven received an undergraduate degree in economics, and the same number held graduate degrees in economics, including six master's and three doctorates. Five of the seven passed through the financial and planning wings of the state bureaucracy on their way to the SECOFI free trade negotiating team, with two each having served in SPP and SHCP and one in the Bank of Mexico.

This new group of state elites based in the Salinas cabinet, in SECOFI as a whole, and within its NAFTA office also had new attitudes about its relationship with the private sector, which had been held at arm's length during most previous trade policy episodes. Based in part on the positive results of the 1987–88 and subsequent stabilization and adjustment pacts, Salinas and Serra decided early on that the direct participation and support of the private sector would be necessary to maximize the chances of success of the NAFTA negotiations and Mexico's potential benefits from the agreement. For its part, much of the business community reacted quite favorably to the changes taking place within SECOFI and to the inclusionary overtures made by the Serra regime. One businessperson involved in the NAFTA negotiations praised the new outlook of the government thusly: "It's a new generation, with different ideas from the past" (interview). Another claimed that in contrast to the new group of SECOFI trade policy makers, "the old generation would not have consulted with the private sector" (interview). The new state elite took bold steps in mid-1990 to bring private sector interests into the fold, incorporating business into the NAFTA negotiations in an unprecedented, official consultative role.

INCORPORATING BUSINESS

The new state elite moved quickly to consolidate the power of the free trade coalition by courting the active support and participation of the business community. This was especially true for the private sector's largest, most dynamic segments that had ties to the international (especially the U.S.) economy and that would be expected to have the most to gain from the free trade agreement.

10 The other two did not have their father's occupation listed.

CACINTE

One of the first steps in this direction was the creation of a new organism to bring together various government and societal groups to discuss and help define Mexico's overall negotiating position. The Advisory Council for the Free Trade Agreement (CACINTE), officially formed at about the same time (September 1990) as SECOFI's Office for the Negotiation of the Free Trade Agreement, was originally to have twenty-one members, including five from the private sector. Jaime Serra and a team from the SECOFI free trade office headed up CACINTE, which also included the leaders of the labor, agricultural, business, and academic sectors (SECOFI documents). Its membership eventually reached thirty people, broken down as follows: five members from the public sector (all from SECOFI), five from labor, four from agriculture, nine from business, and seven from the academic sector. Thus, not counting agriculture among its ranks, business held the largest share of CACINTE representation at 30 percent (SECOFI 1993b). Furthermore, Puga (1993b) reports that the three business organizations devoted exclusively to foreign trade issues also participated in the meetings in an unofficial capacity, and that the most frequent attendees of CACINTE meetings were the business representatives.

The representation of the private sector itself within CACINTE was highly skewed toward the largest groups and firms. The business contingent in this body included (ca. 1992) the presidents of the CCE (Nicolás Madáhuar Cámara), CONCAMIN (Jesús Cevallos Gómez), and CONCANACO (Ricardo Dájer Nahum), as well as Juan Gallardo Thurlow, the Private Sector Coordinator for the Negotiation of the Free Trade Agreement (see below). The remaining five official private sector CACINTE members all came from the exclusive ranks of the powerful Mexican Businessmen's Council (CMHN). The CMHN members present within CACINTE were the then-CMHN president Enrique Hernández Pons, former CMHN and CCE president (and advisor to President Salinas) Claudio X. González of Kimberley-Clark, the Grupo Arancia's Ignacio Aranguren Castiello, Andrés Marcelo Sada of the Grupo Cydsa, and Industrias Bachoco's Enrique Robinson Bours (SECOFI 1993b). More than half of the business representatives in CACINTE came from the ranks of the very top of Mexico's business elite via the CMHN alone.

In contrast, many other business organizations had no direct representation at all on the Advisory Council. One of the most notable omissions is that of CANACINTRA, the principal small- and medium-sized industry business organization. Not only did CANACINTRA lack a representative in CACINTE, but it is also not a voting member of the CCE, the peak organization that presumably represented the business sector as a whole on the council. Although some have argued (with some merit) that CACINTE's basic mission was one of public relations, of simply legitimizing the negotiating process by creating an image of broad societal support for NAFTA (see Puga 1993b), the balance of forces within this body nevertheless suggests two tentative conclusions. First, business concerns were being officially included within the government-sponsored NAFTA negotiating framework. Second, this incorporation exhibited a clear pattern of favoritism toward the very largest sectors of the business community. The government chose to ally itself with the largest and most powerful factions of the private sector when constructing CACINTE.

Coordinating Council of Foreign Trade Business Organizations

Far more important to the consolidation of the free trade coalition were the mechanisms established to facilitate more extensive and closer relations between state policy makers and business during the actual preparation and negotiation stages of the free trade agreement. The Mexican government encouraged the private sector to develop a formal vehicle to incorporate business into the NAFTA negotiations on a more direct, day-to-day level than CACINTE. As the government began preparations for negotiating a free trade agreement with the United States and Canada in the spring of 1990, Jaime Serra issued an invitation to the business community via its peak-level umbrella organization, the CCE, presided over at the time by Rolando Vega. According to several different observers, Serra invited Vega's CCE to organize a team of knowledgeable businesspeople to bring the different sectors of the business community together in order to present a single, unified position to the government negotiators that they could refer to when negotiating the terms of the agreement with the U.S. and Canadian negotiators (interviews with business and government officials). The CCE's response to Serra's proposition was the creation of the Coordinating Council of Foreign Trade Business Organizations (COECE), an ad hoc, offshoot organization designed to coordinate the overall efforts of the private sector in the NAFTA negotiations. On June 11 (the same day that the Bush-Salinas meetings concluded), the CCE officially created COECE and named Juan Gallardo Thurlow the Private Sector Coordinator for the Negotiation of the Free Trade Agreement, "the business representative in support of the negotiations that our government is conducting with the United States, and possibly Canada, to arrive at a free trade agreement" (COECE press release, 18 October 1990).

According to Gallardo, a prominent Mexican businessman whose Grupo Geupec was affiliated with the U.S. multinational firm Pepsi,

COECE's basic purposes were "to support the efforts of the official government negotiators in the definition of the terms to be negotiated" in the free trade agreement, and "to support SECOFI's free trade negotiating office to achieve the best possible trilateral agreement that takes into consideration the interests of the Mexican private sector" (Gallardo 1994b, 137). Gallardo defined COECE's original functions as: (1) to facilitate the participation of the private sector as an advisor to the government; (2) to carry out and present studies of each industrial sector to the government negotiations office; (3) to form groups for consultation and support and to create working groups with the objective of presenting a single negotiating position for each sector; (4) to find out from the sectors themselves what measures would be necessary for them to increase their competitiveness; and (5) to keep the Mexican business community (both before and during the negotiation process), as well as the relevant authorities and the general public of the three signatory countries, well informed of any aspect of the negotiations that they might consider important (ibid., 138).

The first task that COECE faced in 1990 was to organize the researching and writing of a series of sectoral monographs solicited by SECOFI to ascertain the status and perspectives of each sector with respect to the upcoming negotiations. Over time, COECE and its constituent organizations prepared monographs for several different sectors of the economy. SECOFI published a series of several of these studies, first individually as pamphlets and subsequently as a two-volume collection of twenty-one sectoral monographs (see SECOFI 1992). Although most of the information in these studies was relatively basic and nonstrategic, many businesspeople found that the actual act of conducting them served a useful purpose in raising self-awareness among some sectors unaccustomed to this kind of self-examination. For example, even such basic information as the average production costs for a specific industrial sector had not been previously collected for some areas (interviews with business officials). From the government's perspective, the sectoral monographs would give them a somewhat stronger base upon which to formulate and eventually revise their initial bargaining positions during the process of negotiating with their northern counterparts. "In the preparatory work for this [negotiating] process, COECE collaborated with the free trade negotiation office in the formation of our country's initial bargaining position, which was defined based on the diagnostics of the various sectors that make up the national productive activity and that were prepared by the business sector" (Zabludovsky 1994, 109).

The prospective role of COECE during the negotiations themselves, after the completion of the preparatory work, was initially unclear. Following a long tradition of limited business participation, most business-people suspected that their work would be complete by the time the negotiations began, after which time they would not be directly or indirectly involved in NAFTA. But the role of a restructured COECE throughout the negotiations would eventually surpass these low expec-tations. Originally organized into 114 separate sectors (and even some specific products), COECE would eventually divvy up what had become upward of 140 sectors into seventeen to nineteen different groups according to the number of negotiating tables existing at the time (see below for greater detail on the structure of COECE). In essence, COECE created a parallel bargaining unit that mirrored the organization of the Mexican negotiating team run out of SECOFI. Initially, however, even Gallardo did not expect the COECE representatives to have an especially active role in the negotiations: "they will only be consulted by the SECOFI negotiating office in extraordinary or dramatic cases," since the government negotiating team already had COECE's sectoral monographs (*El Economista*, 1 August 1991, p. 22).

After the negotiations actually got under way in June 1991, it gradu-ally became apparent that COECE's private sector representatives would participate actively and directly in the formulation and revision of Mexico's negotiating positions in the various tables. Government and private sector leaders would typically meet together in Mexico immedi-ately preceding a negotiating round to discuss negotiating issues and strategies. For each negotiating round, a team of private sector repre-sentatives would accompany the government negotiators to the various alternating Canadian, Mexican, and U.S. sites. COECE would typically reserve hotel rooms as close as possible to the actual negotiation rooms in order to maintain frequent contact with their government's negotiat-ing teams (interviews with COECE officials). This site soon became known as the "side room," or the "room next door" (*cuarto de al lado*, or *cuarto de junto*).[11] During the negotiating rounds, the COECE repre-sentatives would continue to meet with the government negotiators, nor-mally at the beginning and end of each day of negotiations, in order to receive updates on the progress of the negotiations and to make sugges-tions. While the government negotiators met with the U.S. and Canadian negotiators, the COECE representatives would remain avail-able in the side room for consultations with the negotiators as needed. At the conclusion of each round, government and business leaders would

11 According to one COECE official close to the negotiations, the side room first came into existence in October 1991 in Ottawa, where private sector represen-tatives congregated in the lobby of the hotel where the negotiations were taking place to conduct impromptu meetings amongst themselves and with Mexican gov-ernment negotiators.

normally meet again in Mexico to discuss the results obtained, and COECE would also hold its own internal meetings to inform its members of the progress of the negotiations (interviews with business and government officials). As SECOFI free trade office coordinator Zabludovsky summarized the role of COECE in the negotiations, "COECE participates in the negotiations through a body of advisors, which is consulted by the heads of each group before, during and after the negotiation meetings" (Zabludovsky 1994, 110).

An examination of the institutional background, structure, and organizational membership of COECE reveals a pattern of concentration of power favoring big business within the private sector's negotiating organism. Although the invitation to create COECE and participate in the negotiations came from the government, the private sector had already begun preparations for its role in a possible free trade agreement earlier. Much of the impetus for this appears to have emerged from Juan Gallardo within the Mexican Business Council for International Affairs (CEMAI), Gallardo's organizational home before (and continuing after) the creation of COECE in June 1990. Founded in 1951, CEMAI serves as the CCE's principal internationally oriented business organization, and it provides a variety of services to its membership to promote international economic exchange. These services include personal networking assistance, in which CEMAI representatives help arrange meetings between Mexican businesspeople, businesspeople from other countries, and Mexican and foreign government officials. CEMAI also collects and disseminates a variety of data and information pertinent to its international business members (interviews with business officials, CEMAI n.d.). One of CEMAI's most important functions is its role as a business sector advocate to the Mexican government on international trade issues: CEMAI "lobbies before the Mexican and foreign governments on issues related to Mexico's international trade policy" (CEMAI n.d.).

CEMAI is affiliated with all of the organizations belonging to the CCE, and it also has approximately 200 individual, voluntary, dues-paying members from the private business community. Organizationally, it is divided into approximately sixty bilateral committees, distributed among six geographical areas: Central America and the Caribbean, South America, Europe, Asia and Oceania, Africa and the Middle East, and North America. At the time that the concept of COECE was being contemplated and formed, Juan Gallardo was the president of CEMAI's U.S.-Mexico Committee, the most important of CEMAI's bilateral committees due to the preponderance of the United States in Mexico's foreign trade relations. This committee played a central role in COECE's founding and development. This group had studied the free trade agreement option since at least 1988, and after the March 1990 *Wall Street Journal* story, Gallardo's committee began to make specific plans for the private sector's role in the negotiation of the potential free trade agreement. Beginning in March, meetings were held at the levels of the Committee, of CEMAI, and of the CCE and all of its member organizations to discuss the potential issues affecting the private sector in such an agreement. In late May 1990 the U.S.-Mexico Committee of CEMAI presented a memo to CCE president Rolando Vega and the board of directors of the CCE recommending that the Mexican business sector organize itself to protect its interests in the free trade agreement (interview with business official). About two weeks later, the CCE officially founded COECE and named Gallardo to direct it.

The fact that the internal impetus for the private sector's involvement in NAFTA originated within CEMAI is instructive. The 200-person membership base of CEMAI draws principally from the ranks of the largest and most internationally integrated firms in Mexico. Though its membership lists are not public, according to one person familiar with the membership base, they include firms from the banking, insurance, and automobile sectors, and such individual companies as Nestlé, Volkswagen, Ford, and (Daimler-)Chrysler. At the other end of the spectrum, "there are few linkages between CEMAI and small and medium business" (interview with business official). Juan Gallardo, perhaps the most influential representative of these large, internationally oriented firms within CEMAI, would go on to direct the operations of COECE in NAFTA while maintaining his leadership of the U.S.-Mexico Committee. In sum, the very creation of COECE came at the invitation of the new SECOFI elite and was carried out by the representatives of internationally and U.S.-oriented big business.

The organizational basis of COECE itself also tells us something about the relative weight of different groups within it. COECE was created by, and is institutionally dependent on, the CCE. As the so-called "peak of peak organizations," the CCE incorporates seven business organization members with full voting rights: the Mexican Association of Brokerage Houses (AMCB), the Mexican Association of Insurance Institutions (AMIS), the Mexican Businessmen's Council (CMHN), the National Agricultural Council (CNA), the National Federation of Chambers of Industry (CONCAMIN), the National Chamber of Commerce (CONCANACO), and the Employers Federation of the Mexican Republic (COPARMEX). Also affiliated with the CCE with rights of voice but not vote are the National Association of Importers and Exporters (ANIERM), the National Chamber of Industries (CANACINTRA), National Chamber of Commerce of Mexico City (CANACO), CEMAI, and the National Council of Foreign Trade (CONACEX). Along with

Table 5.3. *Distribution of Membership and Voting Rights in the CCE*

Organization	Principal economic activity of affiliates	Approximate number of affiliates	Percent of total CCE affiliates	Percent of votes
AMCB	Finance	25	0.003	14.3
AMIS	Insurance	59	0.007	14.3
CMHN	Various	37	0.004	14.3
CNA	Agriculture	250,000	27.6	14.3
CONCAMIN	Industry	125,000	13.8	14.3
CONCANACO	Commerce and services	500,000	55.2	14.3
COPARMEX	Various	30,000	3.3	14.3
CCE totals	Various	905,121	100	100

Note: Percentages may not add to 100 due to rounding. Totals for CONCAMIN include CANACINTRA (82,000 members).
Source: Luna and Tirado (1992).

CEMAI, the Center for Fiscal and Legislative Studies (CEFYL), the Center for Social Studies (CES), and the Center for Economic Studies of the Private Sector (CEESP) are the CCE's official instruments in their various individual institutional realms (POEM 1994).

The historical origins of the CCE suggest that COECE's parent organization was founded by some of the largest, most radical segments of the business community (see Chapter 4). The distribution of voting power within the CCE at the time of COECE's creation shows fairly clear patterns of big business (and financial sector) predominance. Any major decisions taken by the CCE must be approved by five of the seven voting members of the board of directors, which is comprised of the presidents of the CCE's member organizations. The small and medium firms' organizations have no direct voting representation on the CCE's board of directors, though CANACINTRA does officially wield a voice within its parent organization, CONCAMIN.[12] Table 5.3 breaks down the distribution of CCE affiliate membership and voting rights among the seven voting constituent organizations. Each organization's vote is counted equally, regardless of the size of that organization's membership base. Thus, the stock brokerage organization AMCB, with only twenty-five

12 CANACINTRA leaders originally opted not to join the CCE at its creation in 1975. Although it did join the CCE as a nonvoting member in the 1970s, Luna and Tirado (1992) note that CANACINTRA's position became increasingly marginalized from the rest of the CCE in the 1980s.

total members, holds as much voting power (one seventh) as CONCANACO, with its approximately half a million members. The 121-person collective membership of the AMCB, CMHN, and AMIS holds just 0.013 percent of the CCE's individual membership base, but three sevenths, or nearly 43 percent, of its voting rights. Furthermore, given the frequent overlap between the memberships of these three organizations, the largest financial-industrial conglomerates in Mexico have double or even triple representation on the CCE board of directors (ibid.). Adding in the totals for COPARMEX, we can see that with just about 3.33 percent of the total CCE affiliate base, these four business organizations together control a simple majority of the voting power on the board of directors. To obtain the five-sevenths' majority necessary to pass major decisions, such as the election of the CCE president, these four would need to recruit just one additional vote from among the presidents of CONCAMIN, CONCANACO, and the CNA, which often leans toward the larger agricultural and agro-industrial concerns. In fact, due partly to this kind of scenario, in 1991 the CCE amended its presidential election process so that each successive president would be nominated in turn by each of the seven voting organizations, beginning with the choice of CONCANACO (Nicolás Madáhuar) for the 1991–93 term and moving next to CONCAMIN's selection (Luis Germán Cárcoba) for 1993–95 (POEM 1994). Despite this change, the organizational profile of the organization that created COECE exhibits a distribution of institutional control that concentrates much power in the hands of large businesses linked to the financial sector.

COECE was created to serve as the representative of the entire Mexican business community for NAFTA. Its membership base was originally designed to be considerably more broad and inclusive than that of the CCE's voting contingent (Johnson Ceva 1998). COECE, like the CCE, was an umbrella organization that brought together business organizations from a wide variety of areas of the economy, in this case for the purpose of promoting a single business voice for the free trade agreement negotiations. Previously, contact between the government and private sector during trade policy episodes had been scattered across the myriad of governmental agencies and business organizations. Encouraged by the positive results of the series of stabilization and structural adjustment pacts initiated in December 1987 in which the CCE led business participation, state and business leaders moved to concentrate their efforts into SECOFI's new free trade negotiation office and the private sector's COECE. The presence of these new offices simplified life considerably and facilitated a smoother, more easily managed relationship between state and private sector leaders during NAFTA.

Figure 5.1 diagrams the institutional relationships among COECE's

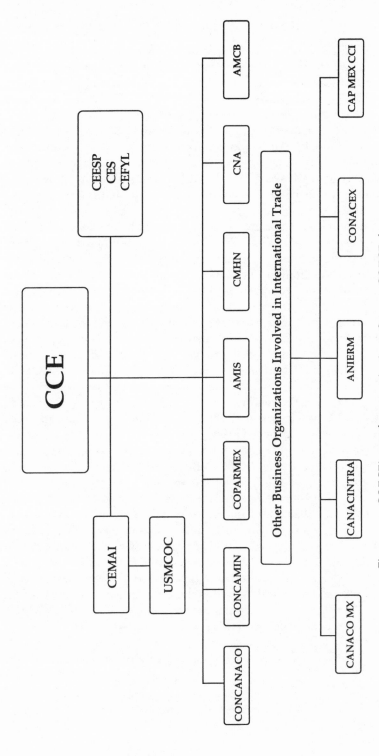

Figure 5.1. COECE's member organizations. *Source:* COECE documents.

member organizations, spearheaded by its parent institution, the CCE. Having been created by the CCE, COECE naturally counted the seven voting CCE member organizations (CONCANACO, CONCAMIN, COPARMEX, AMIS, CMHN, CNA, AMCB) among its membership. It also included the three CCE think-tanks, the CEESP, CES, and CEFYL, as well as the United States–Mexico Chamber of Commerce (USMCOC), and, of course, CEMAI. In addition, it brought in several organizations that were neither voting members nor instruments (such as CEESP) of the CCE, including CANACO, CANACINTRA, ANIERM, CONACEX, and the Mexico Chapter of the International Chamber of Commerce (CAP MEX CCI).[13]

The institutional structure of COECE itself put the CCE at the top, followed by the rest of COECE's member organizations, the leaders of which together made up the directorship of COECE. Figure 5.2 is a schematic representation of the hierarchy and relationships among the various institutional components of COECE. Directly below the business organization directorship is Coordinator General Juan Gallardo, the single voice authorized to speak on behalf of the private sector. CACINTE was also officially affiliated with COECE, inasmuch as Gallardo sits on the business delegation of that group. Moving one level down, we find Guillermo Güémez as the Executive Director of COECE. Güémez was COECE's operational person, in charge of overseeing the daily functions of the private sector's NAFTA participation. Gallardo was COECE's public persona whose picture and statements appeared regularly in the newspapers; Güémez was the person working behind the scenes, making sure that everything ran smoothly and ironing out differences of opinion among COECE's membership.[14] Subsequently a business partner of Gallardo's at Grupo Geupec after the conclusion of the negotiations, Güémez had previously been a director of the National Bank of Mexico (Banamex), one of the two largest commercial banks in Mexico (along with the Bank of Commerce, Bancomer), when called to duty by Gallardo.[15] Gallardo and Güémez put together a small staff that included Guadalupe Albert, Alejandro del Toro, Paulina Hernández, and Carlos Miranda. COECE also had a representative in Washington, Raúl Ortega, who had previously served in the same capacity for CEMAI. The CCE's CEESP provided data and research services for COECE (COECE and SECOFI documents, interviews with business officials).

---

13 All but the Mexico Chapter of the International Chamber of Commerce had voice rights in the CCE.

14 Organizationally, Güémez would be parallel to Jaime Zabludovsky in SECOFI, while Gallardo's government counterpart would be Herminio Blanco.

15 Güémez later served as a member of the Board of Governors of the Bank of Mexico.

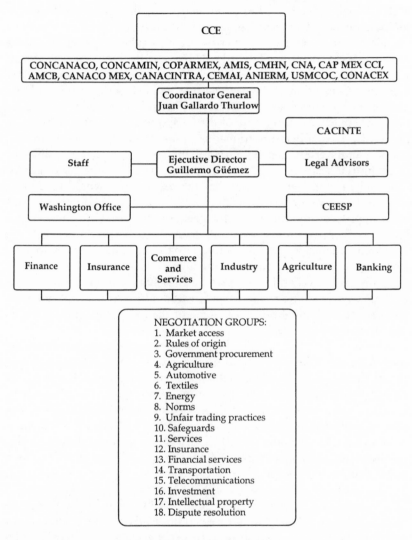

Figure 5.2. The structure of COECE. *Source*: COECE and SECOFI documents.

The real substance of COECE lay among and below its basic six sectoral divisions, or "coordinations," which included sections for finance, insurance, commerce and services, industry, agriculture, and banking. A single coordinator, selected by the appropriate COECE member business organization leaders, headed up each sector's representation (interviews with COECE officials).[16] The coordinators for the six sections were as follows: finance, Carlos Villagómez; insurance, Tomás Ruiz Ramírez; commerce and services, Ruperto Flores; industry, Rodolfo Cruz Miramontes; agriculture, Eduardo Bours; and banking, Patricio Ayala. Below each coordinator is a team chosen by the coordinator to assist with the organization of the negotiations, and below that a series of any number of individual sectors, defined as broadly as mining and as narrowly as apples. As in the case of the CCE, the organizational structure of COECE gave a disproportionately heavy weight to financial groups, whose sectors accounted for three of the six divisions responsible for directing the sectoral efforts of the private sector in the negotiations. Originally, it had been thought that the negotiations would take place on a sector-by-sector basis, which is why COECE first adopted the sectoral approach. By the time the negotiations began in June 1991, however, the trilateral negotiators had opted for a more thematic approach, organizing the negotiations into the series of seventeen to nineteen separate "tables." These tables collapsed the sectoral groups into an assortment of general issue areas, such as market access (tariffs), rules of origin, norms, unfair trading practices, and investment. Negotiators also created individual tables for some of the most contentious sectors: agriculture, automotive, energy, and textiles.

COECE responded to this change by amending its own structure, channeling the different sectoral groups into the new structures of the negotiating groups. A leader was appointed for each of the seventeen original groups, and representatives from the 140-plus individual sectors would participate in the group or groups most relevant to their interests. For most groups, there were approximately eight to twelve business representatives in the official COECE delegation. Most of the day-to-day private sector participation throughout the NAFTA negotiations – both in Mexico and via the side room at the negotiating sites – would occur through these groups (COECE and SECOFI documents, interviews with COECE officials). This reorganization of COECE helped concentrate power within the organization to a certain degree, as the private sector participation in the seventeen original negotiating groups became a bit more exclusive than it had been under the sectoral arrangement. A high degree of personnel turnover also occurred with this transformation. By one count, only forty-two of the original 185 sectoral representatives participated in the newly restructured COECE. With 122 private sector representatives spread across the new groupings, this meant that nearly

---

16 For example, CONCAMIN leadership named the coordinator of the industry section, CONCANACO named the coordinator for commerce and services, the CNA agriculture's, and so on.

two thirds of the COECE negotiation group representatives were new (Puga 1993b; see also Rubio 1992). By most accounts, the bulk of these new representatives came either from individual, almost exclusively large companies or from the business organization leadership. For a businessperson to participate in the negotiations, COECE leadership required certain skills, such as the ability to at least read English and to digest many of the complex economic issues involved in international trade negotiations (interviews with COECE officials). Perhaps more important, a person also simply had to have the time to dedicate to the process, which would have been very difficult for small business owners, almost all of whose time is spent running the day to day operations of their businesses. In contrast, the larger firms and business chambers often have specialists in these areas who devote most or all of their time to such matters. Each sector decided for itself who would represent it in the restructured COECE's negotiating groups, but according to Gallardo "we looked for people who had the time" when naming the sectoral rep-resentatives (Gallardo 1994a, 12). As a consequence, "in short time the [business] representation fell mostly in the hands of the large export firms and the experienced business organization leaders who had the support of the CCE" (Puga 1993b, 68).

The organizational background, membership, and structure of COECE together established the potential for big business predominance in the private sector's NAFTA participation via COECE, an organization ostensibly and officially open to the participation of all segments of the Mexican business community. The next chapter examines exactly how these processes played out during the negotiations, but small and medium business representatives expressed hesitation about the Gallardo/COECE-led business participation in NAFTA early on, before the negotiations even began. According to one CANACINTRA official, "we are concerned about the excessive optimism of the president of COECE" (*El Financiero*, 2 August 1990).

POSSIBLE EXPLANATIONS FOR INCORPORATING BUSINESS INTO THE NEGOTIATIONS

Why did the government incorporate the business community into the negotiating framework in an official capacity? In previous policy episodes, business-government consultation was informal and sporadic. Why did policy makers choose this strategy to consolidate the position of the free trade coalition? This section lays out two complementary reasons for the Mexican government's solicitation and encouragement of the participation of the business community in the NAFTA negotiations. The first of these explanations is a primarily technical one related to the

gathering of information and knowledge. The second has a more structural and political character stemming from state policy makers' need to
attract investment resources to facilitate economic growth and maintain
their hold on power.

Experience and Expertise

The private sector provided business experience and expertise that government negotiators lacked. Most of the government's negotiators were
very young and inexperienced, with far greater expertise in theoretical
economics than practical management. One reason that the government
approached the private sector about participating in the negotiations was
simply to gain access to the technical know-how and sectoral expertise
necessary to negotiate successfully an intricate international trade accord
like NAFTA (interviews with business and government officials). No
matter how brilliant, an inexperienced bureaucrat sitting on the eigh-
teenth floor of the SECOFI building in Mexico City with a Harvard
Ph.D. in economics could not possibly possess all of the detailed knowledge necessary to conduct fully informed, multisectoral negotiations
with her more experienced U.S. and Canadian counterparts. There were
over 11,000 separate Mexican tariff items negotiated in NAFTA. To
avoid inefficient inconsistencies in the final outcome of the free trade
negotiations, the government's negotiating team needed to get information on the specific characteristics of the individual sectors and product
lines from the private sector producers. If, for example, the protective
tariffs on a certain product's inputs are phased out over a fifteen-year
time period, but the market for the output good is opened up in just
five years, it could leave the producers of that product artificially hand-
icapped in the ten intervening years. Similarly, if a certain product
(e.g., silk) is not produced in sufficient quantities in North America, a
strict rule of origin could artificially constrain the production capabilities of the regional producers of any goods (e.g., silk shirts) that use
that product as an input. No one had a better handle on this kind of
information than the private sector, which addressed these issues as a
matter of course.

Interviews with both public and private sector leaders confirm that one
reason the government chose to consult with business was to exchange
this kind of technical information so as to conduct better, more well-
informed free trade negotiations. As one high-level SECOFI official put
it, "it would have been unthinkable and impossible to do all of this
without business" participation (interview). The new, inexperienced
SECOFI negotiators simply did not know enough about the specific
sectors to go it alone in the free trade negotiations. The development of

the monograph series and the passing of information between government negotiators and COECE representatives through the side room at the negotiations highlight this aspect of the new business-state NAFTA relationship.

Searching for Investment

If the government merely needed information from the private sector, it did not necessarily have to remake the institutional structure of business-government relations, as it did when it officially and thoroughly incorporated the private sector into the basic negotiating framework. The corporatist structures of the existing business organizationstate linkages would have been sufficient for that simple task. Furthermore, the government had certainly not found it necessary to take the formal step of including the business sector in the negotiations of the 1979 and 1986 GATT protocols. Why now? There is a more political and structural explanation for the choice to incorporate business into the NAFTA negotiations that complements the technical reasons elaborated above.

Several authors (see Kaufman, Bazdresch, and Heredia 1994, Schneider 1997) credit Mexico's system of concertation (*concertación*) with its relatively greater success in economic stabilization and structural adjustment. Mexico's reforms succeeded politically where others failed because a strong state consulted key interests within a clientelistic, patronage-based political hierarchy. These state capacities date back to the Revolution and the subsequent formation and reform of the PRI in the 1920s and 1930s. But many of these new consultative mechanisms diverge sharply from historical forms of Mexican corporatism. Most important, they now gave an important voice to business. Why? While many pose exit and voice as mutually exclusive choices, they have the potential to be mutually reinforcing. Furthermore, the impact of institutions on economic policy is clear (see Haggard and Kaufman 1995), but institutions mean little outside of the broader political milieu in which they reside. More critical, if we rely on institutions to explain outcomes, how can we explain the changes in the institutions themselves? I do not attempt to build a theory of political institutions; rather, I simply argue that structural-political factors can induce the kinds of institutional changes that facilitate policy change. The ability to exit gave certain segments of business a greater voice in Mexican policy making and promoted shifts in the bureaucracy. In other words, the need to attract investment resources helped instigate the institutional changes in the policy-making process that ceded an expanded role in policy formulation to business in general, but especially to large potential investors.

By 1990, the government still had not managed to solve the many problems associated with the decline in investment that followed the 1982 outbreak of the debt crisis and the mid-1980s oil price collapse. Earlier efforts at economic stabilization had succeeded at lowering annual inflation in the late 1980s, and previous rounds of trade liberalization had already given Mexico one of the more open trade regimes in the developing world. Salinas went to Davos in February 1990 armed with this and other evidence of the coming of the next "Mexican miracle," hoping to attract new investment. Despite the progress made in many areas of economic reform, the Mexican economy still suffered from low levels of productive investment, employment, and economic growth. When his words at Davos fell on deaf ears, Salinas decided to extend and formalize his country's ties to the U.S. market to attract the necessary investment resources to bring Mexico out of its protracted crisis. The consolidation of the free trade coalition via the incorporation of big business as an active partner in the NAFTA negotiations was a crucial element of Salinas's strategy.

The attraction of investment became immediately apparent as one of the foremost goals of the new Salinas administration. Assurances to private investors were sprinkled throughout various government statements, development plans, and speeches from the first moments of the new term. In his December 1, 1988, inaugural speech, for example, Salinas expressed his commitment to adopt the measures necessary to raise investor confidence and attract higher levels of investment into Mexico's economy:

To the businesspeople, I reiterate my promise to generate a propitious environment for private investment and the creation of employment and well-being. I am determined to support the modern entrepreneur who risks his capital and his talent.... We will give clear rules and certainty on the policies of the government. We will simplify regulations that impede production and that only feed the bureaucracies. We will promote flows of foreign investment in the framework of our priorities and with the purpose of generating employment, technological transfer and increases in our exports. I ask businesspeople to invest and reinvest, with a modern and enterprising vision, and to continue to commit themselves to economic stability because it is in the interest of everyone (quoted in Puga 1993a, 181).

Raising the low levels of investment in the Mexican economy soon emerged as one of the very top priorities of the new administration. In the 1990–94 National Program for Industrial Modernization and Foreign Trade, an "insufficient level of investment" is the first problem listed in the first chapter on the problems facing the Mexican economy (SECOFI 1991). The 1989–94 National Development Plan lists the following as its first tool to achieve the broad economic goals of the administration: "to stimulate private investment, national and foreign, by means of clear, certain economic policies, and with an internationally competitive tributary framework" (reprinted in Arriola 1994a).

As the Salinas administration realized, perhaps above all else, private investors want clear, stable rules governing a country's economic policy system. This had been an endemic problem in Mexico, where tariff rates on individual items could and would change regularly not just from one *sexenio* to another, but from one month to the next (interviews with business and government officials). A company that wanted to come in and invest in an export facility to take advantage of Mexico's comparative advantage could not be assured that its access to imported inputs would not be restricted or more costly in the future, or that its broader export activities would not be hindered by future government policy. Investors never knew which economic activities future and seemingly arbitrary changes in policy would favor or hamper. This uncertainty constrained the flow of long-term, productive investment. Even the dramatic reforms adopted since the mid-1980s could be reversed at least as rapidly as they were implemented and as easily as López Portillo had nationalized the banks with his September 1982 executive decree. As one SECOFI official put it, "stability is important. It is very important for Mexican business to know what policy will be 3, 4, 5, 10 years down the road" (interview). One of the primary purposes of NAFTA, therefore, was to give credibility, security, and permanence to the earlier trade policy reforms (Tornell and Esquivel 1995). This would help attract the investment resources of national and foreign private capital controllers. NAFTA will "give permanence to liberalization in Mexico" (interview).

Economist Jaime Ros (1992a) argues that Mexico's pursuit of NAFTA was not so much inspired by the potential trade gains to be had, but rather by the need to raise investor confidence in the Mexican economy and in the stability of the country's new trade policy regime. (In fact, Ros argues that any significant potential trade gains to Mexico would arise only in a world of open capital markets.) The investment logic for pursuing NAFTA is two-fold. First, as an international commitment it would lend greater permanence, credibility, and transparency to Mexican trade policy. Potential investors could now more or less count on knowing what Mexican trade policy would look like in fifteen or twenty years. Second, it would guarantee those who invest in the Mexican economy permanent access to the U.S. and Canadian markets. This should attract new investment by those who want to take advantage of Mexico's preferential access to the world's largest market under NAFTA. In a later work, Ros estimates that "any future increase in the permanent flow of foreign investment can only occur as a result of the possible effects of NAFTA" (1994, 235). The Salinas administration grasped these aspects of NAFTA from the very beginning. In an April 1990 interview Salinas said, "I believe that a trade relationship with the U.S. and Canada on a more certain horizon would give foreign investors in Mexico an additional stimulus to come. It would provide them with a guaranteed access to each of these markets" (*Wall Street Journal*, 4 April 1990). And in their 11 June 1990 statement, Presidents Bush and Salinas emphasized the establishment of "a climate of greater stability and confidence for trade and investment" (reprinted in Arriola 1994a).

As time went on, the Mexican government continued to issue optimistic prognostications of the anticipated investment benefits of the new policy of regional integration. In his March 1991 inaugural address at the Mexican Senate's National Forum of Consultation on Mexico's foreign trade relations, Jaime Serra assured his audience that "the agreement will establish between the three countries clear and permanent rules that will govern trade flows and stimulate productive investment. This will grant certainty and confidence to investors in the planning of their long-term projects. Thus, we will be able to comply with the first rule of competition: the stability of economic policy" (SECOFI 1993c, 12). Serra also predicted that the "general increase in competitiveness that will be derived from the agreement, as well as the climate of certainty that will be established, will stimulate investment, especially in sectors that require long maturation periods" (ibid., 15). These high expectations continued after the conclusion of the negotiations and the approval of NAFTA by the three signatory parties' legislatures. Upon hearing the news of NAFTA's November 1993 passing in the U.S. House of Representatives, Salinas gave a speech in which the first points he mentioned were the creation of the world's largest free trade market, and the fact that the new agreement would "give clear and permanent rules for trade and investment and . . . generate employment and opportunities in our country" (reprinted in Arriola 1994a). Herminio Blanco, Mexico's chief negotiator, wrote hopefully in 1994 that the secure and preferential access to the North American market and the clarity, stability and permanence of economic policy resulting from NAFTA "will generate a vigorous inducement for the accumulation of capital in Mexico" (Blanco Mendoza 1994, 267–68). Tomz (1997) presents evidence that NAFTA's November 1993 approval in the United States House of Representatives and Canadian Prime Minister Jean Chrètien's decision to implement NAFTA eleven days later helped a fictional portfolio of Mexican securities make "abnormally large capital gains" due to NAFTA's positive impact on Mexico's policy credibility (13).

The private sector welcomed these advances intended to elicit investor confidence. Certain segments of the business community had already begun to push for something resembling a free trade agreement with the United States before the government first brought up the possibility publicly in 1990. CEMAI, for example, prepared an "options paper" in 1988 outlining five distinct options for Mexico's future trade relations with the United States: (1) continue under the status quo of the 1987 framework agreement; (2) seek mutual benefits under GATT most-favored-nation status; (3) negotiate individual sectoral agreements; (4) request temporary one-way preferential treatment for Mexico (recognized as a favorable but unrealistic option); and (5) pursue a comprehensive trade and investment agreement, similar to what NAFTA would become (interview with business official). ANIERM, another business organization involved in providing foreign trade services to its private sector membership, first pressured the government to join the GATT in the mid-1970s. It was also one of the few strong proponents of GATT membership in the 1979–80 debates, and later supported Mexico's 1986 accession. During the 1988 presidential campaign, at a time when the possibility of Mexico's formal economic integration with its northern neighbors still seemed remote, ANIERM's leadership presented a document specifically proposing the negotiation of a bilateral free trade agreement with the United States to PRI candidate Salinas (interview with business official). The supportive role of these foreign trade business organizations was confirmed, at least symbolically, in 1990 when Salinas chose CEMAI's annual congress as the location to announce the possible negotiation of a free trade agreement with the U.S. (Puga 1994).

Mexican businesspeople interviewed for this book agreed that the investment imperative was an important determinant of the government's decision to pursue a free trade agreement. In fact, several claimed that the investment motive outweighed the trade motive in NAFTA. Like the government leadership, they too cited the importance of policy stability and market access: "They need to give investment guarantees to foreign and domestic investors. . . . the private sector wants clear rules and stability, and the NAFTA rules are clear" (interview). "The number one objective was to show the world it would have access to the North American market if they invested in Mexico" (interview). Several members of the private sector also realized that trends in international patterns of capital mobility affected their structural leverage, which they could exert over policy. As one Mexican officer of a large multinational corporation viewed the situation, the Mexican state does not have the resources or mechanisms to subsidize foreign capital, so policy instruments, such as NAFTA, become much more important in attracting investment resources: "The competition for foreign capital was the most important reason for the free trade agreement" (interview).

Big Business, the State, and Free Trade

One way for state leaders to ensure private sector confidence in the free trade agreement negotiating process at a time of political and economic instability was to consolidate the free trade coalition by incorporating the business community directly into the negotiations themselves, at least in a consultative role. The incorporation of the private sector into the internal policy-making bureaucracy by the government helped shore up the investor confidence that had been so badly damaged by what the private sector viewed as the arbitrary, unilateral government decision to nationalize the private banking system in 1982. As one COECE representative put it, "they were negotiating our businesses" (interview). To negotiate the livelihood of Mexico's business community without making its members an integral part of the process might have led to much greater private sector resistance and opposition to NAFTA, and might have undermined those aspects of the agreement that were designed to attract foreign and domestic investors into the Mexican economy. By including businesspeople in the negotiations, the government made them part of the process, binding and committing them to NAFTA. According to one SECOFI policy maker, the private sector was consulted "to get business support for NAFTA, and to get them and their interests included in the process" (interview).

What might have happened if the NAFTA negotiations had failed to yield an agreement, or if the private sector had not been consulted? Would investors have fled the Mexican market, or at least not increased their investment to the levels envisioned by state policy makers? Although answers to these kinds of counterfactual questions cannot be definitively determined, several observers sounded ominous notes for the Mexican economy in the case of a failure in the NAFTA negotiations. During the negotiations, when the final fate of NAFTA was still very much in doubt, an independent economic consultant (Vladimiro Brailowsky of the consulting firm Economía Aplicada) predicted that a failure to sign the agreement by the end of 1992 would provoke "definite uncertainty among foreign investors, who might withdraw their resources from the country." This would have negative effects on the capital account, which in turn could put downward pressure on the peso and cause a devaluation, which "would be disastrous for the last three years of the Salinas administration" (quoted in *El Financiero*, 26 March 1992). In terms of the potential effects of the government not incorporating the private sector into the NAFTA negotiations, several business community observers agreed with general sentiments of the private sector participant who stated that "the whole world would disinvest if they were not consulted. It would have brought this country to chaos. . . . There would have been brutal disinvestment" (interview).

Conclusion

At the same time that the PRI government was attempting to attract higher levels of investment into the Mexican economy, it faced mounting electoral challenges from both its right and left (see Chapter 4). These challenges, in a context of low economic growth, high levels of international capital mobility, and a lack of alternative investment resources available to the state, made state policy makers vulnerable and put pressure on them to move in one direction or another to consolidate their political position. The changes in the internal makeup of business (partially caused by previous policy reforms) altered the panorama of available potential partners with whom to ally to strengthen one's political position. Together with a new outlook within the state and SECOFI in particular, these factors encouraged state elites to move toward specific segments of the private sector to consolidate the position of the free trade coalition by formally incorporating them into the negotiations, giving them a more direct, active, institutionalized role in the trade policy-making process.

Some interesting, and testable, implications for the NAFTA negotiations can be deduced from these arguments. If the new generation of policy makers serving in the Mexican government chose to incorporate the private sector in the NAFTA negotiations in part to increase investor confidence and maintain their hold on power, we should expect to see favoritism during the negotiations toward those members of the business community who have the most investment resources to offer the Mexican economy. The most likely candidates would be large, mobile asset controllers, which correspond to the biggest, most internationally oriented national and multinational firms, groups, and conglomerates that link together various financial and industrial business concerns. For the purposes of this study, I refer to these actors collectively as "big business." Thus, my argument would predict that the consolidation of the free trade coalition and the related incorporation of the private sector by the new state elites in the NAFTA negotiations should favor big business. This section has demonstrated the strong influence of big business within the structures through which business participation passed, namely CACINTE, CEMAI, the CCE, and COECE. We should also expect to see big business participating much more actively in the actual negotiations than small and medium business, and its concerns more closely heeded by the government negotiators.

6

Business Participation in the
NAFTA Negotiations

INTRODUCTION

Mexico's negotiation of NAFTA closely reflected the characteristics of the state's negotiating team and its ties to the private sector. These negotiations marked an important turning point in Mexican policy making, opening it up to the participation of limited, powerful elements of the business community. Though many business leaders had initially been highly skeptical of the sincerity of the government's offer to consult with the private sector, a high level of continuous interaction took place between the government negotiators and the COECE representatives during the NAFTA negotiations. According to an announcement by President Salinas in March 1992, government negotiators had already conducted 1,333 meetings with the representatives of the private sector to discuss the negotiating issues, including 522 from the very beginning of the NAFTA process until the initiation of the formal negotiations in June 1991, and 811 meetings through the side room during the negotiations from June 1991 to March 1992 (*El Financiero*, 18 March 1992). The pace of contact picked up as the negotiations progressed. According to SECOFI calculations, by the time the negotiations ended in August 1992, more than 2,600 meetings had been held between the government negotiators and private sector representatives (SECOFI 1993b).

The next section examines the nature, extent, and impact of the interactions that took place during the negotiations through the private sector's "side room" at the negotiating sites. It also analyzes the varying roles of the different strata of the business community, paying particular attention to the wide gap between the levels of participation of small and large business representatives. A brief examination of the negotiations in the textiles sector complements this analysis. The following section looks in greater detail at how these processes unfolded in the negotiations for the automotive sector, one of the most complex and contentious sectors in NAFTA. The chapter then concludes with a brief discussion of the effects of these processes on the new coalition between the state and big business.

THE SIDE ROOM

Virtually everyone interviewed for this project agreed that the participation of the private sector in the NAFTA negotiations was extensive, intensive, and effective. The direct negotiations with the U.S. and Canadian negotiators were clearly a government-to-government affair conducted on the Mexican side solely by the SECOFI-led team. However, over the course of the negotiations many of the private sector participants in the COECE side room developed excellent relationships with their government counterparts. The business representatives communicated frequently with government officials of all levels, from Jaime Serra on down. One mid-level private sector participant went out of his way to praise Serra personally for his accessibility, noting that he had met with him regularly and that the Trade Minister always listened and responded carefully to his concerns and those of his sector (interview). Regular meetings to discuss the overall progress and issues surrounding the negotiations typically took place at least weekly between the top two government negotiators, Herminio Blanco and Jaime Zabludovsky, and the two directors of COECE, Juan Gallardo and Guillermo Güémez.

Most of the detailed, day-to-day contact between the government and business during the negotiations occurred at the level of the individual negotiating groups, each of which had its own side room housing the COECE private sector contingent. According to one SECOFI lead negotiator, the contact between his team and that of the COECE side room was nearly constant. They would meet with the COECE representatives in Mexico before leaving for each negotiating round. Once at the site, they would meet at least once a day with the side room's participants, often both before and after (and even sometimes during) their sessions with the U.S. and Canadian negotiators. Negotiators would inform COECE representatives of the progress of the negotiations and find out what the private sector wanted out of the various negotiating rounds. "We had them at our side the whole time" (interview with SECOFI negotiator). A COECE leader agreed: "We got as close as possible to the negotiations without actually being there" (interview with COECE participant). Often, if the sessions ran late, the government representatives would go meet with the COECE members at two or three o'clock in the morning (interviews with business and government participants). These meetings were intense and numerous. In a single negotiating group, the government's lead negotiator estimated that his team had conducted approximately thirty meetings with the U.S. and Canadian negotiators, and approximately 180 meetings with the Mexican private sector (interview).

This kind of constant, formal contact in trade policy making represented a sharp departure from past patterns of business-state relations and made a strong impression on the private sector. No such system of regular consultation had been employed in any previous trade policy episodes, including the 1979–80 and 1986 GATT negotiations and the post-1987 stabilization pacts. When asked how he would characterize his relations with the government during the negotiations, one COECE leader responded: "magnificent, extraordinary, honest, frank" (interview). Many members of the private sector negotiation team echoed the general sentiments of this business participant: "What was surprising about all of this was the openness of the government to us. There was a climate of confidence, of shared objectives. It surpassed all expectations. Extraordinary, without precedent" (interview).

This high level of trust had not existed at the outset of the negotiations. After decades of conflictual relations with SECOFI and a general distrust of a government that it viewed as encroaching on its territory and unnecessarily interfering with its business operations, the private sector was very reluctant to embrace fully the new generation that professed a willingness to include the business point of view in the negotiations. They had to be convinced that things had changed, that this was a new group with new ideas, and that their own interests and concerns would be respected rather than manipulated. To this end, Serra reportedly instructed all of his lead negotiators to go to great lengths to respect business interests in the negotiations. According to one lead negotiator, "he gave us an order: 'Don't make any decisions without private sector agreement.' Almost all decisions at all levels were taken in consultation with the private sector" (interviews with SECOFI officials). This system of consultation gradually built up greater trust between the government and private sector as the negotiations progressed. Though the government negotiators did not always do exactly what the COECE representatives wanted (they of course had their own ideas and faced constraints from U.S. and Canadian negotiators), "they respected the rule of consulting us on all points of negotiation" (interview with COECE official).

A key turning point in the development of trust between government negotiators and private sector representatives came in early January 1992 when SECOFI gave a copy of the recently completed draft of the text of the agreement to the COECE leadership and solicited the private sector's comments and reaction to it. COECE organized a team of experts and lawyers to review the text, and they compiled an approximately fifty-page document outlining the revisions that COECE wanted to see made to the text. According to one COECE leader, SECOFI adopted approximately 90 percent of the suggestions made in that document. This cemented a firm bond of trust between the government and COECE: "We realized they must be serious if they are letting us do this and actually implementing our changes" (interview with COECE official). Later in the month, Gallardo proclaimed, "we businesspeople do feel well represented in the themes that have been drafted to this point. The private sector is being listened to by SECOFI" (*El Economista*, 15 January 1992).

Validating the increased level of trust that the business representatives developed in the public sector negotiators, COECE appears to have had a noticeable effect on the government's negotiating positions.[1] One COECE person familiar with many different sectors and negotiating groups claimed that, though it varied somewhat by sector, "there was not one single case of total disagreement" between the SECOFI negotiators and the private sector representatives (interview). A SECOFI negotiator estimated that within the general parameters of the negotiations, SECOFI adopted approximately 80 percent of COECE's proposals in formulating and revising its strategies for negotiating with the United States and Canada (interview). On the whole, though the outcome of the negotiations may or may not have favored every one of their specific individual interests, most of COECE's private sector representatives seemed quite satisfied with the incorporation of their views into the government's negotiating positions (interviews with COECE representatives).

WHO WAS THERE, WHO WAS NOT

Broad Trends

Not all segments of the business community participated equally in the NAFTA negotiations. The COECE members most frequently consulted by government negotiators were generally those who would be most likely to benefit from NAFTA, and who controlled the largest number of economic resources. Most of NAFTA's private sector losers did not

---

1 Note that this point does not directly address the actual outcome of the negotiations, which naturally also depend on the positions adopted by the U.S. and Canadian negotiators and the dynamics of the negotiations between the three parties. In this sense, the NAFTA negotiations are a good example of Putnam's (1988) two-level games. In this case, the Mexican government negotiated simultaneously on the domestic level with COECE and on the international level with the United States and Canada.

participate in the negotiations.[2] Many of these actors came from the ranks of the smaller and medium firms, which had only a limited, indirect role in the NAFTA negotiations. The most active participants were those who supported the basic idea of NAFTA, and those from the largest firms and groups. Very often, these two categories overlapped, resulting in an alliance between new state and big business elites to negotiate the free trade agreement with the United States and Canada.

According to numerous participants from both the government and private sector sides of the negotiations, for a businessperson to participate in the NAFTA negotiations, she had to first accept the basic concept of the free trade agreement. If she did not accept that general notion, there really was no place for her in the negotiations (interviews with business and government officials).[3] From a pure efficiency standpoint this made perfect sense. The government had already decided to negotiate a free trade agreement with the support of key members of the private sector – why would either of them want to involve people who would work to obstruct that goal? The consequences of this policy, however, were significant. Similar to what had taken place within the state, this made for a private sector team of free traders. According to one government official, "there was no one against NAFTA in the negotiations" (interview). Another noted that, despite internal differences within COECE as a whole, all members of the private sector who were involved in the negotiations were in favor of the basic concept of NAFTA (interview). Private sector observers agree on this point. One private sector representative claimed, "I never found a single businessperson who was against NAFTA" in the negotiations, while another estimated that 98 percent of the business NAFTA delegation supported the free trade agreement (interviews).

Along with anti-NAFTA private sector forces, most small and medium businesspeople were effectively excluded, or at least greatly distanced, from the negotiating process. This left mostly proxy representatives and big business to staff the private sector's negotiating teams. The basic problem was one of resources and representation. COECE was entirely privately funded, and an essentially volunteer organization. Apart from

2 A few interviewees did claim that business representation was universal, echoing the government official who flatly stated that "everyone was there, everyone was represented" (interview). On the whole, however, most public and private sector participants recognized the disparity in levels of participation.

3 This is not meant to imply that no one from the business community sought protection during the negotiations. On the contrary, many attempted to use long tariff reduction phase-in periods, strict rules of origin, norms, and safeguards to shield themselves from NAFTA's potential impact. The point is that all of this was done within the context of NAFTA, with the general understanding that trade between the three countries would be freed.

the approximately twenty total paid staff members who ran the administrative end of the organization, all of the COECE negotiation representatives worked strictly on a volunteer basis. Members of the COECE negotiation groups paid their own travel expenses to and from meetings and negotiation sites, and none received a salary or any other sort of financial compensation from COECE (interviews with COECE officials). Either they or their employers had to pick up the tab for their participation in the NAFTA negotiations. If anyone could not participate directly, the task fell to the official business organization representatives, whose expenses the respective organizations paid.

The largest, most internationally integrated firms and groups have the greatest number of their own resources to dedicate to these matters, and they very frequently employed them during the negotiations. These kinds of enterprises usually have entire departments devoted to international trade and governmental relations. The staffs and directors of these offices have often studied the issues and formulated negotiating positions well before the government or any private sector organizations solicit them. Most of these businesses sent their own company representatives (usually the directors of the international trade and/or governmental relations departments) to the negotiations. Once there, they would participate directly in the side rooms of whichever negotiating groups were most relevant to their business interests.[4] In the words of one SECOFI official, "the larger firms were readier to participate" (interview).

On the other hand, small and medium firms exhibit a family structure, with the head of the family usually running the daily operations of the business. These kinds of firms often lack the corporate culture and structures that spawn an active role in trade policy. They are less familiar with the issues, and they usually lack the experience in international trade that many of the larger firms enjoy. As one medium-sized entrepreneur described the difference between large and small firms, "big business has prepared people. The small and medium businessperson is unprepared" (interview). Furthermore, and perhaps most important, due to their smaller size, these kinds of firms could not as easily absorb the high costs of participating in the free trade negotiations. Relative to the revenues of a small business, the cost of sending a representative all over North America to follow the free trade negotiations can be substantial. If the

---

4 Collective action problems also favor the largest firms and groups, which are much more likely to be able to overcome the free rider problem since there are many fewer of them. Due to the frequently oligopolistic nature of their markets, it is also often in their narrow self-interests to participate, regardless of what others do. For the thousands of small and medium firms, however, the incentive to free ride the efforts of others usually outweighs the potential marginal benefits of participating. See Olson (1971, 1982).

director of one of these firms vacated his position to spend a year and a half personally participating in the side room negotiations to promote his business interests, his firm would likely go bankrupt. He is also unlikely to be able to hire someone full time to participate directly on his behalf. As one representative of a large private firm recognized, "it was very difficult for a small company to have a full-time representative" (interview).

Because of these problems, the participation of small and medium business was conducted almost exclusively through the business associations and chambers, principally through CANACINTRA. One CANACINTRA leader who participated in negotiations on behalf of small and medium business confirmed that most private sector participants came from the large firms and groups, and that small and medium representation occurred only through the business organizations. This proved to be a difficult task, as these representatives frequently found themselves criticized by their constituents and outweighed by the representatives of big business in the negotiations. This same person confirmed that, although the negotiations were officially open to all, there were numerous complaints from small and medium businesspeople who felt distanced and removed from the negotiations (interview). These organizations, CANACINTRA and its member sectoral associations in particular, have long been denounced for serving more as corporatist mechanisms of government control than as effective representatives of business interests before the state. Many of the potential private sector opponents of NAFTA were channeled into and through these organizations, where their dissent could be controlled and muffled (see Shadlen 1997). In addition, even though bright and capable people led these delegations, the sheer number and scope of the firms and sectors they encompassed limited their ability to represent effectively the broad interests of their entire constituencies. COECE officials recognized the limitations on the representation of the small businessperson in the negotiations: "If he wanted protection, he probably was not well represented. If he wanted access to U.S. markets, he was well represented" (interview with COECE official). As one SECOFI officially reluctantly acknowledged, for some small firms there was a tendency for them "not to have been as well represented as would have been desirable" (interview).

Several businesspeople not directly involved in the negotiations complained early on about of a lack of access to information about the progress and content of the negotiations, as well as about COECE itself (*El Economista*, 26 November 1991). Leaders of CANACINTRA itself criticized the COECE leadership and frequently demanded greater information on the negotiations. Leaders of the CANACINTRA offshoot,

National Association of Manufacturing Industries (ANIT), were more strident in their criticism. In March 1992, ANIT Vice President Francisco Hernández claimed that the negotiations "are not proceeding like the negotiators and some industrialists say they are" (*El Financiero*, 24 March 1992). Luna (1992) notes that "the president of ANIT declared that micro, small and medium businesspeople had not been taken into account, seeing that information only circulated among the representatives of the large businesses that were participating in the peak structures of COECE" (16–17).

The Textiles Negotiations

A good example of the disparate levels of participation of different segments of the business community occurred in the textiles negotiations. Three separate subsectors together comprise the chain of production in the textiles industry: fibers, textiles, and apparel. The chain begins with the production of natural and artificial fibers. The textiles stage of production spins the fibers into yarn and weaves the yarn into fabric. The apparel stage transforms the fabric into the final consumer products.

Within the fibers subsector, the producers of artificial fibers are almost exclusively large national and multinational petrochemical firms with extensive linkages to international markets. Some of the most important firms include Cydsa, Celanese, Resistol, and DuPont. This type of firm typifies the large, modern corporation that made up Mexico's business elite and that was so active in COECE. It devotes numerous resources to international trade and governmental affairs, and started to prepare for the negotiations well before they began. Most of these firms are members of the National Association of the Chemical Industry (ANIQ), one of Mexico's most effective industrial associations. This organization coordinated the overall efforts of the petrochemical and fibers sectors in the NAFTA negotiations.[5] It began its efforts to organize the sector around international market opening in the mid-1970s, making initial contact with its U.S. counterpart, the Chemical Manufacturers Association, in 1976. ANIQ stepped up its organizational campaign in the 1980s, largely in response to the negotiations for the 1987 bilateral textile agreement with the United States. By the time NAFTA rolled around, ANIQ had already experienced some exposure to international trade negotiations, even though it did not participate as extensively in the bilateral agreement as it would in NAFTA (interviews with business officials).

---

5 The nonfiber petrochemicals negotiations were handled primarily through the energy chapter.

The leadership of ANIQ, made up of representatives from the large petrochemical firms, participated in the COECE textiles side room during the NAFTA negotiations. It also urged the individual firms in its sector to create their own working groups and specialists organized along the themes of the negotiations. An internal ANIQ document summarizing the negotiating issues emphasizes this point, and gives the following warning: "BE CAREFUL: Not replaceable with advisors." This meant that the petrochemicals firms should assign their own representatives to the negotiating groups and not depend on ANIQ or independent consultants to do the job for them. The petrochemical companies apparently took this advice to heart, as the major ones each assigned their own individual corporate representatives to the COECE negotiating groups. These representatives were among the NAFTA negotiations' most active participants. The contentious textiles table was heavily politicized throughout the negotiations, due in part to the political weight and media attention attracted by textiles producers in the United States, especially in the southeast. The large, often multinational petrochemical companies coordinated their efforts across the three NAFTA countries to protect their interests long before the negotiations even began. ANIQ and individual company representatives met with their U.S. and Canadian counterparts to share ideas and plan negotiating strategies. By the time COECE formed and the negotiations began, this sector was poised to take advantage of the opening to business participation (interviews with business officials). Although everyone in these groups ostensibly represented the entire sector collectively, one petrochemical sector representative said that "about 95 percent of what I did was push for [my company's] position" (interview).

Representation and participation within the textiles and apparel subsectors was more dispersed. Both of these industries suffered from classic collective action problems. The textiles subsector, which occupies the middle of the chain of production, is much less concentrated than the fibers subsector, with a good number of medium-sized firms. It was represented almost exclusively by its industrial chamber, the National Chamber of the Textile Industry (CANAINTEX). This organization faced a difficult task in coordinating and reconciling the interests of its approximately 1,200 members, whose narrow self-interests varied by product line and current rules of market access, which were not uniform across different goods. The apparel sector is nearly 100 percent micro and small firms, with only a few medium and large firms. The National Chamber of the Apparel Industry (CANIVE) spoke on behalf of its approximately 8,000 member apparel firms. The interests of these producers also varied widely. Mexico's low-cost labor gave them important competitive advantages, but small firm size, the inability to capitalize on economies of scale, and a lack of access to credit and technology eroded many of these cost savings. Assessing and representing the varied interests of the thousands of tiny enterprises presented formidable organizational and substantive challenges. It was much more difficult to reach consensus in both the textiles and apparel negotiations than in the fibers sector.

When no consensus emerged, there were few individual company representatives to defend their interests at the textiles table. More often than not, chamber representatives had to make decisions on their own that inevitably hit some firms harder than others (interviews with business representatives). Furthermore, little official coordination took place between Mexican textiles and apparel producers and their much better organized North American counterparts. Individual U.S. textiles and apparel producers and their trade associations, the American Textile Manufacturers Institute and the American Apparel Manufacturers Association, were among the most active participants in the negotiations. They made frequent formal and informal contact with U.S. negotiators to extract the best possible deal from the Mexicans (interviews with business officials). Facing the U.S. and Canadian firms and the organized teams of the petrochemical companies in the fibers subsector, the textile and apparel subsectors were at distinct disadvantage during the negotiations. Though negotiators made much progress at the textiles table, most of the successful private sector pressure appears to have come from U.S. producers and the large petrochemical firms (interviews with business leaders).

THE AUTOMOTIVE SECTOR NEGOTIATIONS

The automotive sector is the single most important sector in the Mexican economy, aside from petroleum. The industry first moved into Mexico in the 1920s and 1930s, and beginning in the 1960s it began to assume a more prominent role in the domestic economy. Over time, the weight of this industry in the Mexican economy gradually increased, until in 1990 the terminal vehicles sector alone accounted for 2.3 percent of total GDP, 9 percent of manufacturing GDP, and approximately one fourth of all manufactured exports (SECOFI 1992, internal AMIA documents). It also employed approximately 400,000 people in Mexico, about 10 percent of total manufacturing employment. These facts alone make this industry a worthwhile subject of study, as the volume of literature on the automotive sector demonstrates.[6]

6 This treatment is a brief exploration of the automotive negotiations, rather than a general overview or history of the industry in Mexico. For just a few examples of useful studies of this industry, see Bennett and Sharpe (1985), Bennett (1986), Unger (1990), Scheinman (1991, 1993), Comisión Económica para América Latina y el Caribe (1992), Taniura, Schatan, and Máttar (1992), and Studer Noguez (1999).

An additional set of characteristics makes this a particularly interesting sector to analyze in a study of trade policy coalition politics. The negotiations for the free trade agreement in the automotive sector, which includes both automobile producers and auto parts producers, were expected to be among the most contentious. Because of this, and the fact that this was such an important industry in the economies of all three countries, the parties agreed to create a separate negotiating table for the automotive negotiations. The length and difficulty of the automotive negotiations confirmed initial expectations. The automotive table was among the very last to be resolved, holding up the completion of the NAFTA negotiations until August 1992.

Compelling divisions at various levels within the industry also make it a useful case study for exploring the roles that different segments of business play in trade policy coalitions. Similar to the textiles sector, the first and most basic distinction lies within the chain of production, across the two sectors that comprise the industry as a whole. This division juxtaposes the interests of the nearly 100 percent multinational vehicle producers with those of the mostly national Mexican auto parts producers. Five companies comprised the vehicles sector; the parts producers numbered approximately 600 (Scheinman 1991). The relationship between these two sectors has often been conflictual, especially since the 1980s. Both the parts and vehicles sectors were traditionally heavily protected, but the parts sector was much less well integrated internationally. Most parts producers were independent national firms that did not enjoy the vehicle sector's vertical MNC linkages. They had few joint ventures with foreign partners, and many of these companies suffered from a lack of access to new technology or economies of scale. Much of this sector's growth resulted from Mexico's national value-added rules that required a certain percentage (varying over time) of the value added to a product to come from Mexican sources, including the parts producers. Because the parts producers were the vehicle producers' mandated suppliers, the two sectors' positions on certain issues, especially on the national value-added rules, often conflicted.

Important differences also exist within each sector of the automotive industry. For example, just five multinational producers made up the terminal industry: Chrysler, Ford, General Motors, Nissan, and Volkswagen.[7] These five companies are among the very largest private firms in Mexico, consistently ranking at or near the top of the list of the *Expansión* 500 top firms in the country. Together they accounted for nearly 98 percent of Mexico's motor vehicle production in 1990, with

---

7 BMW, Honda, and Mercedes-Benz entered the Mexican vehicles market after NAFTA's 1994 inception.

the remaining 2 percent produced by the makers of trucks, tractors, and buses: Mercedes-Benz, Dina, Kenworth, and Masa (ibid.). The most obvious distinction between the five large automobile MNCs divides them into two camps, with the "Big Three" American producers on one side and the German Volkswagen and Japanese Nissan on the other. Similarly, interesting demarcations also existed within the parts industry. A small number of mostly large, potentially internationally competitive firms with joint venture relationships with mostly U.S. companies contrasted with a much larger number of mostly uncompetitive small and medium parts producers. In general, the larger and more internationally integrated firms in this industry participated more actively and directly in the NAFTA negotiations. The vehicle producers and large parts firms, for example, each sent their own representatives to the negotiations. The small and medium companies participated through their industry association.

The Different Faces of the Automotive Industry

Parallel to the creation of the NAFTA negotiating table for the automotive industry, COECE formed its own private sector automotive negotiating group. Representatives from each of the industry's two sectors – vehicle and auto parts producers – staffed this group. The Mexican Association of the Automobile Industry (AMIA), led at the time by César Flores, coordinated the overall efforts of the five vehicle producers. Flores's task was to attempt to reconcile the interests of the five automobile producers, and to present the sector's views as a collective entity before the Mexican government negotiators. The efforts of the parts producers passed through the offices of the National Auto Parts Industry (INA), a voluntary association of many of Mexico's auto parts producers. Miguel Angel Olea headed up the INA delegation. Like Flores, Olea's task was to bring together the various concerns of the auto parts sector and to present the overall views of his constituency to the SECOFI negotiating team.

The members of these two sectors originally intended to meet first amongst themselves through the offices of AMIA and INA, and then with each other, to negotiate more or less unified positions for their individual sectors and for the industry as a whole. Their representatives would then present position papers to the government negotiators, who would use these recommendations in their sessions with the U.S. and Canadian negotiators. To facilitate this communication, COECE created a side room for the industry and staffed it with ten to twelve representatives of the two sectors (interviews with business and government officials, SECOFI documents).

Irreconcilable differences soon began to divide the two sectors. The central issue upon which the vehicle and parts producers most strongly disagreed was the local content rules. The national value added in production requirements dated back to the series of decrees that had governed the Mexican automotive industry since 1962 (see Bennett and Sharpe 1985). The basic goals of the first 1962 decree, which was successively renewed by new decrees in 1972, 1977, 1983, and 1989, were to promote the development of a domestic automobile industry and to stimulate the growth of local auto parts producers. The principal tools outlined in these decrees to achieve these goals were regulations on the types of parts that vehicle producers could import, limitations on the number of models and lines each company could produce, restrictions on the quantity of imports that the vehicle producers could bring into the country, restrictions on foreign ownership in the parts sector (40% maximum), export requirements, and local content laws. These laws required that approximately 60 to 75 percent (using different measures over time) of the parts and components used in the manufacturing process come from local, Mexican suppliers. The final 1989 decree loosened most of these restrictions and paved the way for NAFTA's trade opening. It brought the Mexican industry more closely in line with its northern neighbors by allowing limited importation of cars and trucks by the auto companies, lifting restrictions on the number of models produced, allowing for greater levels of foreign investment in the auto parts sector, and by changing and lowering the domestic content requirements. After the implementation of this decree in 1990, 36 percent of the total national value added in production (NVAp) – including both labor and parts – of a company's Mexico production would have to come from local sources (United States International Trade Commission 1990, Scheinman 1991, Taniura, Schatan, and Máttar 1992).

The local content restrictions included in the series of automotive decrees helped the Mexican auto parts sector grow rapidly. The total sales of this sector increased from $4.61 billion to $6.57 billion in the 1988–92 period alone, due mostly to increases in domestic sales (Scheinman 1993). These restrictions also caused much friction in the NAFTA negotiations, as the five vehicle producers sought to lower and eventually eliminate the NVAp requirements, while the parts sector struggled to hold onto what it viewed as the single most important policy for its industry (interviews with automotive sector representatives). At the behest of COECE and SECOFI, which wanted the industry to submit a single position on all issues, representatives from the vehicle and parts sectors met together many times to try to iron out their differences. According to several sources involved in the negotiations, the parts sector, led by INA, fought to maintain the level of 36 percent NVAp "at all cost," while the vehicle producers wanted to lower it gradually, eventually phasing it out completely (interviews with automotive sector representatives). Eventually, negotiations broke down. In January 1992, the president of INA, Ernesto Garza, declared that the position taken by the vehicle producers "is radically opposed to ours" (*El Economista*, 20 January 1992).

Because the leaders of these two sectors could not agree on the fundamental issues that divided them, they effectively maintained two separate side rooms for the automotive industry for the duration of the negotiations. One room housed the terminal automobile companies and another the parts producers. The physical separation of the two groups underscores the fundamental differences between their negotiating roles. While the terminal industry was concentrated into just five large producers, two distinct strata made up the parts industry. The first consisted of the largest auto parts companies in the country. The top fifteen firms in the sector accounted for nearly 35 percent ($2.29 billion) of the entire sector's sales in 1992. One firm alone, Spicer, accounted for more than 10 percent ($697 million) of the sector's 1992 total sales (Scheinman 1993).[8] Most of these firms were also members of auto parts business groups and broader multisectoral conglomerates, including the Vitro, Condumex, ICA, and Cifunsa groups. Most of these top firms are also the sector's largest (and virtually only) exporters, and they are also the most likely to have entered into joint ventures with foreign investors, especially from the United States (Scheinman 1991, 1993; Comisión Económica para América Latina y el Caribe 1992; Taniura, Schatan, and Máttar 1992).

In contrast, the remaining 500-plus firms that make up the second strata of the auto parts sector range in size from small to medium, and tend to be much less competitive and internationally integrated. They export far less, are much less likely to have joint venture arrangements with foreign partners, and often depend on the local content requirements of the automotive decrees to stay in business. According to several automotive industry executives, only about fifteen to twenty Mexican auto parts firms – almost exclusively the large ones – were competitive at international standards in the early 1990s. As NAFTA frees imports, eliminates local content laws, and eases restrictions on foreign investment, experts expect most of the small and medium auto parts producers to disappear (interviews). Even before NAFTA, the Mexican auto parts sector's trade account declined from a roughly zero balance in 1989 to a deficit of more than $5 billion in 1992 (Studer 1997, fig. 3).

---

8 I converted Scheinman's peso-denominated data to U.S. dollars using the IMF's (1994) 1992 exchange rate of 3.1154 new pesos per dollar.

The representation and participation of different auto parts producers in the NAFTA negotiations reflected the sector's heterogeneity. As in other sectors, the largest companies and business groups in the auto parts sector normally sent their own representatives to the negotiations. Many of these companies were active exporters integrated with the U.S. market and foreign investors. While they had certainly benefited from the local content laws, their greater international competitiveness made them relatively less dependent on the NVAp regulations than the medium and small firms. Meanwhile, the small firms once again did not have the time, resources, or ability to participate directly in the negotiations. As one participant succinctly described the situation, "the representatives of the auto parts sector were exclusively from the large companies. The small companies simply were not there" (interview). As César Flores, president of AMIA, described the problem for small firms, "we needed people who could talk about taxes, tariffs, rules of origin, unfair trading practices, etc. The small businesspeople did not even have the language that was required" to participate (quoted in Puga 1993b, 66–67). Consequently, INA was left to lobby primarily on behalf of the sector's small and medium firms. Though widely considered to be far more effective than some other organizations such as the CANACINTRA chambers, INA still suffered from the problems inherent in representing hundreds of different companies with somewhat disparate interests (interviews with automotive sector participants). A single organization simply could not thoroughly represent the diverse interests of all the firms within a sector the way that the representatives of the large parts companies and the five automobile producers were able to do on their own.

Interesting cleavages also arose within the motor vehicles sector. Though sharing many interests in common as a sector, the perspectives of the five automobile producers in the Mexican market diverged in one crucial area. It is useful to divide them into two groups according to their region of origin, or the region of their "home" country. The Big Three auto producers formed the North American contingent. Ford first began its Mexican operations in 1925, GM arrived in 1935, and Chrysler came in 1939. From outside the North American region, the two players in the Mexican automobile sector were Volkswagen, which first entered Mexico in 1954, and Nissan, which began in 1956 (AMIA documents).[9] The biggest differences between these two camps arose in the debates on the rules of origin. The parties to a free trade agreement use rules of origin to limit the ability of nonmember third parties to penetrate the

---

9 A handful of other producers came and went over the years, but from 1984 to 1994 these five were the only competitors in the Mexican market.

markets of the member countries by taking advantage of the internal lowering of barriers within a region. Rules of origin require that a certain percentage of a product originate from within the region for it to be able to pass freely between the member countries. Without such rules, a third party producer could export to the member country with the lowest external trade barriers and then gain free access to the other member countries' markets.

The Big Three wanted strict rules of origin, requiring as much as 70 percent regional content. Nissan and Volkswagen, on the other hand, pushed for much looser requirements, as low as 50 percent or less (interviews with automotive sector participants). The Big Three's home location in the North American region would make it easier for them to comply with a strict rule of origin. Based in Japan and Germany, Nissan and Volkswagen imported a higher proportion of their inputs from suppliers in non–North American regions. This put them at a competitive disadvantage under a system of strict rules of origin. Though it was really the only major point of disagreement among the automobile producers, the rules of origin dispute prevented the adoption of a common position for the five companies. SECOFI called for a single unified sectoral position, but months of intense negotiating led nowhere. In March 1991, César Flores of AMIA sent a letter to COECE's Juan Gallardo (with copies to several people in SECOFI) in which he outlined the basic initial positions of each company for the assorted issues in the auto negotiations (AMIA documents). In September 1991, the Big Three put together a common position advocating strict rules of origin around the 65 to 70 percent level. At that point, according to the people who participated in the negotiations, it became clear that no consensus could be reached. Nissan and Volkswagen countered the U.S. firms' position by submitting proposals of their own for lower requirements, along the lines of the 50 percent specified in the 1989 U.S.–Canada Free Trade Agreement (interviews with automotive sector participants).

Despite their differences on the rules of origin question, the five automobile producers together represented probably the most highly concentrated of all the sectors involved in the negotiations, and their representation was fairly uniform in most other areas of negotiation. In addition to AMIA, each of the five companies sent at least one, and often more, middle- to upper-level executive to the automotive side room to participate personally in the negotiations on behalf of their interests. According to many people involved in these negotiations, these representatives were extremely active in virtually all aspects and phases of the negotiations. The auto firms had too much at stake in the negotiations, which would alter the way the entire industry did business, to depend on another organization to represent their own interests along with those of the other firms. As one of these representatives described his role in the automobile negotiations, "we *were* COECE" (interview). These corporate representatives were well received by their SECOFI counterparts. SECOFI brought in several people specially from the Undersecretariat of Industry and Foreign Investment, which oversaw the Auto Decree, because they were most familiar with the auto sector and because the auto companies were most comfortable dealing with them (interview). Even the Undersecretary of Industry and Foreign Investment himself, Fernando Sánchez Ugarte, participated actively in the SECOFI auto negotiating team (SECOFI documents).

The participation of the representatives of the five auto companies reached levels not achieved in any other private sector negotiating groups. Like other sectors, most of these representatives devoted themselves to NAFTA nearly full time, studying the issues, developing company and industry positions, and meeting with their private sector and government cohorts. But some of these representatives actually participated the negotiations themselves, rather than just through the side room. At times the SECOFI negotiators would send one or more of these representatives to sit across the table from the U.S. and Canadian negotiators to help Mexico negotiate some of the most complex aspects of the agreement (interviews with government and business automotive sector participants). In the automotive sector at least, the direct participation of large firms surpassed even the highest expectations that business might have had about its consultative role in the NAFTA negotiations.

The Exertion of Structural Leverage by the Automobile Producers

The high level of participation by the representatives of the auto producers in the NAFTA negotiations partly reflects the structural leverage of these vertically integrated multinational firms that carry so much weight in the Mexican economy. This structural relationship between the auto companies and the Mexican state goes back much further than NAFTA (cf. Bennett and Sharpe 1985), but the patterns of these years highlight it exceptionally well. The negotiations for the 1989 Auto Decree liberalized the Mexican auto market by lowering or removing several nontariff trade barriers, but the prohibition on the import of subcompact cars (defined as having engine sizes of 1800 cc or less) was retained until model year 1993. According to one auto industry expert, the inclusion of this import ban in the decree resulted directly from structural power considerations: "This provision was included as a quid pro quo to both Nissan and Volkswagen for their respective $1 b[illio]n investments to modernise and increase the capacity of their Mexican plants" (Scheinman 1991). The Mexican government also made several other concessions designed to attract new investment in the automotive industry. In exchange for Ford building a new plant in Hermosillo, Sonora, the Sonora state government made infrastructural improvements in local water and energy supplies and highway construction. The federal government also gave Ford a $10 million credit toward machinery and equipment for the new plant (Studer Noguez 1997, 16–17).

My interviews with the representatives of the five automobile producers in Mexico confirm the presence and significance of this structural power relationship. According to one such person, his company began in the mid-1980s to send suggestions to the Mexican government about what sort of policy and infrastructural changes and concessions would be required for the company to undertake investments in ventures such as new plant openings. Another company sent the government a study of the measures taken by other countries, and even states in the United States, to attract foreign capital, so that the Mexican government would know what it was up against in the international competition for capital (interviews).

A third company was even bolder in exerting its structural leverage in its communications with the government. In 1988, before the drafting of the new Auto Decree had begun, this company sent several high-level government officials involved in regulating the automotive sector a document outlining the specific policies that it wanted to see changed in the new Auto Decree upcoming the following year. In exchange, the company offered to invest significant sums in the Mexican economy: "We told them, 'with these policies, we can invest hundreds of millions of dollars'" (interview). Such policies included trade liberalization. The document summarized the company's general viewpoint: "given the comparative advantages, we believe that the Mexican automobile industry has a good opportunity to participate in the international automobile scheme; nevertheless, to promote this greater participation, we believe that the automotive legislation should be more flexible and less protectionist" (anonymous internal auto company document).

This company strongly suggested that investment would increase if the decree adopted these kinds of free-market policy changes. In a section entitled "Requirements for Attracting New Programs" (i.e., investment), the company wrote that it believed

a more flexible and less protectionist law would create the ideal climate for promoting the growth of the domestic market and for improving the participation of Mexico in the international automobile business. Ideally, the automobile industry would be regulated by a reduced number of global parameters, under a system of an open economy, and where self-sufficiency of currency was the principal requirement. The adoption of this new policy would improve the possibilities of attracting new programs to Mexico (ibid.).

In its conclusion, this document predicted that the adoption of these types of changes "would generate new, urgently needed jobs, and stimulate the continuous inflow of new automotive and related technology" (ibid.).

The company requested both general and specific policy changes in this document, including dropping the restrictions on the number of models produced by each company, lowering the national content requirements, freeing up the selection of sourcing, and eliminating the restrictions on foreign investment in the auto parts sector. In the end, this company's 1988 demands very closely resembled the final 1989 Auto Decree. The success achieved with this approach impressed the company's representative: "Before, the government could impose decrees on us. They could not do that this time" (interview).[10]

Some Results of the Negotiations

A full assessment of the actual outcomes of the NAFTA negotiations would have to take into account more than this book attempts to do (see Maxfield and Shapiro 1998). For one thing, it does not directly address the constraints placed on the Mexican negotiators by their U.S. and Canadian counterparts. Neither has it dealt in detail with the domestic pressures on the U.S. and Canadian negotiators that helped determine their own negotiating strategies. For these and other reasons, I concentrate more on the domestic factors affecting the determination of the Mexican negotiating team's bargaining positions in the negotiations. Nevertheless, a brief and admittedly incomplete consideration of the influence of the various segments of the business community on some of the outcomes of the automotive negotiations can be instructive.

Though all five automobile producers enjoy significant economic weight, the results of the rules of origin debate suggest that the Big Three wielded somewhat greater influence in the negotiations than the Volkswagen and Nissan tandem. The final agreement phases in the rules of origin, beginning at 50 percent for the first four years, and then increasing to 56 percent for four more years before ending up with a final 62.5 percent rule of origin. In other words, by 2002, 62.5 percent of the valued added in production must come from within the North American region. Given the original positions of the two groups within this sector, on balance the results seem to favor the Big Three. The Detroit automakers had asked for 65 to 70 percent rules of origin, while

10 Contrast this with the typical experience of one CANACINTRA small business representative, who said he had submitted numerous proposals designed to help his members adjust to the economic opening to government officials, only to receive no response whatsoever (interview).

the non–North American companies had sought to cap it at 50 percent. According to one participant, "the paragraph on rules of origin was basically an agreement among the American companies" (interview). And as someone associated with the Big Three admitted, "perhaps 60 percent would have been more fair" (interview).

Aside from their basic numerical (three vs. two) superiority, the Big Three held two distinct advantages in the negotiations that helped them win this battle. First, as companies with operations in both Mexico and the United States (and Canada), they had "one foot on each side of the border" (interview with automotive sector participant). All three U.S. companies were extremely active in promoting their interests both in Washington and in Mexico City (interviews with automotive sector participants). This gave them influence with both governments that Volkswagen and Nissan did not enjoy. Second, these firms are also more internationally, or at least regionally, integrated. Historically, most automobile manufacturers had principally served the domestic Mexican market. Beginning in the 1980s, however, the export sector of this industry began to grow very rapidly, especially for the U.S.-based firms. The proportion of automotive exports as a share of total exports increased from less than 5 percent in 1983 to approximately 20 percent in 1992 (Studer Noguez 1997, fig. 2). Though Volkswagen is the largest of the five in terms of production, the Big Three export a much greater proportion of their total output. In 1990, the Big Three together exported 185,496 passenger cars (59% of their total production), compared with 67,046 passenger car exports (24% of total production) for Nissan and Volkswagen together (Scheinman 1991). Given the Mexican economy's need for foreign exchange, this gave the Big Three greater economic clout upon which to draw.

The final resolution of Mexico's NVAp regulation in NAFTA reflects in part the relatively weak position of the smaller parts sector compared with the more powerful automobile producers. NAFTA lowered Mexico's national value-added requirement immediately to 34 percent beginning in 1994. Though the parts producers did manage to salvage a five-year grace period during which the NVAp remains at 34 percent, beginning in 1999 it falls by 1 percentage point per year until it reaches 29 percent in the year 2003. In 2004 the NVAp requirements disappear altogether, along with the rest of the provisions of the 1989 Auto Decree (SECOFI 1993a). Furthermore, loopholes in the agreement allow the existing five automobile producers to lower their NVAp requirements below the 34 percent level. The agreement holds these manufacturers to the domestic-content percentage actually achieved in 1992, which for nearly all of them was less than 34 percent. (New entrants, like BMW, Honda, and Mercedes-Benz, must meet the new requirements.) Additionally, the NVAp requirements for incremental increases in production are calculated at progressively lower rates, so that all told, "the average domestic-content requirement quickly drops to 20 percent before going to zero" (Hufbauer and Schott 1993, 38–39).

It is difficult to assess fully the relative weights of the various determinants of the outcomes of the negotiations without reference to the negotiating positions of the United States and Canada, which were likely to oppose Mexico's NVAp requirements on discriminatory grounds. But my interviews suggest that the parts producers were not pleased with the negotiations and their outcome. According to one participant, the parts sector "saw the reduction from 36 percent to 34 percent as a great loss," and another observed that "the producers of auto parts were never satisfied" with the negotiations. This applied with particular force to the sector's many smaller firms, which received an unfavorable prognosis from one participant: "They are condemned to die" (interviews).

THE NATURE OF THE NEW BUSINESS-STATE ALLIANCE

The incorporation of big business into the NAFTA negotiations via COECE and the side room helped consolidate the position of the free trade coalition, which joined together the free trade factions from within the state and business to negotiate NAFTA. This consolidation of the free trade coalition spread beyond the narrow realm of the NAFTA negotiations and the side room, spilling over into other areas. It fostered a new spirit of more overt, public cooperation between big business and the state that deviated from the alliance for profits system of silent partnership and that finally mended many of the wounds that the 1982 bank nationalization inflicted on the business-state relationship.

Over the course of preparing for and negotiating NAFTA, the leaders of SECOFI (Jaime Serra, Herminio Blanco, Jaime Zabludovsky, etc.), and COECE (Juan Gallardo, Guillermo Güémez, etc.) developed close personal relationships that helped generate higher levels of trust between the government negotiators and private sector representatives down the line. Numerous people interviewed from both sides of the business-state relationship agreed that the process of negotiating NAFTA served to form new bonds of trust between government officials and businesspeople. This process reached such a level that several business and government leaders went out of their way to praise the professional manner in which the negotiations were conducted and to mention the close, personal friendships they had developed with some of the people from what they previously considered "the other side."

The politics of NAFTA's approval in the United States offers a good example of this new relationship. Mexico had previously kept a relatively low diplomatic profile in the United States, and often clashed with Washington on key foreign policy issues, such as U.S. policy in Central America in the early 1980s (Grayson 1995). Relative to the level of economic exchange between these two North American neighbors, Mexico expended relatively little diplomatic energy and few resources on protecting its interests in the U.S. political system. The recognition of key shared interests, the importance of NAFTA's successful approval to the Mexican economy, and the rise of the new breed of outward-oriented bureaucratic elite encouraged Mexico to increase its diplomatic presence in the United States. Mexico's efforts at lobbying various branches of the U.S. government, especially Congress, for NAFTA's approval highlight these efforts most clearly. The most comprehensive study to date of Mexico's NAFTA lobbying in the United States calculates recorded earnings by Mexico's biggest foreign agents from 1991 through 1993 at nearly $38 million, which "probably represents only a minority of the Mexicans' total expenditures on the pact." The Mexican government paid more than $32 million of this total; SECOFI alone paid more than $25 million (Eisenstadt 1997, 94, 113). The Mexican government hired lobbyists, contracted a prominent public relations firm (Burson-Marsteller), and employed American lawyers to protect its interests in the U.S. (Center for Public Integrity 1993).

The business community, led by COECE, also involved itself deeply in U.S. politics, for the first time. As early as 1990, the CEMAI/COECE office in Washington began carefully charting the patterns of support and opposition in the U.S. Congress for the 1991 fast-track vote. By October 1990, Raúl Ortega, the CEMAI/COECE representative in Washington, had met with the assistants of forty-three U.S. legislators to discuss NAFTA issues (COECE press release, 18 October 1990; interviews with COECE officials). COECE continued its lobbying efforts during the negotiations, frequently contacting U.S. legislators and their aides, congressional committees, and regulatory agencies (Eisenstadt 1997, 101). COECE also hired its own lobbyist and lawyers in the United States (Center for Public Integrity 1993). From 1991 through the end of 1993, COECE alone spent at least $1.17 million in its NAFTA lobbying campaign in the United States (Eisenstadt 1997, 94). Individual companies, including the Cementos Mexicanos (CEMEX), Alfa, and Vitro groups, paid out an estimated $1 million in lobbying expenses. Finally, the secretive and powerful Mexican Businessmen's Council (CMHN) hired the government's own public relations firm, Burson-Marsteller, for $3.5 million in 1993 (ibid.). All told, private Mexican business spent at least $5.7 million lobbying for NAFTA's approval in the United States.

Among its many lobbying activities, Mexican business sponsored a series of visits to Mexico by U.S. policy makers. The private sector paid for, and COECE organized, "more than half a dozen junkets to Mexico for at least forty-eight congressional aides, three congressional members, and a governor" (ibid., 100). The participants in these visits reportedly spent long working days (and often nights) in crash courses on NAFTA from the Mexican perspective. One of the most intriguing aspects of these visits was the meetings that the participants held with Mexican government officials, including representatives from the labor and environmental arms of the state, and numerous SECOFI officials (Center for Public Integrity 1993). Several people interviewed for this project went to great lengths to emphasize that the Mexican government did not subsidize COECE's participation in the NAFTA negotiations in any way, shape, or form. But the level of cooperation between COECE and the Mexican government did reach such a level that the private sector paid for U.S. politicians to come to Mexico to meet with officials of the Mexican government. The private sector's participation in NAFTA and active cooperation with the government established an active partnership between big business and the state and consolidated the power of the free trade coalition.

7

Conclusion: Mexico in Comparative Perspective

INTRODUCTION

This book argues that trade policy depends on the formation and relative strength of two competing cross-cutting business-state trade policy coalitions: the protectionist coalition and the free trade coalition. In turn, a series of international and domestic-level political and economic variables associated with the external context, the business sector, and the state drive these coalition dynamics. This chapter reviews the argument and evidence presented in previous chapters, places the Mexican case into a larger comparative framework, and offers some potential theoretical and practical implications of this research. The next section provides a brief review of the basic tenets of the argument and the evidence from the Mexican case in order to tie back together the study's theoretical and empirical components and permit an assessment of its explanatory power. The third section compares Mexico with three other cases that undertook varying degrees of economic reform: Argentina, Brazil, and Chile. Some of the most successful reformers shared critical characteristics with Mexico, while those countries that lagged behind in their reform efforts often exhibited very different kinds of coalition dynamics. The fourth section raises some of the study's theoretical implications. It presents contributions that the approach developed in these pages may be able to make to the development of theory in the discipline as a whole, as well as in the subfields of international political economy and comparative politics. The chapter concludes by highlighting some of the study's practical implications for Mexico's recent past and future.

A REVIEW OF THE ARGUMENT AND EVIDENCE

The Mexican trade regime underwent a program of radical liberalization during the 1980s and 1990s. The government dismantled several barriers to inflows of foreign trade, beginning with import licenses and official pricing mechanisms and continuing with sharp tariff reductions. By the end of the 1980s, Mexican imports faced relatively few quantitative restrictions and a fairly low maximum tariff level of 20 percent. The implementation of NAFTA over a varying phase-in period of zero to fifteen years beginning in 1994 has begun to eliminate Mexico's remaining restrictions on imports from Canada and the United States, which together account for more than three fourths of Mexico's foreign trade.

A profound transformation in business-state relations has accompanied these changes in Mexican trade policy. The relationship between the private sector and the state bottomed out after López Portillo's 1982 nationalization of the private banking system. In the late 1970s and very early 1980s, the "balance of power" between these two entities leaned toward the state, and most of the business community felt shut out of the policy process. Over the course of the 1980s, business gained a greater degree of structural power as its leverage increased simultaneously with the state's dependence on private investment. Business also began to seek a more active role in the policy process. As time went on, the relationship between the public and private sectors improved as a newly rising technocratic elite within the state gradually incorporated the concerns and representatives of certain segments of the business community into the policy-making apparatus. This group formed the nucleus of the free trade coalition that would soon overpower the incumbent protectionist coalition to carry out a series of trade reform initiatives. The base of this coalition began to form in the mid-1980s during the initial round of liberalization and Mexico's accession to the GATT. It gained greater strength and institutional representation in the late 1980s as government, business, and labor leaders negotiated the Economic Solidarity Pact. During the NAFTA negotiations of 1991–92, free trading state elites fully incorporated important segments of the business community into the policy process to consolidate the free trade coalition's dominant position in Mexican trade policy making.

Table 7.1 presents a stylized summary of the empirical relationship between the independent, intervening, and dependent variables employed in this study. The formation and relative strength of competing trade policy coalitions is an intervening variable between the dependent variable of trade policy outcomes and the independent (or causal) variables within this framework. I hypothesize that the independent variables directly affect the formation and relative strength of the competing policy coalitions, which then determine policy outcomes. This schematic allows us to evaluate the overall explanatory power of the argument and the relative impact of its different components with greater precision.

Table 7.1. *Snapshots of the Variables by Policy Episode*

Policy episode	Dependent variable: policy outcome	Intervening variable: protectionist vs. free trade coalition	Independent variables							
			International constraints	International opportunities	Business leverage	Business makeup	Business strategies	State vulnerability	State institutions	State initiative
1979–80 GATT	Closure	Protectionist coalition dominant	Weak	Recession in North limits	Low; IFI begins; underdeveloped capital markets in Mexico	Favors ISI interests and small business	Exit dominant; voice incipient	Low structural vulnerability; few credible electoral challenges	ISI interests and ideas prevalent	President courts opposition to opening through public forum
1985–86; GATT	Opening	Banxico and World Bank sponsor; free trade coalition begins to form	Strong; IMF and World Bank; little private lending	Special relationship with U.S.; gives aid; open markets and recovery in North create export incentives	Increase; IFI and growth of dominant private financial and portfolio capital markets	Still favors ISI, but begins to shift toward export sector	Exit and voice combine	Foreign lending cut-off, oil prices fall; Electoral challenges from PAN	Balance shifts over to free traders when President comes on board	State policy begins to create and favor free trade interests in private sector
1987–88 PSE	Faster opening	free trade coalition takes shape	Still strong	World Bank resources support reforms	Increasing	Specific free trade interests emerge, large northern firms	Exit and voice continue	High inflation, low growth and PAN complicate governance	SHCP joins team, free traders strengthen their hand	State seeks out specific business interests and brings into talks
1991–92 NAFTA	Deeper and broader regional opening	free trade coalition consolidate	Some renewal of lending with Brady Plan	Special relationship with and proximity to U.S. offer NAFTA benefits to Mexico	IFI rising; domestic capital markets opened to foreign participation	Concentration rises; balance moves toward large, export-oriented firms	Seek direct role in policy making	High, but inflation falls and growth begins as NAFTA boosts investor confidence; 1988 FDN challenge hurts new regime	Free traders control most important agencies; new young elites in charge of policy bureaucracy	Formally includes new free trade interests and big business into NAFTA via COECE and side room

Big Business, the State, and Free Trade

At the time of the 1979–80 GATT debate, Mexico faced relatively weak international constraints. The ability of organizations like the IMF and World Bank to impose policy conditionality on Mexico was limited because of the prolific financing available from private bank lenders. International opportunities did not provide Mexico with many special resources that it could use to finance trade reform, and the external context of northern recession limited the attractiveness of the export option. Business's structural leverage was still relatively low as international financial integration had just begun to pick up, and Mexico's domestic capital markets remained underdeveloped. The internal balance of forces within the private sector leaned heavily in favor of import-substituting interests, and business did not seek out an active role in policy making, preferring instead to withhold investments and engage in exit to protest unfavorable policies. The vulnerability of the state was relatively low due to its access to low-cost international credit and large oil revenues and to the lack of significant electoral opposition to the PRI. The internal makeup of state institutions resembled that of business, with import-substituting interests and agencies dominating. Finally, in the public debates surrounding Mexico's protocol of accession to the GATT President López Portillo appeared to have changed his mind. Rather than promote GATT entry, he used the debates to help generate opposition to the GATT within both the state and society. This tactic strengthened the hand of the protectionist coalition, which exerted its influence over policy to derail Mexico's entry into the GATT.

During the 1985 unilateral liberalizations and the 1986 GATT accession, Mexico faced a far more constraining international environment. The IMF and World Bank had demanded specific trade policy concessions in exchange for badly needed, scarce balance of payments assistance. Several international opportunities turned in liberalization's favor at the same time. Mexico's special relationship with the United States gave it access to greater sources of external financing than other countries enjoyed, and open markets and economic recovery in the north combined with domestic crisis created incentives for an export-based platform. The structural leverage of business was on the rise, as international financial integration took off and domestic capital markets began to develop. The internal makeup of business still favored import substitution, but took some initial steps toward the export sector. Business began to engage in simultaneous strategies of exit and voice after the 1982 bank nationalization ignited a crisis of confidence in the government. The state became more vulnerable due to its increased reliance on private investment after foreign private credit dried up and oil prices fell, and to the growing electoral challenges to the PRI from the PAN. The internal balance within the state shifted over to the free traders when

Conclusion

President de la Madrid joined the side of the Bank of Mexico and the Ministry of Programming and Budget (SPP) in supporting trade liberalization. The economic policies of the de la Madrid administration helped promote the disproportionate growth of the larger, more internationally oriented mobile asset holders, likely proponents of free trade. These changes gave the free traders within the state a greater number of more powerful potential allies within society. The free trade coalition was still nascent at this point. Trade reforms in 1985 and 1986 were politically sponsored and backed by a small group of technocrats within the Bank of Mexico, SPP, and the World Bank. After these new policies failed to generate significant amounts of new investment and economic growth, this group sought to broaden the coalition within both the state and business in subsequent rounds of reform.

The 1987–88 Economic Solidarity Pact (PSE) negotiations took place within a context of continuing strong external constraints. Additional funding from the World Bank in the form of two Trade Policy Loans contracted in 1986 and 1987 provided more external support for the trade liberalization program of the Mexican government. Business leverage remained high, as international financial integration continued and Mexican capital markets increased their pace of development. Shifts in the internal makeup of business became somewhat clearer as the effects of earlier government policies, including the previous round of liberalization, began to appear in the emergence of specific large, export-oriented interests. The strategies of business continued to combine exit and voice to pressure the state. Capital flight continued in 1987 and 1988 (though the rate of private investment increased sharply in 1988, most likely due to the confidence-raising effects of the first pact), and the PAN continued to challenge the PRI in regional elections. State vulnerability remained high as inflation, low rates of economic growth, and electoral pressures complicated PRI governance. The balance among state institutions continued its shift toward the free traders as Finance and other key ministries joined the free trade coalition. A group of young state elites associated with Carlos Salinas de Gortari's SPP team took the initiative in incorporating specific big business interests into the pact negotiations. The position of the free trade coalition strengthened in both its state and business memberships, and a model for allowing business participation in policy reform was established.

The 1991–92 NAFTA negotiations occurred within an environment of somewhat weaker international constraints, as Mexico's 1989 Brady Plan agreement facilitated some new flows of foreign lending. Mexico still faced stagnation and a large debt burden, but seemed to have survived the worst of the crisis. Mexico's special relationship with the United States and its geographical proximity to the world's largest single market would provide Mexico with a unique opportunity for exports under NAFTA's privileged market access rules that other developing countries did not enjoy. Business leverage rose significantly leading up to these negotiations, as international financial integration picked up speed and Mexican financial and portfolio capital markets developed rapidly as they were opened up to greater levels of foreign participation. Indices of concentration in the Mexican economy suggest that the internal balance of forces of the private sector continued to move in favor of large export-oriented firms, especially northern ones, leading up to the NAFTA negotiations. Business sought out a direct role in economic policy making, based in part on its experience in the PSE negotiations. The state remained fairly vulnerable to business leverage, but by the early 1990s the rate of inflation had begun to slow and economic growth picked up as the PSE began to have an impact and the prospect of NAFTA helped raise investor confidence. Electorally, the position of the PRI had never been more tenuous. In the 1988 presidential elections, a left-leaning coalition gave the PRI its biggest electoral scare since assuming power nearly sixty years before. The PAN also continued to threaten the governing party at the regional level. Within the state, the free traders took over the last remaining significant bastion of opposition to all-out liberalization when a former Finance official, Jaime Serra, took the reigns at SECOFI. The state took a firm initiative in formalizing its alliance with big business and consolidating the position of the free trade coalition when it invited the private sector to organize itself to participate indirectly in the NAFTA negotiations. This invitation, followed by the negotiations themselves, served to formalize and cement the new bonds between the new big business elite and the young generation of outward-looking state elites who together formed the nucleus of the free trade coalition that now had a firm grip on Mexican trade policy.

In assessing the argument's overall explanatory power and the relative causal effects of the different independent variables, it is useful to examine each variable's performance individually in light of the "snapshots" summarized above and in Table 7.1. First, a strong correlation between the relative strength of the two competing trade policy coalitions and policy outcomes is observed across the cases. Only in the 1985 reforms did a relatively weak free trade coalition succeed in imposing trade reform, and it was those reforms themselves that helped strengthen the new free trade coalition in the latter part of the decade and the first years of the following one. For the continuation and acceleration of these reforms to succeed *politically*, a strengthening of the free trade coalition became necessary.

Second, with a few exceptions most of the explanatory variables conform to expectations. The impact of international constraints appears reasonably strong, though the final step in Mexico's trade opening (NAFTA) was undertaken in a less constraining international context. International constraints appear to make some sort of adjustment likely, but they are not determinate. International opportunities helped Mexico along in its path toward liberalization and smoothed some of the bumps along the way by providing politically valuable resources to support the process and by creating some of the external incentives for a shift to an export-oriented model of development. These factors help explain varying responses of different countries to what are often portrayed as identical external stimuli. The international positions of Brazil and Mexico, for example, differ significantly, especially in terms of the distinct international opportunities and conditions each country faces. But these factors still say little about how political actors will respond to external stimuli.

The concept of business leverage helps us understand the ability of business to exert pressure on the state and provides a logic for when and why business may influence policy, but it is less successful in explaining how this influence translates into political efficacy. When will one coalition's constituency become stronger, while another weakens? The internal makeup of business determines the universe of available coalition partners for state policy makers. This variable helps explain much of the relative strength of competing coalitions and helps account for some of the variance between the outcomes in Mexico and other cases. Brazil, for example, had a very different and less internationally oriented business community than Mexico, and its trade reform program also got a much later start and was more tenuous (cf. Lal and Maxfield 1993, Edwards 1995). The approach employed here would link some of this variation to the different bases of societal and business support for free trade that might be observed in the differential rates of participation in and the weight of the free trade coalition in Brazil (see below). The Mexican case, however, demonstrates that potential coalition partners often need to mobilize themselves and exert pressure on the state to participate in policy formation. Business strategies for pressuring the state and for participating in policy correlate fairly closely with the observed results. As business's pressure strategies became more varied and intense, government policy came to reflect many of the demands of the private sector and business representatives were gradually incorporated into the free trade coalition to appease business opposition and boost investor confidence.

The state's vulnerability to business's structural leverage and to electoral challenges illuminates the state's responsiveness to business demands and the state's incentives to incorporate different groups into the free trade coalition. As these kinds of threats to governance mounted, the state moved further along in its efforts to consolidate its hold on power by allying itself with powerful groups, in particular the new big business elite. The development of state institutions and interests also helps explain this shift, as the new generation of trade policy makers was generally more inclined to move in that direction. More fundamentally, this internal balance helps explain the initial round of liberalization in 1985, when the free traders in the state managed to overcome the opposition of the protectionists. This small group eventually found it expedient to expand its base of political allies, within both the state and business. Finally, state initiative in the process of coalition formation appears to be crucial. Effective state policy makers can facilitate the political processes of trade reform and coalition building by favoring certain groups over others, encouraging the growth of particular interests within society, and establishing alliances with those whose power is rising. These processes were especially important in the latter episodes of trade liberalization, those that gave Mexico's new open trade regime more permanence. As Mexico's political system democratizes, the ability of state leaders to recruit powerful societal allies will take on increasing importance.

A COMPARATIVE PERSPECTIVE

Varying international contexts, business participation, and state behavior have led to different processes of coalition formation and strengthening across Latin America and elsewhere.[1] These coalitions, in turn, have exerted varying degrees of control over the policy-making process. Where cohesive governments have succeeded in establishing formal or informal political alliances with outward-oriented, big business, their reform efforts have met with much greater success. The reform programs of Argentina, Brazil, and Chile exhibit interesting variation over time and useful contrasts with the Mexican experience. Argentina and Brazil represent Latin America's late reformers, while Chile led the way with significant neoliberal reforms in the 1970s and 1980s. Today, Chile's reform

---

1 Böhme (1967) discusses Bismarck's construction of the iron-rye coalition in Germany. In the contemporary European context, Zubek and Gentleman (1994) draw interesting parallels between Mexico and Poland. The extensive literature on the East Asian "miracle" underscores the importance of business-state relations from a generally more state-centric point of view. For one example of this literature that compares East Asia and Latin America, see Gereffi and Wyman (1990). Hamilton and Kim (1993, 1995) analyze business-state relations surrounding political and economic liberalization in Mexico and South Korea. Pempel and Tsunekawa's (1979) treatment of the privileged place of business in the Japanese corporatist political system also provides interesting insight into the Mexican case.

Conclusion

coalition is the most broadly based and most well established. The Argentine reform coalition has been successful, but its social and political bases are less secure. Brazil's situation suggests that its reform game is far from over.

Argentina

Carlos Menem managed to forge a similar coalition in Argentina with even stronger economic results than Mexico. Menem, a member of the populist Peronist party, came into office in 1989 facing runaway inflation and a profound crisis of confidence. Menem's predecessor, centrist Radical Party leader Raúl Alfonsín (1983–89), left office under a cloud of 3,000 percent annual inflation and a protracted economic crisis. As Argentina's first democratically elected President after the brutal military dictatorship of 1976–83, Alfonsín had significant political leeway his first few years in office that he drew upon in his attempts to stabilize the economy. Alfonsín's government vacillated between attempts to implement IMF-conditioned structural reform programs and heterodox stabilization programs such as the 1985 Austral Plan (Kaufman 1988). Each of these efforts failed, often leaving the economy in worse shape than before. Alfonsín never established an effective alliance with business or any other powerful social actor, and his policies and policy-making procedures failed to win the confidence of the public or of private investors. Meanwhile, organized labor, a longtime supporter of the Peronist Judicial Party, consistently opposed much of the Radical Party's reform agenda.

By the end of Alfonsín's term, Argentina's economy was far more closed, and far less stable, than Mexico's. Argentina had a maximum tariff of 55 percent in 1987, and its unweighted tariff and paratariff protection averaged 28 percent in 1985. Nontariff barriers covered approximately 32 percent of Argentina's imports in the late 1980s (Edwards 1995, 126). Annual inflation averaged 829 percent from 1984 to 1989, when it topped out at 3,085 percent (Interamerican Development Bank n.d.). Privatization of state-owned enterprises did not begin in earnest until 1989–90. From 1980 to 1992, the Argentine government privatized only forty-five firms, or 15 percent of total state-owned enterprises, and many of these occurred during the 1990 to 1992 period under Menem (Edwards 1995, 171). Real GDP growth stagnated at an annual average rate of –0.52 percent from 1982 to 1990 (calculated from IMF 1997). By the time of Menem's election in May 1989, all public confidence in the government's ability to govern the economy had dissipated (Rock 1995). The situation was so severe that Menem agreed to take office months early, in July 1989, in order to implement a new strategy.

Big Business, the State, and Free Trade

Menem's populist background and charismatic personal style made investors wary, and his campaign platform specified few concrete policies that he intended to adopt. Menem and a series of Ministers of Economy took an aggressive approach to inflation reduction by instituting several plans to control prices in 1989 and 1990, but none proved effective for long (Acuña 1994). Finally, in April 1991, new Minister of Economy Domingo Cavallo implemented the Convertibility Plan, or "Cavallo Plan" (Starr 1997, 83). This new strategy fixed the Argentine currency and made it fully convertible with the U.S. dollar. It also constrained the central bank's ability to print money by requiring it to maintain foreign reserves totaling 100 percent of the domestic monetary base (ibid., 87). Table 7.2 highlights the spectacular success of the plan, which lowered inflation from 2,316 percent in 1990 to 172 percent in 1991 and 25 percent in 1992. Inflation eventually dipped into single digits in 1994, and virtually disappeared from 1996 to 1998, when it averaged 0.47 percent.

Aside from its technical details, one of the principal reasons for the plan's success was the fact that it formed part of a larger economic and political agenda that also included trade liberalization, privatization, and the construction of a new political coalition of support for the Peronist government. Previous Peronist governments had nationalized industries and intervened extensively in the domestic economy. They had also pursued closed-market, protectionist trade policies that favored Juan Perón's urban constituency at the expense of Argentina's more export-oriented rural elite. Eager to assuage business fears, calm inflation, and secure his own political future, Menem quickly established informal contacts with important business groups even before his May 1989 election and his July inauguration (Starr 1997, 101). In one of his first official acts, Menem named Miguel Roig as Minister of Economy. Roig was a representative of the internationally integrated, multinational grain conglomerate Bunge and Born, and his surprise appointment by a Peronist signaled Menem's early intentions to pursue business-friendly policies. Menem also attempted to shift his coalition by reaching out to the main business associations and the principal right-wing party by appointing some of their members to key government posts. After Roig's death in mid-July 1989, Menem consulted openly with Bunge and Born leadership in selecting his successor, Néstor Rapanelli (Acuña 1994). These overtures, combined with the success of the Convertibility Plan, a bold privatization scheme, sharp reductions in trade protection, and Argentina's leadership in establishing the Common Market of the South (Mercosur), brought big business into the fold (Rock 1995). "Ultimately, the internationally-oriented segment of the Argentine private sector became one of the most enthusiastic boosters of the Menem government" (Starr 1997, 102).

Table 7.2. *Inflation and Real GDP growth in Argentina, Brazil, Chile, and Mexico, 1989–1998 (percent)*

Country	1989	1990	1991	1992	1993	1994	1995	1996	1997	1998
Argentina										
Inflation	3,084.6	2,315.5	171.7	24.9	10.6	4.2	3.4	0.2	0.5	0.7
Real GDP growth	−7.2	−1.2	10.2	10.0	6.1	5.8	−3.0	5.6	8.1	4.6
Brazil										
Inflation	1,289	2,938	441	1,009	2,149	2,669	84.4	18.2	7.5	3.0
Real GDP growth	3.2	−4.2	0.3	−0.8	4.2	6.0	4.2	3.0	3.0	0.2
Chile										
Inflation	17.0	26.1	21.8	15.3	12.8	11.4	8.2	7.4	6.1	5.1
Real GDP growth	10.6	3.7	8.0	12.3	7.0	5.7	10.6	7.4	7.6	3.4
Mexico										
Inflation	20.1	26.6	22.7	15.5	9.7	7.0	35.0	34.4	20.7	15.9
Real GDP growth	4.2	5.2	4.2	3.7	1.8	4.6	−6.5	5.5	7.1	4.9

Source: Interamerican Development Bank (n.d.).

Much like the experience of the "revolutionary" party governing Mexico, Menem's efforts to establish ties with big business while maintaining tight control over the organized labor movement and other potential societal opponents of neoliberalism helped him consolidate and extend his hold on power. Menem even managed to get the constitution amended to allow him to run successfully for reelection in 1995, a year in which the economy contracted by 3 percent in reaction to the Mexican peso crisis and "tequila effect" (see Table 7.2). This evidence suggests that left-leaning political parties with links to politically captive labor movements may have distinct advantages in implementing neoliberal economic policies. These policies would be most likely to benefit the constituencies of the more socially isolated but politically powerful right. The Peronists' and the PRI's control of much of the left end of the political spectrum enabled both parties to solidify their holds on power by moving to the right to undercut right wing electoral support and gain the critical investment that they needed for the economy to grow.[2] The risk of such a strategy is that new forces will emerge on the center-left to take advantage of and capture dissent among the ruling parties' historic bases of support. This explains some of the recent electoral successes of the PRD in Mexico and the Radical Party–Frepaso alliance in Argentina. High and rising levels of inequality and unemployment exacerbate these tendencies. The distribution of income in Mexico has worsened as the neoliberal adjustment strategy has progressed (Pastor and Wise 1997, 425), and the rate of unemployment in Argentina has vacillated between 15 and 20 percent in recent years (IMF 1997). Menem's reform coalition, while effective in the short run, was less institutionalized and even narrower than the Salinas coalition in Mexico (see Borón 1995, López 1997). Without a broadening of political support, and as society's memories of hyperinflation fade, Argentina may emulate the social and political backlashes against the degree of economic and political concentration associated with the neoliberal coalition in Mexico (see Thacker 1999b).

Brazil

Brazilian reform efforts lagged behind both Mexico's and Argentina's. Hyperinflation plagued Brazil's economy throughout the 1980s and into the 1990s, and a series of successive attempts to control prices met with only fleeting success. Like Argentina's Austral Plan, President José Sarney's 1986 Cruzado Plan created a new currency and established price

---

2 Gibson (1997) provides a very useful comparison of the PRI and the Peronist Judicial Party.

controls to contain inflation. Both plans significantly lowered inflation in the short term, but continued fiscal deficits put upward pressure on prices. This inertial inflation led to the plans' breakdown (Edwards 1995). Brazil's domestically oriented industrial sector was much larger and stronger than Argentina, Chile, or Mexico's by the end of the 1970s, and this put it in a better position to resist neoliberal reform efforts in the 1980s (see Villareal 1990). The state also played a larger role in the Brazilian economy than most of its Latin American counterparts (see Gereffi 1990). State-owned enterprises accounted for a relatively larger share of total capital accumulation, and the ISI bureaucracy more generally was decisive in domestic policy debates. State interventionism governed much of Brazil's economy throughout the 1980s, as trade policy protected domestic and multinational producers from outside competition and state-owned enterprises remained in government hands. Efforts to adopt market-based reforms did not really begin until the early 1990s, and were not effectively implemented until after 1994.

In addition to the different set of international opportunities facing Brazil (see above and Hagopian 1995, 265), Brazil exhibited stronger domestic political obstacles to reform within the state and business. Inward-oriented producers and their government allies maintained their ISI coalition to resist reform efforts, shun IMF-style policy recommendations, and direct policy formulation and implementation. Even when the power of this group began to decline in the early 1990s, no effective political force managed to coalesce around the idea of market reform. Within the private sector, a decade of economic crisis and a series of incoherent government stabilization plans helped fragment the business community (see Nylen 1992, Weyland 1996). Similarly, the political capacity of the Brazilian state decayed as clientelism and special interests undermined policy cohesion within the new democratic government (Hagopian 1995, Weyland 1997).

Taking office on a "modernizing" platform in 1990, Fernando Collor de Mello made greater progress toward economic reform than his predecessor. But in the end, Collor's initiatives collapsed and another round of hyperinflation ensued. Analyzing Brazilian privatization, Schneider (1992) documents the opening of political space for reform within the state in the early 1990s as a result of bureaucrats' acceptance of the necessity of market-based measures to tame Brazil's hyperinflation. But despite the erosion of political resistance to reform, Collor did not construct a new coalition of public or private support for privatization (ibid., Kingstone 1997b, 8). He faced less strident opposition, but his failure to capitalize on the partial opening and create new policy alliances with state or business actors ultimately defeated his reforms. Within the state, institutions remained weak and political loyalties disaggregated. Parts of the Brazilian business class began to recognize the potential benefits of neoliberal policies, but a series of efforts by different groups to create peak-level business organizations to coordinate business interests and participation in policy making failed (see Payne 1994, Kingstone 1997a, Schneider 1997). Collor's free market policy initiatives were put aside when he resigned shortly before his impeachment on corruption charges in late 1992, and the new Itamar Franco government saw inflation increase to 2,149 percent in 1993 and 2,669 percent in 1994 (see Table 7.2).

The appointment of Foreign Affairs Minister Fernando Enrique Cardoso as Finance Minister in 1993 served a function similar to Cavallo's nomination in Argentina. One of Latin America's most prominent academics before taking a seat in the Brazilian Senate in 1983, Cardoso was known for his work on dependency theory and his concerns for social equity. In 1994, Cardoso initiated the Real Plan, which, like Argentina's Convertibility Plan, employed strict monetary instruments to achieve a remarkable price stabilization. Inflation declined to 84.4 percent in 1995 and 18.2 percent in 1996 before reaching single digits in 1997 and 1998 (see Table 7.2). On the momentum of this burgeoning success, Cardoso won the 1994 presidential elections with a broad-based electoral coalition of support. The success of Cardoso's anti-inflationary policies gave him momentum in his attempts to rebuild the state (see Weyland 1997), and helped boost political support within the government for his broader reform agenda. The business sector had begun a process of transformation that favored newer, more outward-oriented firms at the expense of traditional, import-substituting private elites (Kingstone 1997b). These shifts, along with the Real Plan, helped Cardoso gather greater political backing for neoliberal reform. In addition to cutting inflation, Cardoso opened up Brazil's trade relations, particularly within Mercosur, and carried out an impressive privatization program that included the telecommunications giant Telecomunicacoes Brasileiras, SA (Telebrás). In response to the Asian and Russian crises, Cardoso and his team of advisors have stepped up their efforts at fiscal reform, cutting social security benefits, imposing an employment tax, and laying off employees of state-owned enterprises since late 1997.

Like Menem in Argentina and Salinas in Mexico, Cardoso emerged from the center-left of the political spectrum to adopt policies that favored parts of the business community. Unlike the other cases, however, the relative balance of forces within Brazilian business still favored market closure, although the internal structure of Brazilian business had begun to change. Cardoso and his advisors have also not yet solidified a political coalition with big business leaders, who have been less successful in their attempts to organize to participate in policy making. The policy influence of inward-oriented industrialists has declined, but has not been replaced by effective political leadership, or voice, among the business sector's potential winning segments (see Kingstone 1997a).[3] Mexico's peak level CCE succeeded in influencing and participating in policy debates, but Brazilian business has had no similarly effective peak association. Furthermore, despite the decline in the influence of ISI elites, mobile asset controllers exerted less leverage through the exit option, despite the severity of the economic crisis in Brazil. Investment fell less sharply and recovered more quickly in Brazil than in Mexico (Schneider 1997, 195). The absence of effective business voice and exit strategies gave the state greater room to conduct policy, but the state itself was unable to pursue a coherent policy path until 1994. As Sarney, Collor, and Itamar Franco's aborted attempts at reform demonstrate, the "extraordinary confusion of the new democracy's policy-making process" impeded policy innovation (Kingstone 1997a, 1). Only Cardoso has been able to fill this political vacuum, and the final fate of his reform efforts remains unclear.

After gaining reelection in October 1998 and the approval of $41.5 billion in IMF credits in November 1998, Cardoso attempted to renew pending reform initiatives, many of which had been stalled in congress. Brazil's decentralized federal political system soon presented new hurdles. In January 1999, new Minas Gerais governor Itamar Franco, the former President who appointed Cardoso as Minister of Finance in 1993, declared a moratorium on his state's debt to the central government in Brasilia. This move proved to be the straw that broke of the back of the real, which had been under pressure from investors wary about the Brazilian government's ability to service its debt in the face of crises in Asia and Russia. The government announced an 8 percent devaluation of the real on 13 January (*New York Times*, 14 January 1999). Strong capital flight ensued, Brazil's equity markets tumbled, and within a few days the government let the real float lest it run out of reserves defending the currency against speculative attacks. Though both the real and the Brazilian economy have recovered somewhat at the time of this writing (January 2000), Brazil's reforms remain a work in progress. As new policy initiatives continue to alter the internal makeup of the Brazilian business community in favor of outward-oriented interests and shift the balance of forces within the Brazilian state, neoliberal reformers may have greater success in constructing a more stable coalition of support for reform. Whether or not Cardoso has enough political capital stored up from his success in reducing inflation to

---

3 Many of liberalization's greatest potential losers – micro-, small-, and medium-sized businesses – have virtually no political representation (Nylen 1997).

withstand the belt-tightening imposed by the recent crisis, and whether or not the business community can be organized and incorporated into the governing policy coalition, will go a long way toward determining whether the reform efforts become politically viable over the medium to long term.

Chile

The influence of business-state political coalitions is not limited to competitive political systems. Chile is the only country in Latin America to adopt neoliberalism wholesale before Mexico (Edwards 1995).[4] Chile's reform program began in the 1970s and continued throughout most of General Augusto Pinochet's authoritarian rule (1973–90). In response to what they viewed as the irresponsible socialist policies of Salvador Allende (1970–73), Pinochet and his advisors moved quickly to reestablish a capitalist, investor-friendly economy. Beyond that general goal, his initial plan for the economy was short on specifics. A career soldier, Pinochet brought in the "Chicago boys," a group of monetarist economists based in Santiago's Catholic University and tied to the University of Chicago through an academic exchange program, to advise him on economic policy (Stallings 1989, 183). Pinochet eventually found, however, that a politically isolated technocratic state can impede an economic reform process that depends heavily on the collaboration of private actors. Economic policy has distributional consequences in democratic and authoritarian systems alike, and "not even the Pinochet government could endure isolated from all kinds of societal support indefinitely" (Schamis 1995, 171). Pinochet's market-based policies broke sharply with Allende's interventionism and statism, but they failed to generate sufficient investment for long-term economic growth despite large inflows of foreign savings (Silva 1996a, 304–5). At a time when other Latin American countries were booming, Chile's economic growth averaged 3.9 percent from 1974 to 1981 (calculated from IMF 1997).[5] In 1982, Chile suffered the region's worst economic decline as real GDP fell by 14.1 percent (Interamerican Development Bank, n.d.). Only after the 1982 debt crisis revealed the limitations of Chile's politically isolated, radical neoliberal restructuring program did Chilean state leaders adopt a coalition-building strategy with the business community. Much like the Mexican case, Pinochet and his technocratic advisors found it useful to forge political ties with private actors in the 1980s. Those state leaders

---

4 Bolivia moved toward neoliberalism at roughly the same time as Mexico, in 1985.
5 By comparison, Brazil's real growth averaged 5.7 percent and Mexico's 6.7 percent during the same period (calculated from IMF 1997).

who aligned themselves with powerful private sector actors gained greater political influence and power.

Though Pinochet maintained tight control over the political system, he and his team of Chicago boys eventually established an effective political coalition with big business to make their economic program yield dividends and to strengthen their grip on power after 1982. Pinochet appointed prominent businesspeople to head government ministries, and policy makers consulted regularly with peak-level business organizations, including the Confederation for Production and Commerce (CPC) and several sectoral associations (Silva 1996a, 309). The CPC in particular played a critical role similar to that of Mexico's CCE in coordinating and channeling business input into the policy-making process. This new coalition between state technocrats and large capital interests initiated a series of neoliberal policy measures similar in content to those of the 1970s, but the specific mechanisms used and the method of consultation with key elements of the business community helped Chile recover more quickly from the debt crisis than the rest of Latin America. New Finance Minister Hernán Büchi played a big role in the Chilean state's rapprochement with the private sector after 1985. Policy content came to reflect what Silva (1996b) has called "pragmatic neoliberalism," which combined a general market orientation with mild forms of state intervention. In response to business's political activation, Büchi incorporated many of their general and sectoral concerns into the broader monetarist policy framework (Stallings 1989, 191). Unlike his predecessors, Büchi also consulted regularly with business leaders to get their input and support for government policies (ibid.).

By the end of the 1980s, the media and academics alike were holding Chile up as the model reforming country. Real GDP growth reached 10.6 percent in 1989, with moderate inflation of 17 percent (see Table 7.2). Chilean policies changed only slightly from the 1970s to the 1980s, and the structure of the state itself and Pinochet's ultimate authority over all decision making remained constant. This leads Eduardo Silva to conclude that the shifts in the business-state relationship were responsible for Chile's improved economic performance in the 1980s (1996a, 308). After 1990, the governments of Patricio Aylwin and Eduardo Frei continued many of Pinochet's economic policies and maintained an effective system of consultation with the private sector under a democratic political system. From 1989 to 1998, Chile's annual real growth rate averaged 7.6 percent and inflation 13.1 percent (calculated from Table 7.2). Despite numerous external shocks in the mid- and late 1990s, Chile has also had large inflows of productive investment and a rate of domestic savings similar to the East Asian countries – almost 27 percent of GDP in 1993 (Edwards 1995, 227).

Big Business, the State, and Free Trade

THEORETICAL IMPLICATIONS

The application of a business-state coalitions explanation of trade policy to the Mexican case in the 1980s and early 1990s poses several possible theoretical implications for the study of political science, international political economy, and comparative politics. One possible implication derives from the application of structural power considerations to trade policy. The extent of the structural power of capital controllers over the determination of economic policy by the state is a question that has received an increasing amount of attention in the literature in recent years. Several theoretical and empirical studies of the power of mobile capital controllers over economic policy making have made important advances in our knowledge.[6] But few studies of the structural power relations between business and the state have focused explicitly on trade and trade policy coalition politics. The most common areas of inquiry have been financial policy (see Maxfield 1990) and general macroeconomic policy (see Winters 1996). One reason for this gap in the literature is the difficulty of specifying a structural theory of trade policy interests (Thacker 1997a). If we do not know what structurally powerful actors want, how can we know if they get it? By supplementing indicators of asset mobility with measures of size, economies of scale, and sectoral cleavages (cf. Shafer 1994, 1997), this study broadens the definition of preferences and makes it possible to extend a structural theory to trade. Only after specifying interests in terms of structure can we connect that structure to trade policy.

Implications also flow from this study's more general use of the concept of trade policy coalitions. One weakness in much of the structural power literature has been the insufficient amount of attention it pays to the political mechanisms through which policy is formulated and implemented. Without examining these aspects of the policy process, an assessment of the structural power of different groups cannot directly account for changes in policy. The best that they can hope to accomplish is to assume away the policy process and argue that outputs directly reflect structural power considerations. If a country's policy processes are consistent with this assumption, then such an approach may well provide reasonably accurate policy predictions, but its explanatory power would still be undermined by its neglect of the crucial question of exactly how structural power considerations affect policy. Structure helps show us the *why* of policy, but it tells us very little about *how* actors make and imple-

---

6 In addition to the literature cited in Chapter 2, see Winters (1994) for a useful review of recent works that address these kinds of issues.

ment policy. By incorporating structural power relations into a broader framework of trade policy coalition politics, this study tries to help remedy this problem.

Similarly, without reference to other theoretical constructs (such as structural power relations, the internal makeup of business and the state, and state initiative), an analysis based strictly on trade policy coalitions would be less useful for telling us the underlying causes of policy. Without understanding the essential political and economic motivations for shifts in the makeup and relative strength of competing trade policy coalitions, an approach that simply identified and measured the strength of coalitions would be hollow and would lack the causal connections necessary to explain policy. To say that trade barriers fell because the free trade coalition became stronger begs the question: *Why* did it become stronger? The critical task is to provide a causal explanation of the coalitions themselves.

The relationship between the strength of competing policy coalitions and trade policy outcomes is complex. It is not unidirectional, but rather reciprocal and dynamic. The relative strength of competing policy coalitions helps determine policy, but policies adopted in one time period can alter the values of the variables (e.g., the internal makeup of business) that determine the formation and relative strength of the two coalitions in the next time period. This can occur even if the time lapse between the periods is short. In this sense policy is both a dependent and an independent variable. By incorporating state initiative into the theoretical framework of this study, I hope to provide a plausible account of how such reciprocal causal interactions work.

This study assumes that neither international nor domestic factors can be viewed in isolation from the other. The same domestic dynamics will play out differently in varying international contexts of constraints and opportunities, and two countries with different domestic structures but facing similar international contexts will most likely react differently to that shared context. In this sense, this framework aims to trespass disciplinary boundaries and further blur some of the already fuzzy lines between political science and economics, and between international relations and comparative politics (see Gourevitch 1978). Similarly, neither the state nor society should be analytically separated from the other. One goal of this research has been to identify and explore business-state relations as a crucial nexus between state and society, and to delineate the international and domestic political and economic factors that together determine their formation and strength. Such a strategy detracts from the goal of theoretical parsimony, but I hope that a greater payoff in explanatory power justifies it.

On a final note, the kinds of processes that have given rise to free trade in Mexico are not necessarily ubiquitous, unilinear, or irreversible. To cite just one example, some studies of the effects of international capital mobility can give the impression that these kinds of forces are somehow unstoppable, overpowering, and inevitable. But evidence from patterns of international factor-price movements does not confirm this hypothesis. Theoretically, international financial integration should lead to equalization of international returns to labor and capital, or factor prices. Despite recent trends in globalization of international financial markets, factor prices have not yet converged (Osler 1991). Similarly, the structural power of capital controllers and its effect on policy have not been identical in every country. A quick review of the two basic sets of factors that make up the structural component of this study's argument help show why this is the case.

The international mobility of capital facing a given country depends not only on the external barriers at the level of the international system, but also on country-specific factors such as the characteristics of domestic capital markets and assets. Maxfield (1990), for example, presents a compelling argument on the potential benefits of restricting international capital flows in her comparison of Mexico and Brazil. And recent evidence from Mexico in 1994 and Asia in 1997–98, where an exodus of mobile capital assets surrounding currency crises sent shock waves through the domestic and international economies, highlights the downside of outward capital mobility. Similarly, the state's dependence on private investment varies across time and space. Some of this has to do with international factors, but it is also related to a country's domestic characteristics. Furthermore, because structural power relations are embedded in a broader context of trade policy coalition formation, the remaining causal factors outlined here would shape the impact of any shift in the structural relationship.

The free trade coalition in Mexico is not an unstoppable, immovable, or uniform force. To be sure, the consolidation of the free trade coalition's power in the NAFTA negotiations created a certain momentum in favor of continuing liberal policies, as those policies continue to generate their own political constituencies over time. The continuation of most of these policies since the 1994 peso crisis demonstrates their continued vitality, despite their deleterious social impact in many regions (Pastor and Wise 1997, Sheahan 1997). But the kinds of circumstances that led to the downfall of the protectionist coalition could conceivably lead to a similar eventual demise of the free trade coalition. A consideration of some of the practical implications of this study demonstrates how these kinds of processes can generate a backlash effect that could promote their reversal in the medium to long run.

Conclusion

The political and economic developments that led to the consolidation of the free trade coalition extend to other realms, posing wider implications for the stability of the Mexican system as a whole. The consolidation of the free trade coalition has been part and parcel of a broader phenomenon in the Mexican political economy. This coalition helped concentrate power and wealth in the hands of a small elite centered within the ranks of the state *tecnoburócratas* and big business. This concentration appeared viable in the short run, as the Mexican economy began to stabilize and grow a bit faster in the early 1990s and the political system rebounded from the instability associated with the 1988 presidential elections (see Table 7.2 and Thacker 1999b). But beginning in 1994, the system began to unravel in several places. This section details some of these developments, organizing them according to conflicts within the state, differences between big and small business, and societal opposition to the new big business-state alliance.

The takeover of the uppermost echelons of the state bureaucracy by the new generation of technocratic elites generated a strong, at times violent, backlash from some of the groups who were shut out of the top circles of power that they had previously occupied. Young, mostly U.S.-educated economists and planners dominated the Salinas administration. The older generation, or the "dinosaurs," as they are commonly referred to in Mexico, became further removed from the inner circles of the state hierarchy over the course of the *sexenio*. As the time to nominate the PRI's official presidential candidate approached in the fall of 1993, Salinas appeared to have two distinct courses of action in choosing his successor. Among several potential pre-candidates, four central players attracted most of the attention in the nomination game. Pedro Aspe, the Minister of Finance (SHCP) with a Ph.D. from MIT and impeccable credentials as a free market economist but relatively little political experience, was considered the preferred candidate in international financial circles. Ernesto Zedillo, Minister of Education, like Aspe a member of the Salinas Programming and Budget (SPP) team and a former SPP Minister, was likewise considered to be an excellent economist but an even less experienced politician than Aspe. In contrast, Manuel Camacho, the mayor of Mexico City, was widely considered to be Salinas's most influential political advisor and the most attractive candidate for mending fences with disenfranchised groups within the state and society. Salinas's choice of Luis Donaldo Colosio, the Minister of Social Development (SEDESOL), may have been a compromise between the technocrat Aspe and the *político* Camacho. Like Aspe and Zedillo, Colosio had been a central figure in the SPP clique and was considered to have top-notch technocratic skills. Unlike the other technocrats, however, he had impressive prior political experience. He had been a representative in the Chamber of Deputies for his northern home state of Sonora, and prior to his run at SEDESOL he spent the first three years of the Salinas administration as the head of the PRI, where he led much of the restructuring of the party that purged many of the dinosaurs from its upper ranks. Until that point, the PRI had presented one of the biggest remaining obstacles to the complete takeover of the new generation that Salinas had led to power. Their efforts to simultaneously shift power away from the party (transferring many of its functions over to the executive branch) while "modernizing" it to consolidate their group's political power helped make many enemies for Salinas and Colosio.

While Salinas's selection of Colosio appeared at the time to be a popular one,[7] it also seems to have generated a fierce reaction from those within the party who saw their influence and power eroding. First, several PRI veterans were still pushing for Camacho to replace Colosio as the official candidate as the latter's campaign got off to a slow start. Camacho eventually stated publicly that he would not seek the nomination, and the following day, 23 March 1994, Colosio was assassinated in Tijuana. Although the ultimate motives for the killing have not been fully determined (or at least not publicly disclosed), the most plausible explanation appears to be that a rift within the party led dissident *priístas* to strike out against the party's official candidate and the most visible representative of the new generation in Mexican politics. A single gunman was first arrested at the scene of the murder, but eventually one of the party's security guards, who stood next to Colosio at the time of the shooting, was also arrested for his alleged complicity in the crime. A few days later, Ernesto Zedillo, Colosio's campaign manager, was named to replace the slain candidate on the PRI ticket.

On 28 September of the same year, the Secretary General of the PRI, José Francisco Ruiz Massieu, was assassinated in downtown Mexico City. Ruiz Massieu was also considered a party reformer who had made several enemies. In February 1995, Raúl Salinas de Gortari, the brother of the then former President, was arrested for masterminding the murder of Ruiz Massieu, his and the ex-President's former brother-in-law. In January 1999, Raúl Salinas was convicted and sentenced to fifty years in prison, which an appeals court later reduced to 27 1/2 years (*New York Times*, 22 January, 17 July 1999). While Carlos Salinas was not named as an official suspect (or even mentioned at the time by name by government officials), he later was reported to be residing in New York,

7 The selection of Colosio was widely lauded by the official representatives of the business community (see *El Financiero*, 30 November 1993).

Conclusion

Montreal, possibly Cuba, and Ireland in a sort of self-imposed exile after the devaluation and assassination debacles. Swiss and U.S. authorities have also investigated Raúl Salinas on corruption and drug trafficking offenses. Shortly after Raúl Salinas's arrest in Mexico, the government accused Mario Ruiz Massieu, the late Secretary General's brother and an investigator in the Attorney General's office, of engaging in a cover-up that shielded Raúl Salinas from the investigation of Mario Ruiz Massieu's own brother's assassination. In September 1999, Mario Ruiz Massieu committed suicide while under house arrest in New Jersey awaiting prosecution on drug and money laundering charges in Houston (*New York Times*, 16 September 1999). This series of assassinations, accusations, and arrests breaks with a long-standing unwritten tradition of immunity for high-level party and government officials. It also represents part of a severe political backlash to the kinds of developments within the state that helped consolidate the position of the free trade coalition.

The concentration of power within the private sector has also led to a counterreaction from dissident segments of business, though not nearly as strongly nor as violently as that which occurred within the state. After the December 1994 devaluation of the peso, the government raised nominal interest rates to nearly 100 percent per year in early 1995. This, and the rising inflation that accompanied the devaluation, put a financial squeeze on small and medium businesspeople, most of whom lacked the preferential access to credit that many members of the large business conglomerates enjoyed. Some of these members of the business community, along with middle-class consumer groups, many of whom had seen their monthly credit card payments approach or even surpass the level of their monthly salaries, staged limited credit demonstrations and payment boycotts and organized a debtors group (El Barzón) to protest government policy. They also began to push much more vigorously for a stronger industrial policy in order to compete with the increased foreign trade competition. Many of these segments of the business community felt shut out of the policy process by the big business-state alliance that now governed economic policy making in Mexico, and they began to mobilize some of their forces to act out against it. This dissatisfaction also extended to the electoral arena, where dissident small businesspeople formed an unlikely alliance with the leftist PRD in the 1997 midterm elections (Shadlen 2000). Their participation in the campaign enabled the PRD to extend its influence beyond its traditional unorganized labor constituency. This kind of broad support helped the PRD end the PRI's majority control of the Chamber of Deputies and helped Cuauhtémoc Cárdenas win the first ever election for mayor of Mexico City.

The new alliance between the state and big business also generated a strong negative reaction within certain parts of society shut out of this coalition of political and economic elites. The mutual accommodation between the PRI and the PAN potentially excluded much of Mexican society from the benefits of the new development strategy and the limited political opening. At the same time, the formal collaboration between the private sector and the PRI during the 1994 electoral campaign was more extensive than in years past. For example, first Colosio and later Zedillo received significant support – both financially and otherwise – from business groups in Monterrey and elsewhere.[8] In addition, the PRI moved a bit closer to incorporating the business sector into its official structures. In early March 1994, the PRI officially announced the creation of the party's new business cells, intended to organize business financial and campaign support for the PRI's presidential candidate (*El Financiero*, 8 March 1994). Though these cells did not give business a formal role in the party of a stature equal to that of its official popular, labor, and peasant sectors, they represent a new spirit of public cooperation between the private sector and the PRI and the partial extension of the business-state alliance into electoral politics.

The incorporation of business concerns into the government and party at the expense of the popular, labor, and peasant sectors also contributed to the violent uprising in the southern state of Chiapas on 1 January 1994. The leaders of this rebellion purposefully timed it to coincide with the inauguration of NAFTA, calling for greater democratization of the Mexican political system and the extension of full political and economic rights to the country's indigenous groups and lower classes. The basic issues dividing government and rebel leaders remain unresolved, and continuing instability, along with the PRI's defeat in the 1997 congressional elections, suggest that the stable system of single-party PRI rule may be coming to an end. Anticipating the possibility of these kinds of problems, the Salinas administration initiated a poverty alleviation program (Pronasol), as well as a new agricultural subsidy program (Procampo). These programs met with some success, particularly electorally, to undermine PRD support in areas (such as Cárdenas's home state of Michoacán) that reportedly received large amounts of Pronasol resources in the 1980s (Dresser 1991, Kaufman and Trejo 1997). But these kinds of band-aid measures have not been able to stop the bleeding of the Mexican political system since 1994.

The response of Mexico's leaders to these challenges in the future will partly determine how well the system adapts. Dealing with these issues

---

8 See *El Financiero*, (10 December 1993, 17 February, 8 June 1994) for reports of such support.

will be an extremely difficult task for future administrations. The 1994–95 peso crisis demonstrated the continuing susceptibility of the state to the exertion of structural leverage by the private sector. The government will need to walk a fine line between satisfying the exigencies of mobile capital controllers and containing economic, political, and social unrest. To be sure, major unrest and political instability in Mexico could themselves lead to rapid outflows of valuable investment resources from the Mexican economy and potentially more intractable problems down the line. Recent election results offer a more hopeful prognosis for Mexico's stability. Most observers judged the 1994 presidential elections as some of the technically cleanest in Mexico's history (*El Financiero International Edition*, 29 August 1994), although the ability of opposition parties to compete on equal footing with the PRI was still limited. A newly independent Federal Electoral Institute oversaw the 1997 midterm elections in which the PRI lost its majority control of the Chamber of Deputies for the first time since its founding in 1929. Zedillo's immediate acceptance of the PRI's losses in the 1997 elections and his ability to impose defeat on party leaders bode well for Mexico's 2000 presidential elections. The PRI primary system adopted for the 2000 presidential race and in several local elections in 1998 reinvigorated the party and helped it win back the governorship of Chihuahua from the PAN, the first time the opposition has passed power back to the PRI. If such progress continues, it will enhance the social legitimacy of the entire system and of whichever party wins the presidency in the year 2000, but the possibility of a political backlash within the PRI and within society still threatens Mexico's long-term stability. Powerful elements within the ruling coalition may continue to resist opening both the policy-making process and the political system to the participation of those who have been disenfranchised by the workings of coalition politics.

Appendix: List of Interviewees

I conducted much of the research for this book in a series of loosely structured interviews with government officials, business leaders, academics, and others from the fall of 1993 to the fall of 1994. Interviewees were told that their responses would not be attributed by name, but that their names would appear in a list at the end of the text.[1]

MEXICAN GOVERNMENT OFFICIALS

Ministry of Trade and Industrial Development (SECOFI)

Undersecretariat of International Trade Negotiations/Office for the Negotiation of NAFTA

Name	Position(s)	Dates
Alvarez, Eric	Director General of Sectoral Coordination and the Pacific Rim	1991–94
Cohen, Aslán	Director General of Rules of Origin	1990–93
Espinosa, Enrique	Director General of Trade Linkages with North America (headed negotiations in textiles and apparel, safeguards, unfair trading practices, and technical norms)	1990–92

1 Interviewees provided the information on positions and dates. Several people held positions in more than one organization, in which case all of their relevant positions are listed under the single most pertinent heading. An open-ended date reflects a position that was not necessarily subject to automatic turnover after the 1994 elections, but does not necessarily reflect continued occupancy of a position.

Appendix

Flores Ayala, Jesús María	Head of Advisors to the Undersecretary (headed negotiations in energy and petrochemicals)	1989–92
	Director General of Negotiations with Latin America	1992–94
Gutiérrez, Israel	Headed automotive and agricultural negotiations	
Jasso, Humberto	Area Director in Economic Studies	
de Mateo, Fernando	Director General of Services Negotiations and Coordination with Europe	1987–94
Parra, José	Area Director of Negotiations with Latin America, Advisor to the Undersecretary	1990–94
Ramírez Hinojosa, Norma	Technical Secretary, safeguards and unfair trading practices negotiations	1989–92
Ramos Avalos, Eduardo	Advisor to the Undersecretary, worked on textile and apparel negotiations	1990–94
Ramos Tercero, Raúl	Director General of International Trade Negotiations Policy	1992–94
	Director General of Economic Studies	1990–92
Zabludovsky Kuper, Jaime	Deputy Undersecretary	1993–94
	Deputy Chief Negotiator for NAFTA	1990–93
Zarco, Javier	Director of Analysis and Coordination and Pacific Rim Affairs	1991–94

Coordination of Advisors to the Secretary

Arriola Woog, Carlos	Advisor to the Secretary	1988–94
Ten Kate, Adriaan	Advisor to the Secretary	1992–94
	Worked on market access negotiations	1991–92

Undersecretariat of Foreign Trade

Bravo Aguilera, Luis	Undersecretary of Foreign Trade	1982–88
Patiño Manffer, Ruperto	Director General of GATT Issues	1986–88
	Advisor to the Secretary	1982–86
	Worked in Tariff Office	1976–82

Undersecretariat of Industry

Fernández Pérez, Manuel	Director General of Industrial Development	1989–94

Appendix

Business Organizations

CANACINTRA

Ruiz Galindo Urquidi, Armando	Represented small business in COECE	1990–93
	Spent 10 years in the International Area Has also held positions in ANIERM, CONCAMIN, CANACO-D.F., CEMAI	
Sauceda Alvarez, Carlos	Associate Director	1992–93
	Assistant Director for International Affairs	1987–92
	Associate Secretary, Foreign Trade Cabinet, Presidencia	1985–87
	Director General, Mexican Association for Normalization and Certification (Normex)	1993–

CONCAMIN

Vázquez Ahedo, Gilberto	Director of the Office for NAFTA	1990–

Coordinating Council of Foreign Trade Business Organizations (COECE)

Cruz Miramontes, Rodolfo	Industry Coordinator	1990–93
	President, Commission for Foreign Trade and International Affairs, CONCAMIN	1990–
	President, National Cement Chamber	1989–90
Güémez García, Guillermo	Executive Director	1990–
Muñozcano Alvarez, Luis	Coordinator for the Agriculture Sector	1991–
	Advisor, National Agricultural Council (CNA)	1991–
Ortega Ibarra, Raúl	Managing Director	1990–93
	CEMAI Representative in Washington	1988–90
Zaidenweber, Jacobo	Coordinator for Tariffs, and Textiles and Apparel in negotiations	1991–
	President, U.S.-Mexico Chamber of Commerce	1986–90
	President, CONCAMIN	1983–85
	President of the Board of American Textil, Encajes Mexicanos, and Banorte	

Appendix

Mexican Association of the Automotive Industry (AMIA)

Cuevas, Fausto	Director General	1992–
Flores, César	President	1981–92
	Director General, National Association of Bus, Truck and Tractor Producers (ANPACT)	1992–

Mexican Business Council for International Affairs (CEMAI)

Pangtay, Laura	Coordinating Manager for North America	1992–

National Association of the Chemical Industry (ANIQ)

Rodríguez Sánchez, Leopoldo	Representative for the chemical and petrochemical industries in COECE	1991–92
	President	1986–88
	Associate Director, Girsa (private group)	1989–

National Association of Importers and Exporters (ANIERM)

Simoneen Ardila, Humberto	Executive Vice President	1988–
	Worked on International Trade Negotiations at SECOFI	1986–87

National Chamber of the Apparel Industry (CANIVE)

Lozada S., Miguel	Director General	1985–
Marín, Jorge	President	1992–94
	Treasurer, CONCAMIN	1994–
Miklos, Víctor	President	1990–92
	Vice President	1987–88
	President, Mexico-Hungary Bilateral Committee of CEMAI	1993–
	Director General, Marsol (private firm)	1965–

National Chamber of the Textile Industry (CANAINTEX)

López Avila, César	Assistant Director General Manager of Economic Studies	1990–

Appendix

Private Firms

Bancrecer

Garrido, Celso	Economist	

Celanese Mexicana

Rodríguez Weber, Tomás	Director of Business Unit, Oxo-Solvent Acetyls	1994–
	Director General of the Chemical Industry and Consumer Goods, Undersecretary of Industry, SECOFI	1982–88

Chrysler de México

Mayoral, Claudio	Director of Governmental Relations	1974–

Ford de México

Salazar, Juan Antonio	Vice President, Finance	1991–

General Motors de México

Gelista, Carlos	Director of Public and Governmental Relations	1991–

Grupo Cydsa

Campusano, Manuel	Director of International Negotiations	1990–93

Macro Asesoría Económica (Serfín Financial Group)

Máttar Márquez, Jorge	Associate Director, Sectoral Analysis	1994–

Nissan de México

López Valadez, Gerardo	Director of Public Relations and Legal and Labor Affairs (Nissan since 1990)	1993–

Appendix

	Director General, National Auto Dealers Association (ANDA)	1988–90
	Director of the Automobile Industry, Subsecretariat of Industry, SECOFI	1982–88

Volkswagen de México

Carrillo, Armando	Director of Legal and Governmental Affairs	At VW since 1963

ACADEMICS IN MEXICO

Autonomous Technological Institute of Mexico (ITAM)

Estévez, Federico	Chair, Department of Political Science
Fernández de Castro, Rafael	Chair, Department of International Studies
Heredia, Blanca	Professor of International Studies
Katz, Isaac	Chair, Department of Economics
Kessel, Georgina	Professor of Economics

Center for Development Research (CIDAC)

Rubio, Luis	Director General

Center for Economic Research and Education (CIDE)

Bazdresch, Carlos	Director General
Elizondo, Carlos	Researcher, Political Studies
Mizrahi, Yemile	Researcher, Political Studies

El Colegio de México (COLMEX)

Alba Vega, Carlos	Professor-Researcher of International Studies
Hernández Rodríguez, Rogelio	Professor-Researcher of Sociology

Latin American Institute of International Studies (ILET)

Casar, José	Director

Appendix

Latin American Social Science Faculty (FLACSO)

Cavarozzi, Marcelo	Professor

National Autonomous University of Mexico (UNAM)

Luna, Matilde	Professor of Sociology
Puga, Christina	Professor of Political Science
Tirado, Ricardo	Professor of Sociology
Valdés, Francisco	Professor of Sociology

University of the Americas (UDLA)

Godínez, Víctor	Professor of Economics

JOURNALISTS

El Financiero

Gaona, José Luis	Editor, International Trade

Reforma

Quintana López, Enrique	Associate Director, Business Section	1993–

OTHER

American Apparel Manufacturers Association (AAMA)

Priestland, Carl	Economist	1965–

American Textile Manufacturers Institute (ATMI)

Bremer, Charles V.	Director of International Trade	1985–

Appendix

Market and Opinion Research
International of Mexico (MORI de México)

Basáñez E., Miguel	President

United Nations

Moreno Brid, Juan Carlos	Regional Advisor in Economic Development, Economic Commission for Latin America and the Caribbean (ECLAC)	1989–
Schatan, Claudia	Economic Affairs Officer, ECLAC	

World Bank, Mexico Office

Draaisma, Joost	Economist	1990–

References

Acuña, Carlos H. 1994. Politics and economics in the Argentina of the nineties (or; why the future no longer is what it used to be). In *Democracy, Markets, and Structural Reform in Latin America: Argentina, Bolivia, Brazil, Chile, and Mexico*, ed. William C. Smith, Carlos H. Acuña, and Eduardo A. Gamarra, 31–73. New Brunswick, NJ: Transaction.

Alduncin Abitia, Enrique. 1989. *Expectativas económicas de los líderes empresariales; Determinantes de la inversión privada; Posición competitiva internacional de las empresas líderes de México; 1988–1990*. Mexico, D.F.: Banco Nacional de México.

Alesina, Alberto, and Roberto Perotti. 1993. Income distribution, political instability and investment. NBER Working Paper 4486. October. Cambridge, MA: National Bureau of Economic Research.

Amparo Casar, María. 1992. Empresarios y estado en el gobierno de Miguel de la Madrid: En busca de un nuevo acuerdo. In *México: Auge, crisis y ajuste. I. Los tiempos del cambio, 1982–1988*, ed. Carlos Bazdresch, Nisso Bucay, Soledad Loaeza, and Nora Lustig, 290–312. Mexico, D.F.: Fondo de Cultura Económica.

Andrews, David M. 1994. Capital mobility and state autonomy: Toward a structural theory of international monetary relations. *International Studies Quarterly* 38(2): 193–218.

Arriola, Carlos. 1988. *Los empresarios y el Estado, 1970–1982*. Mexico, D.F.: Miguel Angel Porrúa.

Arriola, Carlos, with the assistance of Rafael Martí. 1994a. *Documentos básicos: Tratado de Libre Comercio de América del Norte*. Mexico, D.F.: SECOFI.

Arriola, Carlos, ed. 1994b. *Testimonios sobre el TLC*. Mexico, D.F.: Miguel Angel Porrúa.

Aspe, Pedro. 1992. Macroeconomic stabilization and structural change in Mexico. *European Economic Review* 36: 320–328.

Baer, M. Delal. 1990. Electoral trends. In *Prospects for democracy in Mexico*, ed. George W. Grayson, 35–61. New Brunswick, NJ: Transaction Publishers.

———. 1991. North American free trade. *Foreign Affairs* 70(4): 132–149.

Baer, M. Delal, and Sidney Weintraub, eds. 1994. *The NAFTA debate: Grappling with unconventional trade issues*. Boulder: Lynne Rienner.

Bailey, John, and Leopoldo Gómez. 1990. The PRI and political liberalization. *Journal of International Affairs* 43(2): 291–312.

References

Bailey, Michael A., Judith Goldstein, and Barry R. Weingast. 1997. The institutional roots of American trade policy: Politics, coalitions, and international trade. *World Politics* 49(3): 309–338.

Baker, Stephen. 1991. The friends of Carlos Salinas. *Business Week*, 22 July, 40–42.

Banco de México. 1993. *The Mexican economy 1993*. Mexico, D.F.: Banco de México.

————. n.d. *Información económica*. Accessed on 1998 June 5 at http://www. banxico.org.mx/public_html/indices/index2.html.

Bank for International Settlements. Various years. *Annual Report*. Basle: Bank for International Settlements.

Bates, Robert H., and Anne O. Krueger, eds. 1993. *Political and economic interactions in economic policy reform: Evidence from eight countries*. Oxford, Eng., and Cambridge, MA: Blackwell.

Bates, Robert H., and Da-Hsiang Donald Lien. 1985. A note on taxation, development, and representative government. *Politics and Society* 14(1): 53–70.

Bazdresch P., Carlos, and Carlos Elizondo. 1993. Privatization: The Mexican case. In *Latin America: Privatization, property rights, and deregulation I*, ed. Werner Baer and Michael E. Conroy. *Quarterly Review of Economics and Finance* 33(special issue): 45–66.

Bennett, Douglas C., and Kenneth E. Sharpe. 1985. *Transnational corporations versus the state: The political economy of the Mexican auto industry*. Princeton: Princeton University Press.

Bennett, Mark. 1986. *Public policy and industrial development: The case of the Mexican auto parts industry*. Boulder: Westview Press.

Bird, Graham. 1995. *IMF lending to developing countries: Issues and evidence*. London: Routledge.

Blanco Mendoza, Herminio. 1994. *Las negociaciones comerciales de México con el mundo*. Mexico, D.F.: Fondo de Cultura Económica.

Böhme, Helmut. 1967. Big-business pressure groups and Bismarck's turn to protectionism, 1873–1879. *Historical Journal* 10(2): 218–236.

Bolsa Mexicana de Valores S.A. de C.V. 1993. *Mexico company handbook: 1993 edition*. Mexico, D.F.: Bolsa Mexicana de Valores, Asociación de Casas de Bolsa A.C.

Borón, Atilio A. 1995. Argentina's neoliberal reforms: Timing, sequences, choices. In *Conversations on democratization and economic reform: Working papers of the Southern California Seminar*, ed. Leslie Elliott Armijo, 215–233. Los Angeles: Center for International Studies, School of International Relations, University of Southern California.

Bravo Mena, Luis Felipe. 1987. COPARMEX and Mexican politics. In *Government and private sector in contemporary Mexico*, ed. Sylvia Maxfield and Ricardo Anzaldúa Montoya, 89–104. Monograph Series, 20, Center for U.S.-Mexican Studies, University of California, San Diego.

Buffie, Edward F., with the assistance of Allen Sangines Krause. 1989. Mexico 1958–86: From stabilizing development to the debt crisis. In *Developing country debt and the world economy*, ed. Jeffrey D. Sachs, 141–168. Chicago: University of Chicago Press.

Bulmer-Thomas, Victor, Nikki Craske, and Mónica Serrano, eds. 1994. *Mexico and the North American Free Trade Agreement: Who will benefit?* New York: St. Martin's Press.

References

Camp, Roderic Ai. 1980. *Mexico's leaders: Their education and recruitment*. Tucson: University of Arizona Press.

———. 1989. *Entrepreneurs and politics in twentieth-century Mexico*. New York: Oxford University Press.

———. 1995a. *Mexican political biographies, 1935–1993*, 3rd ed. Austin: University of Texas Press.

———. 1995b. *Political recruitment across two centuries: Mexico, 1884–1991*. Austin: University of Texas Press.

Cárdenas, Cuauhtémoc. 1990. A conversation with Cuauhtémoc Cárdenas (interview with Jesús Galindo López). *Journal of International Affairs* 43(2): 395–406.

Carrillo Arronte, Ricardo. 1987. The role of the state and the entrepreneurial sector in Mexican development. In *Government and private sector in contemporary Mexico*, ed. Sylvia Maxfield and Ricardo Anzaldúa M., 45–63. Monograph Series, 20, Center for U.S.-Mexican Studies, University of California, San Diego.

CEMAI (Mexican Business Council for International Affairs). n.d. *What is CEMAI?* Informational pamphlet. Mexico, D.F.: CEMAI.

Centeno, Miguel Angel. 1990. The new científicos: Technocratic politics in Mexico 1970–1990. Ph.D. diss., Yale University.

———. 1997. *Democracy within reason: Technocratic revolution in Mexico*, 2nd ed. University Park: Pennsylvania State University Press.

Centeno, Miguel Angel, and Sylvia Maxfield. 1992. The marriage of finance and order: Changes in the Mexican political elite. *Journal of Latin American Studies* 24: 57–85.

Centeno, Miguel A., and Patricio Silva, eds. 1998. *The politics of expertise in Latin America*. London: Macmillan.

Center for Public Integrity. 1993. *The trading game: Inside lobbying for the North American Free Trade Agreement*. Washington, DC: Center for Public Integrity.

Cohen, Benjamin J. 1996. Phoenix risen: The resurrection of global finance. *World Politics* 48(January): 268–296.

Comisión Económica para América Latina y el Caribe (CEPAL). 1992. *Reestructuración y desarrollo de la industria automotriz mexicana en los años ochenta: Evolución y perspectivas*. Santiago: United Nations, CEPAL.

Cordera, Rolando, and Carlos Tello. 1981. *México: La disputa por la nación. Perspectivas y opciones del desarrollo*. Mexico City: Siglo Veintiuno Editores.

Cronin, Patrick. 1994. Domestic versus international influences on state behavior: Trade liberalization in Mexico. Paper presented at the Latin American Studies Association XVIII International Congress, Atlanta, GA, 10–12 March.

Dávila Villers, David R., ed. 1996. *NAFTA, the first year: A view from Mexico*. Lanham, MD: University Press of America.

Davis, Diane E. 1992. The politics of economic liberalization in Mexico: Explaining the North American Free Trade Agreement. Paper prepared for the 1992 American Sociological Association Annual Meetings, Pittsburgh, PA, 20–23 August.

del Castillo V. 1996. NAFTA and the struggle for neoliberalism: Mexico's elusive quest for First World status. In *Neoliberalism revisited: Economic restruc-*

References

turing and Mexico's political future, ed. Gerardo Otero, 27–42. Boulder: Westview Press.

Domínguez, Jorge I., ed. 1997. Technopols: Freeing politics and markets in Latin America in the 1990s. University Park: Pennsylvania State University Press.

Dornbusch, Rudiger. 1990. Mexico's economy at the crossroads. Journal of International Affairs 43(2): 313–326.

Dresser, Denise. 1991. Neopopulist solutions to neoliberal problems: Mexico's National Solidarity Program. La Jolla: Center for U.S.-Mexico Studies.

Edwards, Sebastian. 1995. Crisis and reform in Latin America: From Despair to Hope. New York: Oxford University Press.

Eisenstadt, Todd A. 1997. The rise of the Mexico lobby in Washington: Even further from God, and even closer to the United States. In Bridging the border: Transforming Mexico-U.S. relations, ed. Rodolfo O. de la Garza and Jesús Velasco, 89–124. Lanham, MD: Rowman & Littlefield.

Elizondo, Carlos. 1993. The making of a new alliance: The privatization of the banks in Mexico. Documento de Trabajo 5, Estudios Políticos. Mexico, D.F.: Centro de Investigación y Docencia Económicas.

———. 1994. In search of revenue: Tax reform in Mexico under the administrations of Echeverría and Salinas. Journal of Latin American Studies 26(1): 159–190.

Escobar Toledo, Saúl David. 1987. Rifts in the Mexican power elite, 1976–1986. In Government and private sector in contemporary Mexico, ed. Sylvia Maxfield and Ricardo Anzaldúa M., 65–88. Monograph Series, 20, Center for U.S.-Mexican Studies, University of California, San Diego.

Evans, Peter B. 1979. Dependent development: The alliance of multinational, state and local capital in Brazil. Princeton: Princeton University Press.

Evans, Peter B., Dietrich Rueschemeyer, and Theda Skocpol, eds. 1985. Bringing the state back in. Cambridge, Eng.: Cambridge University Press.

Fernández Aldecua, María José. 1993. El gremio bursátil y los nuevos empresarios financieros. Proyecto Organizaciones Empresariales en México (POEM), Cuadernos 6. Facultad de Ciencias Políticas y Sociales, Instituto de Investigaciones Sociales. Mexico, D.F.: Universidad Nacional Autónoma de México.

Frieden, Jeffry. 1988. Classes, sectors and foreign debt in Latin America. Comparative Politics 21(1): 1–19.

———. 1991a. Debt, development, and democracy: Modern political economy and Latin America, 1965–1985. Princeton: Princeton University Press.

———. 1991b. Invested interests: The politics of national economic policies in a world of global finance. International Organization 45(4):425–451.

———. 1995. On the primacy of international influences. In Conversations on democratization and economic reform: Working papers of the Southern California Seminar, ed. Leslie Elliott Armijo, 346–348. Los Angeles: Center for International Studies, School of International Relations, University of Southern California.

Frieden, Jeffry A., and Ronald Rogowski. 1996. The impact of the international economy on national policies: An analytical overview. In Internationalization and domestic politics, ed. Robert O. Keohane and Helen V. Milner, 25–47. Cambridge, Eng.: Cambridge University Press.

Gallardo, Juan. 1994a. La apertura llegó para quedarse: Entrevista con Juan Gallardo, realizada por Beatriz Mariscal Hay. Examen 56 (January): 12–13.

References

———. 1994b. La Coordinadora de Organismos Empresariales para el Comercio Exterior. In *Testimonios sobre el TLC*, ed. Carlos Arriola, 135–144. Mexico, D.F.: Diana and Miguel Angel Porrúa.

García, Brígida. 1988. *Desarrollo económico y absorción de fuerza de trabajo en México*. Mexico, D.F.: El Colegio de México.

Garrett, Geoffrey. 1995. Capital mobility, trade, and the domestic politics of economic policy. *International Organization* 49(4): 657–687.

Garrett, Geoffrey, and Peter Lange. 1991. Political responses to interdependence: What's "left" for the left? *International Organization* 45(4): 539–564.

Garrido N., Celso. 1991. ¿Reforma económica neoliberal en México? Nuevo pragmatismo en las relaciones entre mercado e intervención política pública. In *Cambio estructural y modernización educativa*, ed. Teresa de Sierra N., 15–34. Mexico, D.F.: Universidad Pedagógica Nacional, UAM-Azcapotzalco, Consejo Mexicano de Ciencias Sociales A.C.

———. 1992. *La evolucíon del actor empresarial mexicano en los ochentas*. Proyecto Organizaciones Empresariales en México, Cuadernos 4. Facultad de Ciencias Políticas y Sociales, Instituto de Investigaciones Sociales. Mexico, D.F.: Universidad Nacional Autónoma de México.

———. 1993. Los grupos privados nacionales en México. Reporte de Investigación No. 156, Serie II. Mexico, D.F.: Universidad Autónoma Metropolitana, Unidad Azcapotzalco.

Garrido Noguera, Celso, and Enrique Quintana López. 1987. Financial relations and economic power in Mexico. In *Government and private sector in contemporary Mexico*, ed. Sylvia Maxfield and Ricardo Anzaldúa M., 105–126. Monograph Series, 20, Center for U.S.-Mexican Studies, University of California, San Diego.

———. 1988. Crisis del patrón de acumulación y modernización conservadora del capitalismo en México. In *Empresarios y estado en América Latina: Crisis y transformaciones*, ed. Celso Garrido N., 39–60. Mxico, D.F.: CIDE, Fundación Friedrich Ebert, UNAM, UAM-Azcapotzalco.

George, Susan. 1990. *A fate worse than debt: The world financial crisis and the poor*. New York: Grove Weidenfeld.

Gereffi, Gary. 1983. *The pharmaceutical industry and dependence in the Third World*. Princeton: Princeton University Press.

———. 1990. Big business and the state. In *Manufacturing miracles: Paths of industrialization in Latin America and East Asia*, ed. Gary Gereffi and Donald L. Wyman, 90–109. Princeton: Princeton University Press.

Gereffi, Gary, and Donald L. Wyman, eds. 1990. *Manufacturing miracles: Paths of industrialization in Latin America and East Asia*. Princeton: Princeton University Press.

Gibson, Edward L. 1997. The populist road to market reform: Policy and electoral coalitions in Mexico and Argentina. *World Politics* 49(3): 339–370.

Gil Díaz, Francisco, and Manuel Zepeda Payeras. 1991. Mexico's recent experience regarding commercial openness. Mimeo, March 1991.

Gilly, Adolfo. 1990. The Mexican regime in its dilemma. *Journal of International Affairs* 43(2): 273–290.

Gilpin, Robert. 1987. *The political economy of international relations*. Princeton: Princeton University Press.

Goldstein, Judith. 1993. *Ideas, interests, and American trade policy*. Ithaca: Cornell University Press.

References

Goldstein, Judith, and Robert O. Keohane, eds. 1993. *Ideas and foreign policy: Beliefs, institutions and political change.* Ithaca: Cornell University Press.

Golob, Stephanie R. 1992. A "New World Order"? Mexico's free trade decision. Paper presented at the Latin American Studies Association XVII International Congress, Los Angeles, CA, 24–27 September.

———. 1999. Crossing the line: Sovereignty, integration, and the free trade decisions of Mexico and Canada. Ph.D. diss., Harvard University.

Goodman, John B., and Louis W. Pauly. 1993. The obsolescence of capital controls? Economic management in an age of global markets. *World Politics* 46(1): 50–82.

Gourevitch, Peter. 1978. The second image reversed. *International Organization* 32(4): 881–912.

———. 1986. *Politics in hard times: Comparative responses to international economic crises.* Ithaca: Cornell University Press.

Grayson, George. 1995. *The North American Free Trade Agreement: Regional community and the new world order.* Lanhan, MD: University Press of America.

Grayson, George W., ed. 1990. *Prospects for democracy in Mexico.* New Brunswick, NJ: Transaction Publishers.

Grindle, Merilee S., and John W. Thomas. 1991. *Public choices and policy change: The political economy of reform in developing countries.* Baltimore: Johns Hopkins University Press.

Haggard, Stephan. 1985. The politics of adjustment: Lessons from the IMF's Extended Fund Facility. *International Organization* 39(3): 505–534.

Haggard, Stephan, and Robert R. Kaufman. 1989. The politics of stabilization and adjustment. In *Developing country debt and the world economy,* ed. Jeffrey D. Sachs, 263–274. Chicago: University of Chicago Press.

Haggard, Stephan, and Robert R. Kaufman, eds. 1992. *The politics of economic adjustment: International constraints, distributive conflicts, and the state.* Princeton: Princeton University Press.

———. 1995. *The political economy of democratic transitions.* Princeton: Princeton University Press.

Haggard, Stephan, and Sylvia Maxfield. 1996. The political economy of financial internationalization in the developing world. In *Internationalization and domestic politics,* ed. Robert O. Keohane and Helen V. Milner, 209–239. Cambridge, Eng.: Cambridge University Press.

Hagopian, Frances. 1995. Does sequence matter? Simultaneous transitions and politics in Brazil. In *Conversations on democratization and economic reform: Working papers of the Southern California Seminar,* ed. Leslie Elliott Armijo, 262–273. Los Angeles: Center for International Studies, School of International Relations, University of Southern California.

Hall, Peter A. 1995. The political economy of Europe in an era of interdependence. Paper prepared for presentation to the Seminar on the State and Capitalism since 1800, 24 February.

Hall, Peter A., ed. 1989. *The political power of economic ideas: Keynesianism across nations.* Princeton: Princeton University Press.

Hamilton, Nora. 1982. *The limits of state autonomy: Post-revolutionary Mexico.* Princeton: Princeton University Press.

Hamilton, Nora, and Eun Mee Kim. 1993. Economic and political liberalization in South Korea and Mexico. *Third World Quarterly* 14(1): 109–136.

References

———. 1995. State-business relations in Mexico and South Korea. In *Conversations on democratization and economic reform: Working papers of the Southern California Seminar*, ed. Leslie Elliott Armijo, 314–321. Los Angeles: Center for International Studies, School of International Relations, University of Southern California.

Handelman, Howard, and Werner Baer, eds. 1989. *Paying the costs of austerity in Latin America*. Boulder: Westview Press.

Helms, Brigit. 1985. Pluralismo limitado en México. Estudio de un caso de consulta pública sobre la membresía del GATT. *Foro Internacional* 26(2): 172–189.

Heredia, Blanca. 1992a. Mexican business and the state: The political economy of a "muddled" transition. Departamento de Estudios Internacionales, Instituto Tecnológico Autónomo de México.

———. 1992b. Profits, politics, and size: The political transformation of Mexican business. In *The right and democracy in Latin America*, ed. Douglas A. Chalmers, Maria do Carmo Campello de Souza, and Atilio A. Boron, 277–302. New York: Praeger.

———. 1994. Making economic reform politically viable: The Mexican experience. In *Democracy, markets, and structural reform in Latin America: Argentina, Bolivia, Brazil, Chile, and Mexico*, ed. William C. Smith, Carlos H. Acuña, and Eduardo A. Gamarra, 265–295. New Brunswick: Transaction.

———. 1996. Contested state: The politics of trade liberalization in Mexico. Ph.D. diss., Columbia University.

Heredia, Carlos. 1994. NAFTA and democratization in Mexico. *Journal of International Affairs* 48(1): 13–38.

Hernández Rodríguez, Rogelio. 1986. La política y los empresarios después de la nacionalización bancaria. *Foro Internacional* 27(2): 247–265.

———. 1987. Los hombres del presidente de la Madrid. *Foro Internacional* 28(1): 5–38.

———. 1990. La conducta empresarial en el gobierno de Miguel de la Madrid. *Foro Internacional* 30(4): 736–764.

———. 1991. Los problemas de representación en los organismos empresariales. *Foro Internacional* 31(3): 446–471.

Hirschman, Albert O. 1970. *Exit, voice, and loyalty: Responses to decline in firms, organizations, and states*. Cambridge, MA: Harvard University Press.

———. 1981. Exit, voice, and the state. In *Essays in trespassing: Economics to politics and beyond*. Cambridge, Eng.: Cambridge University Press.

———. 1986. Exit and voice: An expanding sphere of influence. In *Rival views of market society and other recent essays*. New York: Viking.

Hoshino, Taeko. 1993. The ALFA Group: The decline and resurgence of a large-scale indigenous business group in Mexico. *Developing Economies* 31(4): 511–534.

Hufbauer, Gary Clyde, and Jeffrey J. Schott. 1992. *North American free trade: Issues and recommendations*. Washington, DC: Institute for International Economics.

———. 1993. *NAFTA: An assessment*. Washington, DC: Institute for International Economics.

INEGI (Instituto Nacional de Estadística e Informática). 1993. XIII Censo industrial: Resultados Definitivos, Resumen General. Mexico, D.F.: Instituto Nacional de Estadística e Informática.

References

———. 1994. *Anuario estadístico de los Estados Unidos Mexicanos, 1993.* Mexico, D.F.: Instituto Nacional de Estadística e Informática.

Interamerican Development Bank. n.d. *IDB economic and social database.* Accessed on 1 October 1999 at http://database.iadb.org/esdbweb/scripts/12186P61.CSV.

International Monetary Fund (IMF). 1994. *International financial statistics yearbook.* Washington, DC: International Monetary Fund.

———. 1997. *International financial statistics yearbook.* Washington, DC: International Monetary Fund.

Jenkins, Gilbert. 1989. *Oil economists' handbook*, vol. 1, *Statistics*, 5th ed. London and New York: Elsevier Applied Science.

Johnson Ceva, Kristin. 1998. Business-government relations in Mexico since 1990: NAFTA, economic crisis, and the reorganization of business interests. In *Mexico's private sector: Recent history, future challenges*, ed. Riordan Roett, 125–157. Boulder: Lynne Rienner.

Kahler, Miles. 1989. International financial institutions and the politics of adjustment. In *Fragile coalitions: The politics of economic adjustment*, ed. Joan M. Nelson, 139–159. New Brunswick: Transaction Books.

———. 1992. External influence, conditionality, and the politics of adjustment. In *The politics of economic adjustment: International constraints, distributive conflicts, and the state*, ed. Stephan Haggard and Robert R. Kaufman, 89–136. Princeton: Princeton University Press.

Kahler, Miles, ed. 1986. *The politics of international debt.* Ithaca: Cornell University Press.

Katzenstein, Peter J., ed. 1978. *Between power and plenty: Foreign economic policies of advanced industrial states.* Madison: University of Wisconsin Press.

Kaufman, Robert R. 1988. *The politics of debt in Argentina, Brazil, and Mexico: Economic stabilization in the 1980s.* Berkeley: Institute of International Studies, University of California, Berkeley.

———. 1989. Economic orthodoxy and political change in Mexico: The stabilization and adjustment policies of the de la Madrid administration. In *Debt and democracy in Latin America*, ed. Barbara Stallings and Robert R. Kaufman, 109–126. Boulder: Westview Press.

Kaufman, Robert R., and Guillermo Trejo. 1997. Regionalism, regime transformation, and PRONASOL: The politics of the National Solidarity Programme in four Mexican states. *Journal of Latin American Studies* 29: 717–745.

Kaufman, Robert R., Carlos Bazdresch, and Blanca Heredia. 1994. Mexico: Radical reform in a dominant party system. In *Voting for reform: Democracy, political liberalization, and economic adjustment*, ed. Stephan Haggard and Steven B. Webb, 360–410. New York: Oxford University Press.

Keohane, Robert O., and Helen V. Milner, eds. 1996. *Internationalization and domestic politics.* Cambridge, Eng.: Cambridge University Press.

Kessel, Georgina, ed. 1994. *Lo negociado del TLC: Un análisis económico sobre el impacto sectorial del Tratado Trilateral de Libre Comercio.* Mexico, D.F.: ITAM and McGraw Hill.

Killick, Tony. 1995. *IMF programs in developing countries: Design and impact.* London: Routledge.

Killick, Tony, ed. 1984. *The quest for economic stabilisation: The IMF and the Third World.* London: Heinemann Educational Books.

References

Kingstone, Peter R. 1997a. Corporatism, neoliberalism, and the failed revolt of big business in Brazil: The case of IEDI. Prepared for the annual meeting of the American Political Science Association, Washington, DC, 28–31 August.

———. 1997b. The limits of neoliberalism: Business, the state, and democratic consolidation in Brazil. Prepared for the XX International Congress of the Latin American Studies Association, 17–20 April.

Klesner, Joseph L. 1994. Realignment or dealignment? Consequences of economic crisis and restructuring for the Mexican party system. In *The politics of economic restructuring: State-society relations and regime change in Mexico*, ed. María Lorena Cook, Kevin J. Middlebrook, and Juan Molinar Horcasitas, 159–91. San Diego: Center for U.S.-Mexican Studies, University of California.

———. 1997. Dissolving hegemony: Electoral competition and the decline of Mexico's one-party-dominant regime. Paper prepared for the Annual Meeting of the American Political Science Association, Washington, DC, 28–31 August.

Kraft, Joseph. 1985. *The Mexican rescue*. New York: Group of Thirty.

Krugman, Paul R., ed. 1986. *Strategic trade policy and the new international economics*. Cambridge, Eng.: Cambridge University Press.

Lal, Deepak, and Sylvia Maxfield. 1993. The political economy of stabilization in Brazil. In *Political and economic interactions in economic policy reform: Evidence from eight countries*, ed. Robert H. Bates and Anne O. Krueger, 27–77. Cambridge, Eng.: Blackwell.

Lindblom, Charles E. 1977. *Politics and markets: The world's political-economic systems*. New York: Basic Books.

———. 1982. The market as prison. *Journal of Politics* 44(2): 324–336.

Loaeza, Soledad. 1992. The role of the right in political change in Mexico, 1982–1988. In *The right and democracy in Latin America*, ed. Douglas A. Chalmers, Maria do Carmo Campello de Souza, and Atilio A. Boron, 128–141. New York: Praeger.

López, Juan J. 1997. Private investment response to neoliberal reforms: Implications of the Argentine case, 1989–96. Prepared for delivery at the 1997 meeting of the Latin American Studies Association, Guadalajara, Mexico, 17–19 April.

Luna, Matilde. 1992. Las asociaciones empresariales mexicanas y la apertura externa. Paper presented at the Latin American Studies Association XVII International Congress, Los Angeles, CA, 24–27 September.

———. 1995. Entreprenuerial interests and political action in Mexico: Facing the demands of economic modernization. In *The challenge of institutional reform in Mexico*, ed. Riordan Roett, 77–94. Boulder: Lynne Rienner.

Luna, Matilde, and Ricardo Tirado. 1992. *El Consejo Coordinador Empresarial: Una radiografía*. Proyecto Organizaciones Empresariales en México, Cuadernos 1. Facultad de Ciencias Políticas y Sociales, Instituto de Investigaciones Sociales. Mexico, D.F.: Universidad Nacional Autónoma de México.

Luna, Matilde, Ricardo Tirado, and Francisco Valdés. 1987. Businessmen and politics in Mexico, 1982–1986. In *Government and private sector in contemporary Mexico*, ed. Sylvia Maxfield and Ricardo Anzaldúa Montoya, 13–43. Monograph Series, 20, Center for U.S.-Mexican Studies, University of California, San Diego.

References

Lustig, Nora. 1998. *Mexico: The remaking of an economy*, 2nd ed. Washington, DC: The Brookings Institution.

Magee, Stephen P., William A. Brock, and Leslie Young. 1989. *Black hole tariffs and endogenous policy theory: Political economy in general equilibrium.* Cambridge, Eng.: Cambridge University Press.

Mahon, James E., Jr. 1996. *Mobile capital and Latin American development.* University Park: Pennsylvania State University Press.

Mares, David R. 1985. Explaining choice of development strategies: Suggestions from Mexico, 1970–1982. *International Organization* 39(4): 667–697.

Maxfield, Sylvia. 1987. Introduction. In *Government and private sector in contemporary Mexico*, ed. Sylvia Maxfield and Ricardo Anzaldúa Montoya, 1–12. Monograph Series, 20, Center for U.S.-Mexican Studies, University of California, San Diego.

———. 1989a. International economic opening and government-business relations. In *Mexico's alternative political futures*, ed. Wayne Cornelius, Judith Gentleman, and Peter H. Smith, 215–236. Monograph Series, 30, Center for U.S.-Mexican Studies, University of California, San Diego.

———. 1989b. National business, debt-led growth, and political transition in Latin America. In *Debt and democracy in Latin America*, ed. Barbara Stallings and Robert R. Kaufman, 75–90. Boulder, CO: Westview Press.

———. 1990. *Governing capital: International finance and Mexican politics.* Ithaca: Cornell University Press.

Maxfield, Sylvia, and James H. Nolt. 1990. Protectionism and the internationalization of capital: U.S. sponsorship of import substitution industrialization in the Philippines, Turkey and Argentina. *International Studies Quarterly* 34(1): 49–81.

Maxfield, Sylvia, and Ben Ross Schneider, eds. 1997. *Business and the state in developing countries.* Ithaca: Cornell University Press.

Maxfield, Sylvia, and Adam Shapiro. 1998. Assessing the NAFTA negotiations: U.S.-Mexican debate and compromise on tariff and nontariff issues. In *The post-NAFTA political economy: Mexico and the western hemisphere*, ed. Carol Wise, 82–118. University Park: Pennsylvania State University Press.

Middlebrook, Kevin J. 1995. *The paradox of revolution: Labor, the state, and authoritarianism in Mexico.* Baltimore: Johns Hopkins University Press.

Milner, Helen V. 1988. *Resisting protectionism: Global industries and the politics of international trade.* Princeton: Princeton University Press.

Milner, Helen V., and Robert O. Keohane. 1996. Internationalization and domestic politics: An introduction. In *Internationalization and domestic politics*, ed. Robert O. Keohane and Helen V. Milner, 3–24. Cambridge, Eng.: Cambridge University Press.

Mizrahi, Yemile. 1992. La nueva oposición conservadora en México: La radicalización política de los empresarios norteños. *Foro Internacional* 32(5): 744–771.

Nelson, Joan M., ed. 1990. *Economic crisis and policy choice: The politics of adjustment in the third world.* Princeton: Princeton University Press.

Nylen, William R. 1992. Liberalismo para todo mundo, menos eu: Brazil and the neo-liberal solution. In *The right and democracy in Latin America*, ed. Douglas A. Chalmers, Maria do Carmo Campello de Souza, and Atilio A. Boron, 259–276. New York: Praeger.

References

——. 1997. Small business and democratization in Brazil. Prepared for the annual meeting of the American Political Science Association, Washington, DC, 28–31 August.

Olea Sisniega, Miguel Angel. 1990. Las negociaciones de adhesión de México al GATT. *Foro Internacional* 30(3): 497–535.

Olson, Mancur. 1971. *The logic of collective action.* Cambridge, MA: Harvard University Press.

——. 1982. *The rise and decline of nations: Economic growth, stagflation, and social rigidities.* New Haven: Yale University Press.

Osler, Carol. 1991. Explaining the absence of international factor-price convergence. *Journal of International Money and Finance* 10(1): 89–107.

Pastor, Manuel. 1987. *The International Monetary Fund and Latin America: Economic stabilization and class conflict.* Boulder: Westview Press.

Pastor, Manuel, and Carol Wise. 1994. The origins and sustainability of Mexico's free trade policy. *International Organization* 48(3): 459–489.

——. 1997. State policy, distribution and neoliberal reform in Mexico. *Journal of Latin American Studies* 29(2): 419–456.

Pastor, Robert A. 1990. Post-revolutionary Mexico: The Salinas opening. *Journal of Interamerican Studies and World Affairs* 32(3): 1–22.

Pauly, Louis. 1997. *Who elected the bankers? Surveillance and control in the world economy.* Ithaca: Cornell University Press.

Payne, Leigh A. 1994. *Brazilian industrialists and democratic change.* Baltimore: Johns Hopkins University Press.

Pempel, T. J., and Keiichi Tsunekawa. 1979. Corporatism without labor? The Japanese anamoly. In *Trends toward corporatist intermediation*, ed. Philippe C. Schmitter and Gerhard Lehmbruch, 231–270. Beverly Hills: Sage.

Pfeffermann, Guy P., and Andrea Madarassy. 1992. *Trends in private investment in developing countries 1993: Statistics for 1970–91.* Discussion Paper Number 16, International Finance Corporation. Washington, DC: World Bank.

Presidencia de la República, Unidad de la Crónica Presidencial. 1992. *Diccionario biográfico del gobierno mexicano.* Mexico, D.F.: Fondo de Cultura Económica.

POEM. 1994. *Organizaciones empresariales mexicanas. Banco de datos.* Proyecto Organizaciones Empresariales en México (POEM), Cuadernos 8. Facultad de Ciencias Políticas y Sociales, Instituto de Investigaciones Sociales. Mexico, D.F.: Universidad Nacional Autónoma de México.

Poitras, Guy, and Raymond Robinson. 1994. The politics of NAFTA in Mexico. *Journal of Interamerican Studies and World Affairs* 36(1): 1–35.

Pozas, María de los Angeles. 1993. *Industrial restructuring in Mexico: Corporate adaptation, technological innovation, and changing patterns of industrial relations in Monterrey.* Translated by Aníbal Yáñez. San Diego: Center for U.S.-Mexican Studies, UCSD, in association with El Colegio de la Frontera Norte.

Przeworski, Adam, and Michael Wallerstein. 1988. Structural dependence of the state on capital. *American Political Science Review* 82(1): 11–29.

Puga, Cristina. 1993a. *Mexico: Empresarios y poder.* Mexico, D.F.: Facultad de Ciencias Políticas y Sociales, UNAM; Miguel Angel Porrúa.

——. 1993b. Las organizaciones empresariales mexicanas de comercio exterior. In *Organizaciones emresariales y Tratado de Libre Comercio*, ed. Cristina Puga, 49–71. Proyecto Organizaciones Empresariales en México

References

(POEM), Cuadernos 7. Facultad de Ciencias Políticas y Sociales, Instituto de Investigaciones Sociales. Mexico, D.F.: Universidad Nacional Autónoma de México.

————. 1994. Los industriales mexicanos en una época de cambio (La negociación del TLC). Paper presented at the Latin American Studies Association XVIII International Congress, Atlanta, GA, 10–12 March.

Putnam, Robert D. 1988. Diplomacy and domestic politics: The logic of two-level games. *International Organization* 42(summer): 427–460.

Remmer, Karen. 1986. The politics of economic stabilization. *Comparative Politics* 19(1): 1–24.

————. 1990. Democracy and economic crisis: The Latin American experience. *World Politics* 42(3): 315–335.

Rey Romay, Benito, ed. 1992. *La integración comercial de México a Estados Unidos y Canadá: ¿Alternativa o destino?* 3rd ed. Mexico, D.F.: Siglo Veintiuno Editores.

Riner, Deborah L., and John V. Sweeney. 1998. The effects of NAFTA on Mexico's private sector and foreign trade and investment. In *Mexico's private sector: Recent history, future challenges*, ed. Riordan Roett, 161–187. Boulder: Lynne Rienner.

Rock, David. 1995. The transition in Argentina. In *Conversations on democratization and economic reform: Working papers of the Southern California Seminar*, ed. Leslie Elliott Armijo, 213–214. Los Angeles: Center for International Studies, School of International Relations, University of Southern California.

Rodríguez, Victoria E., and Peter M. Ward, eds. 1995. *Opposition government in Mexico*. Albuquerque: University of New Mexico Press.

Rodrik, Dani. 1989. Credibility of trade reform – A policy maker's guide. *World Economy* (March): 1–16.

————. 1991. Policy uncertainty and private investment in developing countries. *Journal of Development Economics* 36(1): 229–242.

————. 1992a. The limits of trade policy reform in developing countries. *Journal of Economic Perspectives* 6(1): 87–105.

————. 1992b. The rush to free trade in the developing world: Why so late? Why now? Will it last? Prepared for the World Bank research project on Political Economy of Structural Adjustment. Revised April.

————. 1997. Sense and nonsense in the globalization debate. *Foreign Policy* (107): 19–36

Roett, Riordan. 1996. The Mexican devaluation and the U.S. response: Potomac politics, 1995-style. In *The Mexican Peso crisis: International perspectives*, ed. Riordan Roett, 33–48. Boulder: Lynne Rienner.

————. 1998. Mexico's private sector: Recent history, future challenges. Boulder: Lynne Rienner.

Rogowski, Ronald. 1989. *Commerce and Coalitions: How trade affects domestic political alignments*. Princeton: Princeton University Press.

Rogozinski, Jacques. 1993. *La privatización de empresas paraestatales*. Mexico, D.F.: Fondo de Cultura Económica.

Ros, Jaime. 1992a. Free trade or common capital market? Notes on Mexico-US economic integration and current NAFTA negotiations. *Journal of Interamerican Studies and World Affairs* 34(2): 53–91.

————. 1992b. On the political economy of market and state reform in Mexico. Prepared for a conference on Democracy, Markets, and Structural

References

Reform in Contemporary Latin America, organized by the North-South Center, University of Miami, and CEDES, Buenos Aires, 25–27 March.

―――. 1994. Financial markets and capital flows in Mexico. In *Foreign capital in Latin America*, ed. José Antonio Ocampo and Roberto Steiner, 193–239. Washington, DC: Inter-American Development Bank.

Rubio, Luis. 1988. The changing role of the private sector. In *Mexico in transition, implications for U.S. policy: Essays from both sides of the border*, ed. Susan Kaufman Purcell, 31–42. New York: Council on Foreign Relations.

―――. 1992. *¿Cómo va a afectar a México el Tratado de Libre Comercio?* Mexico, D.F.: Fondo de Cultura Económica.

Sachs, Jeffrey D., ed. 1989. *Developing country debt and the world economy*. Chicago: University of Chicago Press.

Salas-Porras, Alejandra. 1992. Globalización y proceso corporativo de los grandes grupos económicos en México. *Revista Mexicana de Sociología* 54(2): 133–162.

Samstad, James G., and Ruth Berins Collier. 1995. Mexican labor and structural reform under Salinas: New unionism or old stalemate? In *The challenge of institutional reform in Mexico*, ed. Riordan Roett, 9–37. Boulder: Lynne Rienner.

Sánchez Ugarte, Fernando. n.d. La política industrial de hoy: La industria mexicana ante la apertura (1987–93). Mimeo, SECOFI.

Scheinman, Marc N. 1991. *Mexico's motor vehicle industry: Prospects to 2000*. Special Report No. R301. London and New York: Economist Intelligence Unit.

―――. 1993. *Mexico automotive industry outlook: Taking off with NAFTA*. A Special Report from Ward's Communications. Detroit: Ward's Communications.

Schamis, Hector E. 1995. On the relationship between political and economic reform: The Chilean experience. In *Conversations on democratization and economic reform: Working papers of the Southern California Seminar*, ed. Leslie Elliott Armijo, 164–178. Los Angeles: Center for International Studies, School of International Relations, University of Southern California.

Schneider, Ben Ross. 1992. Privatization in the Collor government: Triumph of liberalism or collapse of the developmental state? In *The right and democracy in Latin America*, ed. Douglas A. Chalmers, María do Carmo Campello de Souza, and Atilio A. Borón, 225–237. New York: Praeger.

―――. 1994. Presentation made at the Latin American Studies Association XVIII International Congress, Atlanta, GA, 10–12 March.

―――. 1997. Big business and the politics of economic reform: Confidence and concertation in Brazil and Mexico. In *Business and the state in developing countries*, ed. Sylvia Maxfield and Ben Ross Schneider, 191–215. Ithaca: Cornell University Press.

―――. 1998. The material bases of technocracy: Investor confidence and neoliberalism in Latin America. In *The politics of expertise in Latin America*, ed. Miguel A. Centeno and Patricio Silva, 77–95. London: Macmillan.

―――. 1999. Why is Mexican business so organized? Mimeo, Northwestern University, March.

Schneider, Ben Ross, and Sylvia Maxfield. 1997. Business, the state, and economic performance in developing countries. In *Business and the state in*

References

developing countries, ed. Sylvia Maxfield and Ben Ross Schneider, 3–35. Ithaca: Cornell University Press.

Secretaría de Comercio y Fomento Industrial (SECOFI). 1991. *Programa nacional de modernización industrial y del comercio exterior, 1990–1994.* Mexico, D.F.: SECOFI.

———. 1992. *Tratado de Libre Comercio en América del Norte: Monografías.* Vols. 1 and 2. Mexico, D.F.: SECOFI.

———. 1993a. *Tratado de Libre Comercio de América del Norte: Texto oficial.* Mexico, D.F.: SECOFI.

———. 1993b. *Tratado de Libre Comercio entre México, Canadá y Estados Unidos.* Mexico, D.F.: SECOFI.

———. 1993c. *El Tratado de Libre Comercio: México, Canadá, Estados Unidos.* Mexico, D.F.: SECOFI.

Shadlen, Kenneth. 1997. Corporatism and the organization of business interests: Small industry and the state in postrevolutionary Mexico. Ph.D. diss., University of California, Berkeley.

———. 2000. Neoliberalism, corporatism, and small business political activism in contemporary Mexico. *Latin American Research Review* 35(2): 73–106.

Shafer, Michael. 1994. *Winners and losers: How sectors shape the developmental prospects of states.* Ithaca: Cornell University Press.

———. 1997. The political economy of sectors and sectoral change: Korea then and now. In *Business and the state in developing countries*, ed. Sylvia Maxfield and Ben Ross Schneider, 88–121. Ithaca: Cornell University Press.

Shafer, Robert J. 1973. *Mexican business organizations: History and analysis.* Syracuse, NY: Syracuse University Press.

Sheahan, John. 1997. Effects of liberalization programs on poverty and inequality: Chile, Mexico, and Peru. *Latin American Research Review* 32(3): 7–37.

Sidell, Scott R. 1988. *The IMF and Third-World political instability: Is there a connection?* New York: St. Martins.

Sikkink, Kathryn. 1991. *Ideas and institutions: Developmentalism in Brazil and Argentina.* Ithaca: Cornell University Press.

Silva, Eduardo. 1993. Capitalist coalitions, the state, and neoliberal economic restructuring: Chile, 1973–1988. *World Politics* 45(4): 526–559.

———. 1996a. From dictatorship to democracy: The business-state nexus in Chile's economic transformation, 1975–1994. *Comparative Politics* 28(3): 299–320.

———. 1996b. *The state and capital in Chile: Business elites, technocrats, and market economics.* Boulder: Westview Press.

Smith, Peter H. 1979. *Labyrinths of power: Political recruitment in twentieth-century Mexico.* Princeton: Princeton University Press.

———. 1991. Tensions within the national political elite. Paper presented at the Latin American Studies Association XVI International Congress, Crystal City, VA, 4–6 April.

Solórzano, María del Carmen. 1993. *La Asociación Mexicana de Casas de Bolsa y la reestructuración del sistema finaciero mexicano (1980–1992).* Proyecto Organizaciones Empresariales en México (POEM), Cuadernos 6. Facultad de Ciencias Políticas y Sociales, Instituto de Investigaciones Sociales. Mexico, D.F.: Universidad Nacional Autónoma de México.

Stallings, Barbara. 1989. Political economy of democratic transition: Chile in the 1980s. In *Debt and democracy in Latin America*, ed. Barbara Stallings and Robert R. Kaufman, 181–199. Boulder: Westview Press.

References

Stallings, Barbara. 1992. International influence on economic policy: Debt, stabilization, and structural reform. In *The politics of economic adjustment: International constraints, distributive conflicts, and the state*, ed. Stephan Haggard and Robert R. Kaufman, 41–88. Princeton: Princeton University Press.

Stallings, Barbara, and Robert R. Kaufman, ed. 1989. *Debt and democracy in Latin America*. Boulder: Westview Press.

Starr, Pamela. 1997. Government coalitions and the viability of currency boards: Argentina under the Cavallo Plan. *Journal of Interamerican Studies and World Affairs* 39(2): 83–133.

Stepan, Alfred. 1985. State power and the strength of civil society in the Southern Cone of Latin America. In *Bringing the state back in*, ed. Peter B. Evans, Dietrich Rueschemeyer, and Theda Skocpol, 317–343. Cambridge, Eng.: Cambridge University Press.

Story, Dale. 1982. Trade politics in the Third World: A case study of the Mexican GATT decision. *International Organization* 36(4): 767–794.

———. 1986. *Industry, the state, and public policy in Mexico*. Austin: University of Texas Press.

Studer Noguez, María Isabel. 1997. Economic sovereignty in the global integration strategies of Ford Motor Co. Prepared for the 38th annual conference of the International Studies Association, Toronto, Ontario, Canada 19–21 March.

———. 1999. How global is Ford Motor Company's global strategy? In *Non-state actors and authority in the global system*, ed. Richard A. Higgott, Andreas Bieler, and Geoffrey R. D. Underhill. London: Routledge.

Taniura, Taeko, Claudia Schatan, and Jorge Máttar. 1992. *Intra-industry and intra-firm trade between Mexico and the United States: The autoparts, electronics and secondary petrochemical industries*. Joint Research Programme Series No. 97. Tokyo: Institute of Developing Economies.

Teichman, Judith. 1992. The Mexican state and the political implications of economic restructuring. *Latin American Perspectives* 19(2): 88–104.

———. 1996. Economic restructuring, state-labor relations, and the transformation of Mexican corporatism. In *Neoliberalism revisited: Economic restructuring and Mexico's political future*, ed. Gerardo Otero, 149–166. Boulder: Westview Press.

Ten Kate, Adriaan. 1992. Trade liberalization and economic stabilization in Mexico: Lessons of experience. *World Development* 20(5): 659–672.

Thacker, Strom C. 1996. From silent to active partner: Big business, the state and free trade in Mexico. Ph.D. diss., University of North Carolina, Chapel Hill.

———. 1997a. Big business, the state, and free trade in Mexico: Interests, structure, and political access. Paper presented at the annual meeting of the American Political Science Association, Washington, DC, 28–31 August.

———. 1997b. The political economy of free trade in Mexico: Business-state coalitions and international context. Paper presented at the annual meeting of the International Studies Association, Toronto, Ontario, Canada, 18–22 March.

———. 1999a. The high politics of IMF lending. *World Politics* 52(1): 38–75.

References

―――. 1999b. NAFTA coalitions and the political viability of neoliberalism in Mexico. *Journal of Interamerican Studies and World Affairs* 41(2): 57–89.

Tomz, Michael. 1997. Do international agreements make reforms more credible? Prepared for the the annual meeting of the American Political Science Association, Washington, DC, 28–31 August.

Tornell, Aaron. 1995. Are economic crises necessary for trade liberalization and fiscal reform? The Mexican experience. In *Reform, recovery, and growth: Latin America and the Middle East*, ed. Rudiger Dornbusch and Sebastian Edwards, 53–73. Chicago: University of Chicago Press.

Tornell, Aaron, and Gerardo Esquivel. 1995. The political economy of Mexico's entry to NAFTA. NBER Working Paper 5322. Cambridge, MA: National Bureau of Economic Research.

Trejo Reyes, Saúl, and Gustavo Vega Cánovas. 1987. El ingreso al GATT y sus implicaciones para el futuro de México. *Comercio Exterior* 37(7): 519–526.

Unger, Kurt. 1990. *Las exportaciones mexicanas ante la reestructuracion industrial internacional: La evidencia de las industrias quimicay automotriz.* Mexico, DF: Fondo de Cultura Económica.

United States International Trade Commission. 1990. *Review of trade and investment measures by Mexico and future prospects for future United States-Mexico relations. Phase I: Recent trade and investment reforms undertaken by Mexico and implications for the United States.* Investigation No. 332–282, April. Washington, DC: USITC.

Valdés Ugalde, Francisco. 1994. From bank nationalization to state reform: Business and the new Mexican order. In *The politics of economic restructuring: State-society relations and regime change in Mexico*, ed. María Lorena Cook, Kevin J. Middlebrook, and Juan Molinar Horcasitas, 219–242. San Diego: Center for U.S.-Mexican Studies, University of California.

―――. 1996. The private sector and political regime change in Mexico. In *Neoliberalism revisited: Economic restructuring and Mexico's political future*, ed. Gerardo Otero, 127–147. Boulder: Westview Press.

―――. 1997. *Autonomía y legitimidad: Los empresarios, la política y el estado en México.* Mexico, D.F.: Siglo Veintiuno Editores.

Vega Cánovas, Gustavo. 1991a. Bilateral or plurilateral free trade in North America: Economic and political implications for Mexico. Ph.D. diss., Yale University.

Vega Cánovas, Gustavo, ed. 1991b. *México ante el libre comercio con América del norte.* Mexico, D.F.: El Colegio de México and Universidad Tecnológica de México.

―――. 1993. *Liberación económica y libre comercio en América del Norte: Consideraciones políticas, sociales y culturales.* Mexico, D.F.: El Colegio de México.

Velasco Arregui, Edur. 1993. Industrial restructuring in Mexico during the 1980s. In *The political economy of North American free trade*, ed. Ricardo Grinspun and Maxwell A. Cameron, 163–175. New York: St. Martin's.

Villareal, René. 1990. The Latin American strategy of import-substitution: Failure or paradigm for the region? In *Manufacturing miracles: Paths of industrialization in Latin America and East Asia*, ed. Gary Gereffi and Donald L. Wyman, 292–320. Princeton: Princeton University Press.

von Bertrab, Hermann. 1997. *Negotiating NAFTA: A Mexican envoy's account.* Westport, CT: Praeger.

References

Ward, Peter M., and Virginia E. Rodríguez, eds. 1995. *Opposition government in Mexico*. Albuquerque: University of New Mexico Press.

Weintraub, Sidney. 1990. *A marriage of convenience: Relations between Mexico and the United States*. New York: Oxford University Press.

Weyland, Kurt. 1996. *Democracy without equity: Failures of reform in Brazil*. Pittsburgh: University of Pittsburgh Press.

———. 1997. The Brazilian state in the new democracy. Prepared for the XX International Congress of the Latin American Studies Association, Guadalarjara, Mexico, 17–19 April.

Williamson, John, ed. 1983. *IMF conditionality*. Washington, DC: Institute for International Economics. Distributed by MIT Press.

Williamson, John, and Stephan Haggard. 1994. The political conditions for economic reform. In *The political economy of policy reform*, ed. John Williamson, 527–596. Washington, DC: Institute for International Economics.

Winters, Jeffrey A. 1994. Power and the control of capital. *World Politics* 46(3): 419–452.

———. 1996. *Power in motion: Capital mobility and the Indonesian state*. Ithaca: Cornell University Press.

Wise, Carol, ed. 1998. *The post-NAFTA political economy: Mexico and the western hemisphere*. University Park: Pennsylvania State University Press.

World Bank. Various years. *World debt tables*. Washington, DC: World Bank.

Zabludovsky, Jaime. 1990. Trade liberalization and macroeconomic adjustment. In *Mexico's search for a new development strategy*, ed. Dwight S. Brothers and Adele E. Wick, 173–193. Boulder: Westview Press.

———. 1994. El proceso de negociación del Tratado de Libre Comercio de América del Norte. In *Testimonios sobre el TLC*, ed. Carlos Arriola, 107–125. Mexico, D.F.: Diana, Miguel Angel Porrúa.

Zubek, Voytek, and Judith Gentleman. 1994. Economic crisis and the movement toward pluralism in Poland and Mexico. *Political Science Quarterly* 109(2): 335–359.

Index

235

Index

Index

Harvard University, 45, 132, 154
Hermosillo, 179
Hernández Galicia, Joaqúin ("La Quina"),
  126
Hernández Pons, Enrique, 141
Hernández, Francisco, 169
Hernández, Paulina, 150
Honda, 181

ICA, 175
import licenses, 81
import-substituting industrialization
  (ISI), 1, 5, 79, 80, 136, 137, 197,
  198
Inbursa brokerage group, 116
India, 41
Industrias Bachoco, 141
Institutional Revolutionary Party (PRI), 4,
  18, 42, 53, 85, 102, 104, 106, 107,
  108, 118, 119, 120, 121, 122, 126,
  132, 155, 161, 189, 190, 196, 205,
  206, 208, 209
Interior, Ministry of, 81
international capital mobility, 26, 28, 30,
  47, 51, 71, 91, 102, 161, 204
international financial institutions (IFIs),
  21, 22
international financial integration, 27, 28,
  29, 39, 47, 50, 71, 91, 204
International Monetary Fund (IMF), 6, 8,
  20, 21, 22, 41, 43, 47–51, 63, 83, 105,
  188, 189, 190, 193, 197
investment crises, 71–75

Jalisco, 120
Japan, 172, 177

Kennedy School of Government, 132
Kenworth, 173
Kimberley-Clark de México, 126, 141

labor, 4, 17, 18, 32, 44, 78, 86, 104, 106,
  122, 126, 127, 141, 170, 174, 184,
  186, 193, 196, 204, 207, 208
Labor, Ministry of, 81
Larrea, Jorge, 116
Latin America, 7, 11, 128, 129, 192, 197,
  198, 200, 201
Latin American Integration Association
  (ALADI), 128, 192
Law to Promote Mexican Investment and
  Regulate Foreign Investment (Foreign
  Investment Law), 57
Legorreta, Agustín, 86, 87, 128
López Portillo, José, 2, 52, 53, 68, 80, 81,
  82, 87, 105, 110, 111, 131, 157, 186,
  188

macroeconomic policy, 1, 11, 15, 20, 26,
  87, 109, 202
Madáhuar Cámara, Nicolás, 141
Marcelo Sada, Andrés, 141
Masa, 173
Massachusetts Institute of Technology
  (MIT), 45, 205
Menem, Carlos, 193, 194
Mercedes-Benz, 173, 188
Mexican Association of Brokerage Houses
  (AMCB), 56, 146, 147, 148, 150
Mexican Association of Insurance
  Institutions (AMIS), 146, 148, 150
Mexican Association of the Automobile
  Industry (AMIA), 171, 173, 176, 177
Mexican Business Council for
  International Affairs (CEMAI), 145,
  147, 150, 159, 161, 171, 176, 183
Mexican Businessmen's Council (CMHN),
  103, 104, 141, 146, 148, 150, 183
Mexican Stock Exchange (Bolsa Mexicana
  de Valores, S.A. de C.V), 56, 100,
  101
Mexico Chapter of International Chamber
  of Commerce (CAP MEX CCI), 150
Mexico City, 95, 98, 154, 205
Mexico state, 120
Michoacán, 119, 120
Middle East, 145
Miranda, Carlos, 150
mobile capital assets, 19, 26, 51, 30, 31,
  33, 71, 85, 88, 91, 204
Monterrey business groups, 100, 105
Monterrey Technological Institute
  (ITESM), 138, 139
Monterrey, 88, 95, 208
Montreal, 207
multinational corporations (MNCs), 99,
  100, 142, 161, 169

National Action Party (PAN), 42, 85, 106,
  107, 121, 188, 189, 190
National Agricultural Council (CNA),
  146, 148, 150
National Association of Chemical Industry
  (ANIQ), 169, 170
National Association of Importers and
  Exporters (ANIERM), 80, 82, 146, 150,
  159
National Association of Manufacturing
  Industries (ANIT), 169
National Auto Parts Industry (INA), 173,
  175
National Autonomous University of
  Mexico (UNAM), 109, 132, 134, 135
National Bank of Mexico (Banamex),
  54

237

Index

Index